THE *Essential*
CHARLES
FILLMORE

THE *Essential* CHARLES FILLMORE

Collected Writings of a Missouri Mystic

With Commentary by James Gaither

Unity Village, Missouri

First Edition 1999

The Essential Charles Fillmore is a member of the Charles Fillmore Reference Library.

To receive a catalog of all Unity publications (books, cassettes, compact discs, and magazines) or to place an order, call the Customer Service Department: (816) 969-2069 or 1-800-669-0282.

The publisher wishes to acknowledge the editorial work of Michael Maday, Raymond Teague, and Joanne Englehart; the copyediting and proofreading of Kay Thomure, Shari Behr, and Deborah Dribben; the production help of Rozanne Devine and Jane Blackwood; and the marketing efforts of Allen Liles, Jenee Meyer, and Sharon Sartin.

Cover design by Gretchen West. Cover photo from the Unity Archives.

Library of Congress Cataloging-in-Publication Data
Fillmore, Charles, 1854–1948.
    [Selections. 1999]
    The essential Charles Fillmore : collected writings of a Missouri mystic / [edited] with commentary by James Gaither.
       p.   cm.
    Includes index.
    ISBN 0-87159-240-1 (hardcover)
    1. Unity School of Christianity—Doctrines.   I. Gaither, James, 1951–   . II. Title.
    BX9890.U505F554   1999
    289.9'7—dc21   99–23600
                                         CIP

Canada BN 13252 9033 RT

TABLE
OF CONTENTS

ACKNOWLEDGMENTS

THIS BOOK is the result of the suggestions, efforts, and encouragement of a community of faith, not of just one person. Obviously, heartfelt appreciation must go to Charles Fillmore whose lifework is central to this book. In addition, those who followed him into Unity ministry have kept his work alive and made it a significant element in the lives of multitudes over the last century. I want to thank all those Unity teachers, especially those who taught me, and acknowledge their contributions to the development and continuence of an important spiritual work.

More specifically, I need to thank those who helped in various ways to bring this book together. I want to thank the Reverend Michael Maday, editor of Unity Books; the Reverend Nancy Clark; and Neal Vahle for their helpful suggestions and encouragement. I want to thank the Reverend Carolyn Stewart, librarian at Unity School of Christianity, for her help in finding some of the pieces included in this volume. Thanks also to the Reverend Orren Evans for his valuable work of putting much of Charles Fillmore's work into computer format. His work greatly facilitated the process of getting this book into print-ready form. Finally, I must thank my wife Chris for her patience and encouragement not only during the time I was working on this project, but through all our years together.

INTRODUCTION

CHARLES FILLMORE may have been the greatest religious innovator since the apostle Paul. With virtually no formal education, Fillmore effectively developed a Christian perspective that synthesized religion, philosophy, and science. What is more, this new form of Christianity called "Unity" is no mere intellectual edifice but has proven itself to be a practical spiritual discipline for people of all socioeconomic classes, all around the world.

This book is an attempt to provide an overview of Fillmore's major themes and ideas in a systematic and accessible way. He wrote on metaphysics and theology for almost 60 years, so a complete collection of his writings would require several volumes. Some of his writings are difficult to read and understand, because they assume the reader has an extensive familiarity with his thought world. This book includes a brief exposition of Fillmore's thought world, as an aid to readers not familiar with the historical and theological context in which Fillmore wrote. The selections in this book are some of Fillmore's simplest and clearest explanations of his views. The selections are arranged according to classic categories of metaphysics and theology in an attempt to help the reader study Fillmore's teachings as a whole system.

CHARLES FILLMORE: A TWENTIETH-CENTURY ST. PAUL?

The parallels between Charles Fillmore and St. Paul are striking.

1

Paul adopted a new religious sect, Christianity, and expressed it in terms of the paradigms of the day: the resurrected-redeemer mystery schools, Gnosticism, Greek philosophies, and Judaism. For example, Paul's explanation of "the Lord's Supper" fits the mystery-school idea of a worthy initiate participating in a sacred meal representing the body of a resurrected redeemer: "Let a man examine himself, and so eat of the bread and drink of the cup. For anyone who eats and drinks without discerning the body eats and drinks judgment upon himself" (1 Cor. 11:28-29).[1] The idea of a secret wisdom, or *Gnosis,* from the Supreme God is reflected in this passage from Paul: "But we impart a secret and hidden wisdom of God, which God decreed before the ages for our glorification" (1 Cor. 2: 7).[2] In Acts, we find Paul quoting Greek philosophers to Athenians in an attempt to convert them: "Yet he is not far from each one of us, for 'in him we live and move and have our being' [Epimenides]; as even some of your poets have said, 'For we are indeed his offspring [Aratus]'" (Acts 17: 27-28).[3]

As we shall see in his writings, Fillmore adopted a new religious perspective called "New Thought" and "Christian Science" and expressed it in terms of *Christian theology,* which included for him, *mysticism, yogic practices, esoteric spirituality, idealist metaphysics,* and *post-Einsteinian physics.*

Paul used the most effective technology of his day—ships, Roman roads, and letters—to spread his message throughout the Roman Empire. Fillmore used the most effective technology of his day—radio, recording equipment, and printing presses—to spread his message throughout America, Europe, Australia, and parts of Africa.

Paul and Charles Fillmore both believed they had guidance from the Ascended Christ Jesus.[4] Both believed that a "new creation" was soon to emerge. Both were effective organizers. Both were reputed to be spiritual healers, who themselves had minor physical afflictions. Both interpreted sacred writings as metaphors for a deep underlying, spiritual reality. Both honored and assimilated the tradition from which their new religion emerged but did not allow the old tradition to take precedence over their new vision.

As one might expect for two religious visionaries who lived nearly two millenia and half a world apart, there are also significant differences between St. Paul of Tarsus and Charles Fillmore of Kansas City. Paul lived in a time of political oppression and religious persecution, and so suffered and was imprisoned for his faith. Fillmore lived in a time and place of much greater political and religious freedom, and so endured criticism but not any severe repercussions from the surrounding culture. Paul worked mainly with men and expressed some of the gender bias of his time. Fillmore worked with his wife Myrtle as an equal partner and had more women associates and students than men. Living in intolerant times, Paul was himself somewhat intolerant of deviation from his understanding of the gospel. Living in a time of liberty, Fillmore, though strong in his personal convictions, encouraged his students and associates to think and explore the inner life for themselves.

Charles Fillmore is reputed to have believed that he was a reincarnation of Paul.[5] Considering the parallels between the two men, that belief, if not literally true, has at least an element of figurative truth to it.

Regardless of how one feels about this comparison between St. Paul and Charles Fillmore, there are other good reasons to give serious consideration to the writings of Charles Fillmore.

A SPIRITUAL THERAPY FOR THE SCIENTIFIC AND SECULAR AGE

Our modern "idols and gods" are technology, information, wealth, and sex. None of these "idols" are inherently evil, but worship of them has exacerbated alienation of individuals from themselves, their families, society, government, and humanity itself. New Thought, for which Charles Fillmore was one of the most inspiring and able spokespersons, may well provide a helpful therapy for some of the problems rooted in these modern obsessions.

We live in an age in which technology has outstripped our ability to adapt our values to our powers. Medical science can keep us alive beyond a point at which we can discern any worthwhile quality of life; thus individuals and families are faced with excruciatingly difficult decisions about continuation of medical treatment. Technological production has virtually replaced craftsmanship and its concomitants— pride and satisfaction in work. Workers have virtually become extensions of machines and production processes. We connect through telephones, computers, and fax machines rather than through personal presence and conversation. Thus machines have become mediators between human beings, much as in the past priests served as mediators between human beings and God. Military technology has given us a capacity to annihilate all life, while our ability to transcend cultural and religious differences is little better than it was during the Crusades of the Middle Ages.

Television, telephone, telegraph, radio, printing press, communication satellite, and computer convey unassimilable quantities of information around the planet. Information is useful when it can be assimilated and evaluated, but the sheer quantity of information available today has resulted in a world of narrow specializations. Specialization creates subcultures whose members can communicate with each other, but not with those outside the group.

Laws are written in such specialized language that only lawyers have a hope of understanding them and nonlawyers must resignedly entrust themselves and their rights to the knowledge and judgment of "experts." Government policy experts control the flow of information to the public they are supposed to serve, so that citizens die or lose loved ones in wars they don't understand. Tax dollars are spent on an array of programs so complex that even the legislators who design the programs can't foresee the consequences.

All humans must understand the nature of our environment In order to make wise decisions about use of natural resources, but specialization in knowledge of nature conceals from rather than reveals to the nonspecialist the impact of our behavior on our environment. So we try to sort out the conflicting rhetoric of environmentalists who warn of impending doom and conservative sceptics who assure us there are no serious problems.

Business and government obsessively pursue efficiency without regard to the needs in the real world for flexibility, creativity, and human emotional needs. Layers of administrators and managers produce reams of policies, procedures, plans, and reports to the point that productivity is measured by quantity of paper rather than quality of product and service. Filling out forms, following policies, and attending meetings seem higher priorities than careful reflection, individual imagination, and joy of working.

The healing arts are so compartmentalized and specialized that human feelings and needs are usually ignored in treatment of the body or "controlled" with chemicals or "processed" without reference to physical needs. This is not a fault of the health care professionals but rather a product of excessive information specialization to the exclusion of treating the person as a whole.

Anyone who pays any attention at all to the electronic and print media knows that we live in an age obsessed with wealth and sex. These social neuroses tempt us to judge others by their sexual attractiveness and financial portfolio. Individuals who fit our culture's notions of sexual attractiveness are continually tempted to use that quality to accumulate wealth and power. We are fascinated by the lives and opinions of the beautiful, rich, and famous, while we virtually ignore our teachers—those who devote their lives to perpetuating the greatest achievements and highest values of our culture. By ignoring these teachers, we not only deprive ourselves of wisdom and beauty, we also forget history instead of learning from it.

In short, we live in an age that urgently requires, not more information and technology, but deeper wisdom; not greater competitiveness, but greater compassion. We need to seriously reflect on the nature of virtue and intangible values like justice, freedom, beauty, and happiness. We need to explore the relationship of attitudes and emotions to physical health and the possibilities of mental autonomy over our own bodies. We need to find new ways to see each other, ways that emphasize the spiritual and human rather than usefulness for personal gratification. We need more soul communication and less electronic communication. We need reconciliation of religions, philosophies, and science—rejoicing in both their unity of thought and diversity of expression. We need ways to find more profound intuitions and a greater global unity of spirit, mind, and heart. That is what Charles Fillmore's teachings offer us.

Fillmore developed an approach to meditation that might best be described as a kind of Christian yoga. Practiced with persistence, his methods can increase our ability to control our physical health, access deeper levels of our conscious-ness, and cultivate in a systematic way the primal virtues and powers that have enabled our species to flourish.

His philosophy is rooted in Idealist metaphysics, the theory that the universe is a phenomena of mind, rather than matter. While several great philosophers, such as Bishop

George Berkeley and G. W. F. Hegel, had advocated philosophical Idealism which influenced New Thought,[6] the philosophers did not produce practical methods for transformation and healing. The New Thoughters, including Fillmore, worked out the practical implications and methods. A significant aspect of the New Thought form of Idealism is a principle of self-respect based on a theology of the omnipresence of God and an inner divinity in all humanity.

Charles Fillmore was one of many New Thoughters to advocate "principles of prosperity" based on the use of mind to attract wealth. Rather than advocating a self-centered accumulation of riches for riches' sake, Fillmore's concept of prosperity is rooted in a consciousness of appreciation and thanksgiving for what we have, an awareness of our creative power to generate wealth, and good stewardship of resources based on considering all humanity to be our family.

Fillmore's aim in developing and practicing spiritual discipline went beyond the cultivation of spiritual virtues and powers. He wanted to attain mystical union with the Mind of God and transform his body. To what degree Fillmore succeeded in his higher aims, I cannot say. I do know that the Unity teachings have benefited millions of people (including me) and that the possibilities of spiritual transformation are greater than any of us have yet accomplished.

AN ARCHETYPAL AMERICAN LIFE

The biography of Charles Fillmore reads like an American archetype. From his birth in a log cabin near an Indian reservation to adventures in the American frontier in the worlds of gold miners, railroad men, mule-team drivers and real estate speculators, Fillmore's early life reflected a persistent self-reliance and struggle against the odds imposed by nature. Then there was his romance and spiritual partnership with his wife Myrtle that began with "love at first sight" on his part. Undoubtedly, Myrtle was a full partner in the development of Unity teachings and practices and a major influence on Charles' spirituality. Finally, there was Charles' spiritual awakening, in which he moved from a healthy scepticism to a determined experimentalism to a whole-hearted, dedicated practical mysticism.

It is difficult to say what impact growing up near an Indian reservation had on Fillmore. As a very young child, Charles was once kidnapped by a tribe, but was safely returned the same evening. Charles later reported that he always felt that he was used in some kind of religious ceremony by the tribe. Whatever the truth of the matter, it is possible that his experience growing up among Native Americans opened his young mind to spiritual traditions other than the predominant American Christian ones of his time. Growing up, playing with Native American children probably also opened him to perspectives and traditions beyond the usual scope of the European-American culture.

A skating accident in his youth left him with an injured hip and leg. The leg stopped growing and eventually Fillmore had to wear a leg brace and a four-inch extension on his shoe. The condition was accompanied by chronic pain. Strangely enough, this injury proved to be a blessing to Fillmore in several ways. It strengthened his character, for he refused to let it hinder him, thereby developing persistence and determination that served him well throughout his life. The condition also helped stimulate his interest in the "Mind Cure" or "New Thought" movement of his time. First it was Myrtle Fillmore who experienced enthusiasm for and healing from New Thought. Her experience certainly was the key factor inspiring Charles' exploration of that movement. Yet if Charles had not himself been in need of healing, it is unlikely that his exploration would have been as determined and intense as it was.

His use of the methods of "Mind Cure" proved therapeutic for his condition in a way that the medical practices of the time did not. He was relieved of chronic pain, and his leg grew in strength and length, providing him with the practical verification he sought for New Thought methods. His injury and recovery may also have taught him both compassion for the physically challenged and faith in the power of Spirit to cure anything. Finally, the regeneration of his leg may well have inspired his faith in the idea of total body regeneration that was to permeate his theology and metaphysics.[7]

NEW THOUGHT: RELIGION AS THERAPY

The New Thought religion that Charles Fillmore adopted and developed emerged in a period of pervasive religious experimentation in America. The nineteenth century saw the rise of the Church of Jesus Christ of Latter-day Saints (the Mormons). Joseph Smith, the founder of the Mormon Church, attempted to resolve the theological controversies of frontier revivalism through a new "revealed" book that wove Christian doctrines into a purported history of pre-Columbian America. Revivalistic fervor generated an anticipation of the millennium and various second advent churches such as the Seventh-Day Adventists. There was also a number of religious communal experiments including the Oneida community and the Shakers. There was some interest in Swedenborgianism, which was based on the writings of the brilliant eighteenth-century scientist-theologian Swedenborg, who claimed the power to communicate with the spirits of the departed in the angelic and demonic realms. The discovery of methods to induce hypnotic-trance states by Mesmer and his followers, along with Swedenborg's influence, culminated in the Spiritualist movement. Out of Spiritualist groups and interest in Eastern religions, Theosophy emerged.[8]

The nineteenth century was also the heyday of Transcendentalism, which proved to be an important influence on the New Thought movement. Ralph Waldo Emerson was the Transcendentalist who was the most influential on New Thought teachers including Fillmore. Some of the ideas espoused by Emerson that still very much characterize Unity and New Thought are self-reliance and independent thinking; the oversoul; Divine Mind as the origin of all things; prayer as "contemplation of Truth" in the Silence (an idea Emerson himself probably got from the Quakers), rather than as begging God for favors; a "Law of Compensation" that operates here and now, not just in the afterlife; knowledge through intuition; good as absolute reality and evil as "privation" or mere negation of the good; Jesus as seer and revelator of the divinity in all humanity. Indeed, these Emersonian themes are so fundamental to New Thought that some have maintained that Emerson is the true founder of the New Thought movement.[9]

However, the distinctive feature of New Thought and Christian Science was not the Idealist philosophy reflected in Transcendentalism, significant and pervasive as that philosophy was. The distinctive feature was rather the practice of what was originally and aptly called "Mind Cure." The New Thoughters used metaphysical arguments, affirmations, and meditations to promote psychosomatic healing. These metaphysical healers maintained that the body is, in reality, an idea in God Mind and in the human mind. They further held that the body is perfect in God Mind and only appears to be ill or imperfect in the human or "mortal" mind. They asserted that if we can align our minds with the divine idea of our body, we will be cured.[10]

Their methods affected cures in enough cases to attract believers and begin new religious movements. Their healings were reported not only in their own literature but also in the popular media and even in William James' classic treatise *The Varieties of Religious Experience.*[11] These healing religions preceded and undoubtedly inspired to some degree both the Pentecostal healing revivals and the serious medical study of psychosomatic healing.

The New Thoughters eventually expanded the application of their philosophy to the areas of success, prosperity, relationships, and mysticism.

Since the "Mind Cure" movement was the main influence on Charles Fillmore's work, it is worthwhile here to briefly sketch the history of that movement.

The first advocates of both New Thought and Christian Science were students and patients of Phineas Parkhurst Quimby (1802-1866). Quimby was a New England man who became interested in the phenomena of "mesmerism."

Mesmerism was a practice that originated in the work of a Viennese physician named Franz Anton Mesmer (1734-1815). Mesmer formulated a theory that gravitational and magnetic fields have a significant effect on human health. Working with magnets, Mesmer discovered that he could cure some patients who did not respond to the conventional medical treatments of his time. Mesmer and his followers also discovered that when passing magnets over their patients, the patients would sometimes go into a trance state. The trance phenomena led to public demonstrations of mind reading and other peculiarities that were then called "clairvoyance." Because of the startling new nature of mesmeric phenomena, public fascination with mesmerism rapidly swept through Europe and America.

Quimby witnessed public demonstrations of mesmerism and decided to try his hand at it. He became so successful as a mesmerist that he gave up his clock-making trade to practice mesmerism full time. Quimby had little formal education but had a very inquisitive mind. He designed a number of experiments to test the theory behind mesmerism and, as a result of his experiments, concluded that the phenomena of mesmerism was produced not by changes in magnetic fields, but rather by mind influencing mind. A similar conclusion had been reached by a royal commission of distinguished scientists in Mesmer's time, but their report dismissed the phenomena as imagination unworthy of further consideration. About the same time Quimby was reaching his conclusions, other mesmerists were arriving at similar conclusions and renaming their work "hypnosis."

But Quimby did not rest in the conclusion that the healing and other effects of mesmerism were just imagination and suggestion. He wanted to know how it was possible for the imagination to have such startling physiological effects and for the mind to communicate seemingly directly with other minds. His reflections led him to the conclusion that mind is substance and the body is, in effect, composed of "thought particles." He came to believe that all illnesses are effects of false opinions. He further came to believe that there is a higher Intelligence or Wisdom that can work through us to correct our errors and thereby heal us.

Quimby's metaphysical and theological theories were an important part of his method. In order to change the patient's belief and produce a cure, he had to change the patient's metaphysical belief from a soul-matter dualism to a spiritual monism. In other words, if the patient believed in physical causes of physical illness, the patient would not believe in mental causes of physical illness and hence would not believe in mental cure for physical illness. By convincing the patient that all cause is spiritual or mental, Quimby could then proceed to work with the patient's beliefs and set up an expectation of healing.

Part of that process involved working with the patient's beliefs about God, salvation, and the meaning of illness.

Many of Quimby's patients believed that God sent illness as punishment for sins or as suffering to prepare them for heaven. Quimby argued that God as loving Father would not send illness for any reason, and therefore the illness must have other causes.

Quimby's religious concept of a higher Intelligence seems to have emerged from the fact that he could go into a "clairvoyant" state and receive information about his patients' feelings and experiences. Evidently, in that state he also experienced guidance for working with his patients and a sense of love as an all-pervading presence. He took the source of this information to be God and Christ, not as beings outside himself but as his own true Self and the true Self of everyone. Quimby came to the conclusion that he was healing people by changing their beliefs, just as Jesus had. The New Thought and Christian Science Christology—Christ as true Self of everyone and Jesus as the historical person who best expressed the Christ—go back directly to P. P. Quimby.

Quimby did not claim to be equal to Jesus, nor to be the second coming of Christ. However two of his disciples, Warren Felt Evans, the first Mind Cure writer, and Mary Baker Eddy, the founder of Christian Science, published opinions about Quimby that compared him favorably to Jesus. Evans wrote that Quimby "seemed to reproduce the wonders of Gospel history."[12] Mary Baker Eddy wrote: "P. P. Quimby stands upon the plane of wisdom with his truth. Christ healed the sick, but not by jugglery or with drugs. As the former speaks as never man before spake and heals as never man healed since Christ, is he not identified with truth, and is not this the Christ which is in him?"[13]

Quimby's students went on to develop modifications of his metaphysical and theological theories and therapies.

Evans developed a concept of three phases of mind: the conscious, the subconscious, and the Christ mind (later called "superconscious" by Fillmore and others). Evans also added Swedenborgian concepts of correspondences between specific spiritual ideas and specific parts of the body. Fillmore developed this approach in his system of the "twelve powers of man." Evans attempted to show similarities among religious and philosophical systems, including Western philosophical idealism, Hindu metaphysics, Hermetic and Kabbalistic esotericism, biblical concepts, Transcendentalism, and others.

Although initially Mrs. Eddy acknowledged Quimby as her healer and teacher, as she began to develop a following, her story changed. She claimed Christian Science as a divine revelation to her, denying that Quimby had any significant influence and claiming that Evans and others stole her ideas. While her diminishment of Quimby's influence seems overstated, she still deserves great credit for her contributions to New Thought. She was the first to perceive and fill the need for an organization to perpetuate the new mental-spiritual therapy. She found ways to simplify and convey the new approach to capture the public's attention. Of Quimby's students, Mrs. Eddy was the most conspicuous in spreading the new ideas.

Two other Quimby disciples, Julius and Anetta Seabury Dresser, also had a significant impact on spreading the new ideas. Feeling that Mrs. Eddy did not give Quimby the credit he deserved, the Dressers began their own teaching and healing practice. When Mrs. Eddy accused them of plagerism, they also began to publish their version of the history of "Mental Science." The Dressers operated as closely as they could to Quimby's ideas and methods. They were also instrumental in organizing New Thought as a movement of independent practitioners and an alternative to the more authoritarian structure of the Christian Science church. Furthermore, the Dressers' sons, Horatio Dresser and David

Seabury, became significant intellectual influences on the developing movement.

Horatio Dresser's works were published in Unity magazines for over 60 years, which indicates he had some influence on the Fillmores and the Unity movement. Dresser's emphasis on the Silence, oneness, mysticism, and his attempts to meld scientific and idealist metaphysical theories have certainly been recurrent themes in Unity literature.

Charles and Myrtle Fillmore's thoughts and practices were influenced not only by the writings of Evans and Eddy, but also by Ursula Gestefeld and Emma Curtis Hopkins. Gestefeld left the Christian Science organization because she could not accept every detail of the doctrines and found Mrs. Eddy's direction of that organization unbearably authoritarian. Hopkins found Evans' universalizing approach more to her liking than the restrictive dogmatism of Mrs. Eddy's Christian Science. Mrs. Hopkins also aligned herself with the goals of traditional mysticism, which emphasizes experiencing or merging with God.

Mrs. Hopkins started her own school and trained not only the Fillmores, but also either trained or strongly influenced many other distinguished New Thought leaders such as the cofounder of the Divine Science Church, Nona L. Brooks; Ernest Holmes, who founded Religious Science; poetess Ella Wheeler Wilcox, and popular New Thought author H. Emilie Cady.[14]

TRADITIONAL AND ESOTERIC INFLUENCES ON CHARLES FILLMORE

As far as I can tell, Charles Fillmore did not reject any of the essential traditional Christian doctrines. It is his interpretations and explanations of those doctrines that have produced some resistance in mainstream Christian theologians and driven self-appointed "cult-hunters" to distraction. Since

Unity students are free to accept or reject both traditional doctrines and Fillmore's interpretations of those doctrines, Unity representatives freely express their own views but are often hestitant to speak for what Unity as a movement believes.

Charles Fillmore believed in the Trinity; Jesus Christ as Lord and Savior; the Virgin birth; the Crucifixion, Resurrection, and Ascension; eternal life, the resurrection of believers, heaven, and hell. Fillmore's interpretations of those doctrines and Unity students' free expression of their own beliefs have provoked resistance to Unity among other Christian sects.[15]

While Fillmore seems to have had some acquaintance with Church history and Christian mysticism, his approach to understanding the Bible was rooted in his Idealist metaphysics and the writings of Swedenborgians, Theosophists, and Rosicrucians. He took the scriptures very seriously as revelations concealing a "spiritual science" for attaining the consciousness and power demonstrated by Jesus Christ. Fillmore not only believed all the miracles attributed to Jesus and the Apostles, but also that following Jesus meant claiming one's own divinity and working through prayer and meditation to reproduce those miracles, including the Ascension. His purpose for metaphysical Bible interpretation was to uncover the spiritual science of raising soul and body to the same state as the ascended Jesus.

As you read Fillmore's work, you will see references to building an immortal body and "regeneration." Fillmore concluded from his personal experiences, his Bible study, and his metaphysical principles that following Jesus all the way meant healing sickness and, ultimately, "ascending." "Ascension," "regeneration," and "building an imperishable body" all meant approximately the same thing to Fillmore. Just as Jesus was no longer visible to his disciples after the

Ascension, those who follow Jesus in building the regenerated-immortal-ascended body would not be visible to those who were still in sense consciousness or "unregenerated" consciousness.

This idea of a regenerated body is pervasive as a goal in Fillmore's writings. There are some, a minority in Unity, who still take this idea seriously. It is certainly not necessary to believe in Fillmore's theory of regeneration to derive insight and benefit from his teachings. Unity students are free to believe what makes the most sense to them on this subject.

How did Charles Fillmore arrive at his approach to the Bible? If one accepts, as Fillmore did, the metaphysical premise that the universe is mind, then ultimately every person and event is understood as consisting of thoughts. If one further accepts the premise that God is Universal Mind, the original source of all ideas, then those ideas can be understood as reflecting the true nature of God. Building on these premises, if the divine nature is revealed through human history, then the Bible can be understood as revealing God Mind. If one takes it that the Bible is an allegorical revelation of God Mind, rather than a literal revelation, one important key to God Mind would then be to understand the allegorical meaning.

Why take the Bible as allegorical, rather than as literal? Fillmore was influenced by a number of factors in his acceptance of the Bible as an allegory. Probably the most significant factor was that New Thought and Christian Science, which so profoundly influenced him, already had established an allegorical interpretation tradition.

Charles Fillmore voraciously studied the esoteric metaphysical writings of the late nineteenth century. Spiritualist, Theosophical, New Thought, and Rosicrucian writers influenced each other to such an extent that at times it is difficult to determine which "school" is being represented. For example, while it was characteristic of New Thought writers to interpret the Bible as allegorically containing principles of spiritual healing, Theosophical writers like John Hamlin Dewey did much the same thing.[16] Dewey and Rosicrucian writer F. B. Dowd advocated ideas about regeneration of the body that Fillmore adopted and reworked in his own books. It was from Dowd's book *The Temple of the Rosycross* that Fillmore got the idea to use the winged globe as the symbol for Unity School.[17]

Those metaphysical groups had been influenced, mainly through Swedenborg, by a tradition of allegorical interpretation in Church history that goes back at least to Philo Judaeus of Alexandria, a Jewish philosopher who was a contemporary of Jesus.

Early Christian theology was heavily influenced by Philo's approach. Clement of Alexandria, Origen,[18] and Augustine of Hippo[19] who, like Philo, lived in North Africa, followed Philo's perspective on the Bible. Allegorical interpretation was common place among Christian theologians up through the late Middle Ages and into the Reformation period. The attempt to take the Bible as literally as possible emerged after the Reformation[20] and so is actually a fairly recent development.

Another significant factor that led Swedenborg, Fillmore, and others to allegorical Bible interpretation was the emergence of scientific theories and discoveries during the Reformation era that opposed the literal biblical view of the universe. Scientific cosmology shifted from the view that the earth was the center of the solar system to the view that the sun was the center. On the basis of such biblical passages as the story of God making the sun stand still for Joshua, both the Catholic and Protestant branches of Christianity resisted the Copernican theory. The Church also resisted the scientific claim that the sun existed before the earth, which claim directly contradicted the biblical creation story in Genesis 1. More significantly, the new scientific perspective described a cosmos that evolved and moved according to physical laws rather than by the direct intervention of God.

The scientific concepts of evolution and law are prominent in Charles Fillmore's writings. His metaphysical interpretation of the Bible allowed him to accept scientific truths without rejecting the Truth of the Bible. He took the concept of evolution and interpreted the Bible as an allegory for human consciousness evolving from a "fallen" state to a divine state. He took the concept of law and applied it to the Bible as an allegory for spiritual and mental laws. The concept of the Bible as allegory for human consciousness anticipated the theory of Carl Jung that human mythology symbolizes primordial archetypes in the collective unconscious of humanity. The concept of mental and spiritual laws foreshadowed developments in physics that have led some physicists to postulate that the universe is more like a Great Mind than a Great Machine.[21] Since the roots of the ideas found in Fillmore's writings can be found in nineteenth-century religious literature, one might well ask, "In what sense is Fillmore an *innovative* religious thinker?" In essence, Fillmore's genius was the ability to synthesize and systemitize without dogmatizing. He found ways to take ideas from the seemingly incompatable thought worlds of science, Christian tradition, occult religion, and philosophical idealism and tie them together in a coherent and intelligible world view. He was able to communicate that world view to a fairly wide range of people in terms of practical application to issues of health, prosperity, and happiness.

Even though Fillmore had a strong conviction that his views were true, he made no attempt to dogmatically impose his views on his students. He attracted students through the spiritual healing work that he did with his wife Myrtle, and they no doubt could have insisted on "orthodoxy" as Mrs. Eddy had done with her followers. Instead, the Fillmores challenged their students to find their own authority and accept only what they could demonstrate in their own experience. That freedom of thought and pragmatic epistemology still thrives in the Unity movement today.

Fillmore's writings should be read in the spirit in which they were written, as expressed in one of his favorite passages from Paul: "Whatsoever things are true, whatsoever things are honest, whatsoever things are just, whatsoever things are pure, whatsoever things are lovely, whatsoever things are of good report; if there be any virtue, and if there be any praise, think on these things" (Phil. 4:8 KJV). You may find it beneficial to contemplate the ideas that seem true to you. I hope you will try some of the prayer, meditation, and other practical ideas that appeal to you. I believe you will discover, as many have, that there will be very positive effects on your feelings, your experiences, and your health.

CRITERIA FOR SELECTION OF ARTICLES

The chapters and articles contained in this collection were chosen on the basis of three criteria: range, accessibility, and practicality.

I have attempted to include articles that represent the full range of Fillmore's theology and metaphysics. By "full range," I do not mean every topic and idea Fillmore ever wrote about, but rather every recurrent theme and fundamental idea.

Furthermore, I have tried to select the most accessible, the clearest, and best-written pieces on each subject. Fillmore spoke and wrote for almost 60 years. He wrote monthly articles for almost the full extent of those years, and nine books were published under his name in that time. Most of the selections in this volume are taken from the books, because in my judgment his books do represent his best and most significant work. If Fillmore or the editors of Unity Books had thought that some other of Fillmore's magazine articles gave a better representation of his thought, surely they would have used those articles or published another work containing them. There is a great deal of interest to be found in Fillmore's magazine articles that has not been published in his books. For the most part, however, no significant new ground is covered in those articles.

Finally, I have selected what seem to me the most practical articles. I have tried to include articles that give practical advice on working with thought and principles to improve one's experience. I have, for the most part, avoided articles that dwell on detailed Bible interpretation or cosmological explanation. The exceptions, of course, are the articles that deal with the topics of Bible interpretation and cosmology.

My aim in collecting these articles in one volume is to provide an overview of Charles Fillmore's thought and some of his best writing. My hope is that this particular collection will be of use to those just beginning their study of Unity, those who have long been studying Unity, those who have an interest in religious studies, and those who are simply curious about this relatively new spiritual movement called "Unity."

Part One

EPISTEMOLOGY: HOW TO KNOW THE TRUTH

EPISTEMOLOGY: HOW TO KNOW THE TRUTH

WHAT IS TRUTH? How can we know? What is the nature of knowledge? Are there limits to what we can know? Philosophers have been attempting to answer these and related questions for thousands of years. From these questions have emerged mathematics and science. The study of these questions is the area of philosophy called epistemology. Every area of knowledge has epistemological aspects. Charles Fillmore's metaphysics also has an epistemological aspect, and that is the theme of this first section of articles.

Science, as a description of nature, involves a method for obtaining knowledge that is based on metaphysical premises. Science maintains that the universe is lawlike, as opposed to consisting of purely random events; this is one metaphysical premise of science. Another premise is that the universe is physical, consisting of objects moving in space and time, as opposed to consisting of, for example, dreams or mental projections. Science observes objects and events to discover laws. In science, the observer participates in events by setting up conditions for observation. In observing the subatomic level of nature, scientists must bombard and move some particles with other particles, thus changing what is observed by the very act of observation. Thus the scientific epistemological ideal of an uninvolved observer is unobtainable. Still, the scientific method has produced a wide range of useful results, which we call scientific knowledge.

Psychology uses scientific method, but the nature of psychological study has two aspects that force modification of methods used in physics, chemistry, and other natural sciences. Psychology involves reports of subjective, unobservable states, and so to some extent psychology relies on verbal reports of the "objects" of study. Natural scientists do not ask their objects of study to tell how they feel or what they believe. The second problematic aspect of psychological study is that many of its elements of study are not reducible to physical states and events. Psychologists are concerned with beliefs, desires, and emotions, which must be stated in natural language rather than in terms of mathematically measurable terms like *mass, length, velocity,* and so on. Thus physical behavior and physiological states cannot be directly correlated with psychological states. Psychology can discover and report probabilities, but it cannot discover "laws" of the type found in physical sciences.[1]

Epistemology for philosophical metaphysics is even more problematic than psychological epistemology, for metaphysics attempts to describe the universe in the most general categories. Metaphysical descriptions must account for the nature of being, both physical and psychological. Furthermore, metaphysics is concerned with the existence and nature of God and so must have a *theological* epistemology as well. These complications for the scientific understanding of metaphysics make the notion of metaphysical knowledge seem unobtainable and tempt us to relegate metaphysics to the category of mere speculation.

For about 2000 years, metaphysicians and theologians relied on two basic methods to obtain metaphysical knowledge: Socratic and Aristotelian.

The Socratic method attempts to draw knowledge from the soul by means of asking questions. The presupposition of this method is that the soul contains, in memory from various incarnations or in the soul's basic structure, the knowledge sought. Socrates believed in reincarnation and soul memory of truth experienced while not in a body. He believed that this knowledge could be remembered by a process of asking questions, attempting answers, questioning the answers, and so forth, until one arrives at an answer that satisfies all questions.[2] This dialectical method is helpful in arriving at mutually agreed upon definitions and in revealing beliefs and other psychological states and events. However, Socratic dialectic, to the degree it relies on observations of the world, is less precise that the scientific method and so subject to false conclusions based on faulty observations.

The Aristotelian method, like the Socratic method, attempts to identify and define basic categories and terms. However, rather than attempting to draw memories from the soul, the Aristotelian method attempts to logically deduce truths from general observations. But again, Aristotelian thinkers made general observations of the world without a method as precise as the scientific method. Consequently, many of their general observations were faulty and so their deductions were unsound.

In the seventeenth-century C.E., the English philosopher Francis Bacon proposed new models for knowledge in science and metaphysics. Bacon critiqued the Aristotelian method as jumping too quickly to conclusions based on imprecise observations. Bacon advocated specialized, careful, detailed, inductive observation of nature. His proposals, refined and acted upon by others, became the basis of modern science. Bacon also proposed that understanding of metaphysical categories could only be attained after the other sciences had accumulated extensive accurate knowledge. Bacon also maintained that extensive knowledge of history, society, and psychology would be necessary to draw conclusions about metaphysics. His basic idea is that knowledge of nature must precede knowledge of metaphysics. He wrote:

> Let the investigation of forms, which are . . . eternal and immutable, constitute *Metaphysics*; and let investigation of . . . (all of which have reference to the common and ordinary course of nature . . .) constitute *Physics*. And to these let there be subordinate two practical divisions: to Physics, *Mechanics*; to Metaphysics, what (in a purer sense of the word) I call *Magic*, on account of the broadness of the ways it moves in, and its greater command over nature.[3]

In the nineteenth-century c.e., a philosophy called pragmatism and instrumentalism emerged. The pragmatists—notably C. S. Peirce, William James, and John Dewey—advocated a view of knowledge based on what works in experience. They argued that the success of the scientific method was based on its applicability to experience and that the criteria of results in experience could be applied to semantics, ethics, theology, and metaphysics.

Charles Fillmore's epistemology is very much in the spirit of the Baconian and pragmatic approaches to knowledge. Fillmore drew his conclusions from experimentation with and observation of his own psychological states in relation to his own physical states and experiences. When he spoke of his teachings as "practical Christianity," he meant that his propositions about theological and metaphysical truths could be demonstrated to be true in personal experience. That is also why he thought of his approach to religion as "scien-

tific." Furthermore, Fillmore held that concepts about God
and metaphysics must be consistent with observations of
science and the spiritual *experiences* of people of all faiths. I
emphasize the word *experiences* because Fillmore did not hold
that all religious dogma or beliefs must be in agreement. His
primary concern was to explain experiences and reconcile
them with scientific and metaphysical theories. He was not
trying to convince people that all religious beliefs are true.

Fillmore's epistemological ideas can be observed in the
articles included in this first section.

The first article, "Not an Answer, but an Opportunity," was
written in 1894 in response to a critique of a fellow New
Thoughter. The article is noteworthy for two reasons: (1) it
indicates Fillmore's instinctive, pragmatic approach to semantics—if the terms used in discussions have no practical
consequence in experience, it makes no practical difference
which term is used (note that for Fillmore, there was a practical difference regarding which terms he used), and (2) the
article contains Fillmore's account of how he began his inner
quest for the Truth about God. The passage in this article
where Fillmore says, "In this babel I will go to headquarters,"
is rightfully famous among Unity students. Here we see that
silent receptivity to intuitions from Divine Mind is a key element of Fillmore's epistemology.

The second article, "The Pure Reason and Honest Logic of
Practical Christianity," was written in 1918 and expresses
Fillmore's reconciliation of deductive and inductive logic in
metaphysics. The essential points in this article can be sum-
marized as follows: (1) "pure reason" deduces from the nature of First Cause, which is known intuitively; (2) God is
First Cause, All-Good, All Life, Intelligent Principle of the
universe; (3) holding to the Truth about God in thought and
words links us with God, produces harmony in experience,
and gives us a causative power of our own; (4) holding

thoughts and words in opposition to God's attributes produces inharmonious conditions; (5) since God is the Real, thoughts and conditions opposed to God's attributes are false and unreal; (6) these propositions and this way of reasoning from First Cause to personal experience are true *because* thinking this way produces the practical effects of health, happiness, and harmony. In other words, the propositions and logic are true, not purely as a matter of deduction but primarily as a matter of experience or induction.

Fillmore's claims about ancient schools indicate his interest in esoteric religious writings of his time and suggest a fascinating area for historical research. However, he unfortunately does not document his claims here and so that aspect of the article does not support his views and must be considered a rhetorical device. His claim that the propositions and mode of reasoning are supported by practical demonstration in experience is not really rooted in ancient history, but rather in his own healing experiences.

The next article, "Faith Precipitations," is from *Atom-Smashing Power of Mind* and first appeared in a *Unity Magazine* article in 1946. This article is included in this section for two reasons: (1) it describes Fillmore's own experience of metaphysical healing, which was a significant factor in his "pragmatic" approach to epistemology, and (2) it indicates the way Fillmore used scientific analogy in discussing metaphysics. It is also interesting to note that Fillmore described the regeneration of his leg in terms of electricity, since there is some evidence that changes in electrical patterns are involved in the regeneration of limbs of creatures like the salamander ("naturally occurring") and frogs (artificially induced by scientists).[4]

Fillmore's internal physical sensations of "electricity" and the visible evidence of the regeneration of his leg were important factors in his conclusion that the body could be completely regenerated and thereby never die. This idea of regeneration shows up in "Faith Precipitations," "Unity of Religion and Science," and many other chapters of this book. The idea of body regeneration is the speculation of a spiritual visionary. Space flight, submarines, and cloning were once science fiction. Genetic engineering to extend life is now a scientific speculation that may, nevertheless, eventually be achieved. Perhaps Fillmore's speculation should not be arbitrarily dismissed. Even if the body cannot be made immortal through prayer and meditation, it may be that life could ultimately be greatly extended through mental and spiritual disciplines.

"Unity of Religion and Science" was an address Fillmore gave to the 1933 World Fellowship of Faiths in Chicago. Here we see Fillmore's vision of a coherent epistemology for metaphysics, based on insights from both science and religion.

Chapter 1

NOT AN ANSWER, BUT AN OPPORTUNITY (1894)

J N A QUESTION in the October number [of *Thought* magazine], I referred to the possibilities of accomplishment through the "Word of Faith." In an article headed "Not a Criticism but a Correction," in the issue of *Freedom* dated Nov. 7th, Helen Wilmans objects to my use of the words God, Father, etc., therein. She says, "Why not credit the power spoken of to *man's* creativeness and the source of supply to nature instead of God?"

Mrs. Wilmans' criticism is very kindly in tone and does not demand an answer, because anyone can see that we differ in the use of words only. However, it gives me an opportunity to say that a great deal hinges on *Words*, and their use is worthy [of] our careful consideration.

Three factors are involved in every manifestation from formless to form, viz: understanding, image and will. Man as a whole is Mind, and he evolves his environments through the impulse of the will working upon ideas or mental images. The images or ideas we entertain are the patterns upon which we build our world and all things in it. Thus the one important factor is the character of the pattern. The

Lord told Moses to make all things according to the "pattern shown in the mount"—state of high understanding.

The spoken word is in itself a mere effect—a vibration of the ether—but it is associated with certain ideas which are called up in the mind when the word is articulated. For instance, the word *water*, if spoken to a Chippewa Indian, would not call up the image of a transparent liquid, because that image is reflected onto his mentality only when he hears or thinks of the word *minne*. Thus the image of a thing with its various qualities and *limitations* is established in the mind of each individual by education. Now Mrs. Wilmans wants me to say "Nature" instead of "the Father." She says: "God is not intelligence; God or the principle of life (ignorantly and unscientifically called God) is the Law of Attraction existing in intelligence and one with it. Intelligence is the *manifestation* of the law. Therefore all visible substance is intelligence or mind."

This may do very well for Mrs. Wilmans, who has educated herself to image or mentally see life, love, wisdom, etc., when the word *nature* is formulated, but the race has not been so educated. Nature is the name of the "blind force" of the materialistic school and will carry to the average mentality just such an image.

When I say that all things are waiting my Word of Faith when sent forth into the bounteous bosom of the Omnipresent Father-Mother, I see in imagination a loving parent; I am thrilled through and through with a living presence and I know in my soul that the very atmosphere about me is luminous with intelligence. I feel no such presence when I invoke *nature*; on the contrary a cold, hard, lonely feeling sweeps over me and I seem alone in a wilderness of blind forces with no star to guide me. Grant that this is all in my own mind, and that we get just what we recognize, would not my image evolve the preferable consciousness?

But I would go further than this—I would affirm that what I call the Father has conscious existence as the Principle of Wisdom (the Mother Principle is Love), and what I feel is not only that Principle within me recognizing its own, but also the Oversoul without springing to meet my desire. That Oversoul is not a principle that has to come forth from "intelligent principle" to "conscious intelligence," but it now holds this planetary system and all things, In the mighty arms of an intelligence that is conscious as we are conscious. Who can for a moment contemplate the order and harmony of the visible heavens and then doubt that a being is at work who guides it all with an omnipotent hand that *knows*—as we know in degree.

I am satisfied that all making manifest of that which is potential in the Principle of Being is done through man, and I will for convenience call this Omnipresent Oversoul the Larger Man. Now man as represented by our human race is an infant in the realization of his true status in Being, and when guided alone by his impulses his path seems rugged—we call it learning by experience.

But there is a shorter, easier way than this. This way is the recognition by each of us that there is an Oversoul, a consciousness universal to everyone on this planet, that knows the road and when its guidance is daily asked will point out the very shortest possible route.

The recognition of this Oversoul does not in any way nulify the universal law that every man gets only what he recognizes or affirms. The Oversoul does not *give* man anything, but it does through its Wisdom, or Father power, point the way so that man avoids many hard experiences in demonstrating the inherent powers of the God-man.

But we should not overlook one important factor in existence—the freedom of every man. We are free to "go it alone," or ask for guidance, just as we prefer, and we get exactly what we ask for, and in exact proportion to the persistency and patience with which we ask. I have in a measure proven this in my own experience, and it may not be out of place to mention here that portion pertaining to my acquaintance with the Oversoul.

To begin with, I was not biased on the God question by an orthodox education. Born and raised in the wilderness of the west, my religious education was quite limited. God was an unknown factor in my conscious mind and always has been until the past few years. I was always drawn to the mysterious and occult, however, and in youth took great interest in Spiritualism and, afterward, in branches of the Hermetic philosophy.

Seven years ago I had my first instruction in Christian Science. I was much interested and took lessons of all the different schools. For a time I was mentally disturbed by the many conflicting statements about Truth, who had it, etc., made by the various teachers. The muddle was so deep that for a time I was inclined to ridicule, yet I could not get away from the evidence of a great power back of the flood of contradictory statements. Neither could I understand why there should be so many divisions and schools, and such assortment of opinions about an exact science. I noticed, however, that all the teachers and writers talked a great deal about the omnipresent, omniscient God, who is Spirit and accessible to everyone. I said to myself, In this babel I will go to headquarters. If I am Spirit and this God they talk so much about is Spirit, we can somehow communicate, or the whole thing is a fraud.

I then commenced sitting in the silence every night at a certain hour and tried to get in touch with God. There was no enthusiasm about it; no soul desire, but cold calculating business method. I was there on time every night and tried in all conceivable ways to realize that my mind was in touch with the Supreme Mind. In this cold, intellectual attitude one can easily understand why I did not seem to get any conscious result, but I kept at it month after month, mentally affirming words that others told me would open the way, until it got to be a habit and I rather enjoyed it. However, a time came when I began to observe that I was having exceedingly realistic dreams. For months I paid no attention to them, my business at the time being of the earth earthy—buying and selling real estate. The first connection that I remember to have observed between the dreams and my affairs was after closing the purchase of a piece of property. I remembered that I had dreamed the whole transaction some months before. After that I watched my dreams closely and found that there was a wider intelligence manifesting in my sleep than I seemed to possess in the waking state, and it flashed over me one day that this was the mode of communication that had been established in response to my desire for information from Headquarters. This has been kept up ever since with growing interest on my part, and I could fill a large book with my experiences. Everything which it is necessary for me to know is shown to me and I have times without number been saved from false steps by this monitor. Again and again I have had mapped out the future along certain lines for months and years ahead, and the prophecies have so far never failed, although I have sometimes misinterpreted the symbols which are used.

My friends have often said to me: "If you can so clearly see the future, why not make it financially profitable by taking advantage of the rise and fall of real estate, stocks, etc.?" In my ignorance this same thought was mine until I learned that the law of God is no respecter of persons. To ask or use the higher Wisdom to get away [help gain] the possessions of my fellows would surely be travesty on justice. God assists no one to take advantage of another in the selfish competition of the world. Yet there are undeveloped resources in the Universal Storehouse and the promise is that "All that the Father hath is mine." They who cleanse their minds from the selfish and limited ideas of the world shall become so at-one with the Universal Wisdom that they will realize this Truth so practically that their every wish shall be gratified in ways that transcend all so-called established laws. This is promised me when I, as "Joseph the Dreamer," realize that I am one with my dreams and thus disappear into the next degree of consciousness—Jesus Christ. This completes the genealogy from Adam asleep to Adam awake, and the God-Man stands revealed.

I can distinguish no difference between my symbolic dreams and those of Jacob, Joseph, and other Bible characters. This is one of the many ways by which the Lord, or Higher Consciousness, communicates with the lower, and is just as operative today as it was centuries ago. This, however, is *a* way and not the *only* way. I know many people who are in communication with the Lord through direct inspiration. I also have this to an extent but have not found it so reliable as the dream state on account of the ever active intellect thrusting in its limited perceptions.

I write in the first person and give these details of my experience in finding the Lord in order that others who are looking outside themselves may take heart and know that He is the indwelling presence of their souls, and that they can communicate with Him in more ways than one. My experience has satisfied me that there is an Oversoul, or Universal Spirit, whose relation is similar to that of our parents—with intelligence, love, and power indefinitely extended. The point of contact between it and man is the mind, and the mental attitude of every individual locates him in conscious touch with this Universal Wisdom, or ignorant of its presence. Man is perfectly free to recognize the

Lord and know Him through the mind, or he is just as free to deny His existence and be void of such knowledge.

When man aspires to know the Lord and asks for the higher guidance, and at the same time shows a willingness to drop his own narrow personality and come into the broader views of the Spirit, he finds that instead of the Lord being a ruler over him, He is his servant. "Not I but the Father in me, he doeth the works," said Jesus, and so every man that willingly lays down his narrow personal prejudices and circumscribed ideas, discovers that he really has nothing to do of himself—he has but to quietly, gently *know* the right relation of things in the Silence of his own Spirit, and the Oversoul does the work, just as Jesus said.

I see clearer every day that the existence of this Universal Father must be made manifest in the lives of those who claim to know Him. Doctrines and arguments have ceased to be operative. If I have found God I must demonstrate God; and to do this I shall have no time to worry about what my brother is doing. I shall cease to be a reformer—if by that is meant one who is in the arena *battling* for the right—because the Spirit does not battle for anything. The Spirit demonstrates Truth as it goes along, and its fruits are love and peace. Men and women from the so-called best to the very worst are doing as well as they know how. If they are doing ill it is because they are ignorant of a better way, for if they knew better they would certainly do better. Everyone does what he thinks will bring the best results. If I can show him a better way and *demonstrate it in my life,* I shall have his attention. If my way is a theory, based upon argument or traditional authority, it will meet with doubt and tardy recognition.

But the world is ready for demonstrations. The people are eagerly looking for those who can *prove* in actual works the presence of the indwelling Spirit.

The more I study humanity the more clearly I see that they are all seeking Truth. I have never had any trouble in finding a ready market for the little Truth which I have put forth. I find that we are not living in an age of bigotry and intolerance. People are free and are earnestly seeking the right road. All that is needed is a piling up of evidence in works, by those who claim to have the Truth. . . .

As for myself I refuse to [any] longer consider life a struggle or a battle. I am not opposing any[thing], nor have I any opposition. If this doctrine which I advocate is true it will prove [itself] in my works. If it is not true I can never make it so by argument. But the Father has shown me that I can demonstrate its highest claims in my life and affairs. I have faith to believe that I can because I have in a measure done so, and the end is not yet.

Chapter 2

THE PURE REASON AND HONEST LOGIC OF PRACTICAL CHRISTIANITY (1918)

"THERE IS NOTHING NEW under the sun." Modern metaphysics is merely a revival of the philosophies taught by the wise of an almost forgotten past. The principles that underlie existence are being again brought to the attention of men. The race is again entering the cycle of knowledge, and we catch once more the light of pure reason and honest logic.

But few people have come into the light, therefore, as yet, pure reason is an almost unknown quantity. Consequently, when strict deductive methods are introduced into religion and logical conclusions are reached from a stated premise, the average believer is at sea. Church people have been taught that certain relations exist arbitrarily, no matter how opposed these relations may be to the logic necessary to cause and effect.

In order to arrive at a mutually harmonious and correct conclusion, the result of a logical argument, we must have a premise or point of beginning upon which we can all agree.

Logic in its strictest sense is the only accurate method by which we can arrive at truth, and that system of philosophy or religious doctrine which does not admit of the rules of perfect logic in reaching its conclusions from a stated premise, must be outside the pale of pure reason and in the realm of man-made dogma. *Logic* and *logos* are almost synonymous terms, and the highest Scriptural authorities tell us that all things were made by the *logos*—ratio—reason, and *oratio, word* or *speech*. Hence the *word* of *reason* or the *reasonable word* is the very foundation of the universe. Therefore to know accurately about the reality of things, we must disregard all appearances as indicated by the five senses, and go into *pure reason*—the Spirit from which was created everything that has permanent existence.

Practical Christianity and Truth stand upon the same foundation and are interchangeable terms. Practical Christianity is not a theory having origin in the human mind; nor is it a revelation to humanity from some prophet whose word alone must be taken as unquestioned authority. It is in this respect totally different from the other religious systems of the world, because it does not in any respect rest its authority upon revelation. It has no dogmas nor creeds, nor are its students expected to believe anything which they cannot logically demonstrate to be true. Thus it is the only system of religion before the people today which because of a universal appeal to pure reason in man, can be applied and accepted by every nation under the sun.

It takes as the basis of its doctrine a fundamental truth that is known alike by savage and civilized, and from that truth, by cold, deductive reasoning, arrives at each and every one of the conclusions which are presented. Thus it does not in any manner partake of the popular idea of religion, as a vague something which has to be accepted on faith and which must be believed regardless of inconsistencies. On the contrary, it invites the closest mental scrutiny, and the analytical logician will find a new world open to him in following the sequential deductions which this science of pure reasoning evolves.

This system of deductions from intuitively ascertained facts is not new, nor are its conclusions new, for the historian tells us that similar methods of arriving at the fundamental truth of things were in vogue thousands of years ago. And long before the historical period, legend and tradition report the existence of temples where pure reason was taught. History also tells of similar schools that existed five thousand years before Christ.

It is recorded that before entering these ancient schools the student was required to drop his preconceived notions and prejudices, that he might learn to think freely from cause to effect, entirely disregarding the phenomenal world and all of its testimonies. To "beware of the illusions of sense" was enjoined upon all who were seeking Truth, and the same law holds good today. You will find, if you are faithful in following the line of argument here presented, that a principle will be disclosed to you which will demonstrate itself in an unmistakable manner. The logical deductions from the premise stated may not come to your full comprehension at once, because of certain intellectual limitations into which the race has plunged itself. Men have been so long divorced from logic and pure reason that they are confused when a clear-cut proposition is stated and carried to a conclusion along the lines of perfect sequence. To think in an independent, untrammeled way about anything, is foreign to the habit of the races of the Occident. Our lines of thought and act are based upon precedent and arbitrary authority. We boast much of our freedom and independence, but the facts are that we defer to custom and tradition. Our whole civilization is based upon man-made opinions. We have never thought for ourselves in religion, consequently we do not know how to think accurately and consecutively upon any proposition. We have not been trained to draw conclusions each for himself from a universal pivotal Truth, and consequently we are not competent to pass judgment upon any statement so predicated. Our manner of deciding whether or not certain statements are true or false is to apply the mental bias with which heredity, religion or social custom has environed us, or else fly to some man-made record as authority.

In the study of Practical Christianity all such temporary proofs of Truth are swept aside as chaff. We entertain nothing in our statements of Truth that does not stand the most searching analysis, nothing that cannot be practically demonstrated.

In order to carry on an intelligent, rational line of argument, it is necessary to find a mutual starting point which is universally accepted as true. There may be many pivotal points chosen from an intellectual standpoint that would doubtless be accepted as reasonably true, but upon close analysis they will usually be found resting upon another and anterior so-called truth. For instance, we might agree that ponderable objects always fall toward the earth, yet the question quickly arises, "What causes them to fall?" The ready answer is, "Gravity, of course." "But what is gravity?" Thus we are led back and back until we are lost in First Cause, or God. So in agreeing upon a statement as the basis of an argument of universal nature, we must be careful to get one that has no anterior. There can be but one basis of being, and consequently but one basis of being's movements and forms. This basis is First Cause, or God. When we have fully agreed that everything of which we are cognizant can be traced in its last analysis to God, and no farther, we have a basis upon which to rest a doctrine that cannot be successfully opposed; its deductions are logical and they can be demonstrated. This is exactly what is claimed for this Science of Christ: that it is not only a system of philosophy which cannot be disputed by the rational mind, but that it also demonstrates in the world of phenomena that its conclusions are true.

Now, having decided upon God, or Primal Cause, as the basis of our system, the next step is to decide upon the nature of this Primal Cause. It is safe to assert that in all the world not a single person of intelligence can be found who would say that God is anything but good. It requires no exhaustive reasoning to arrive at this conclusion, for it is the ready response of the intuitive faculty of all mankind, which it is always safe to count as correct. Even those who think that evil actually exists as a principle, claim that God is *All-Good* but that He allows His opposite, the devil, to possess part of His kingdom to accomplish certain ends.

Having agreed that God, or the Primal Cause of all things, is the only safe basis on which to predicate an argument that deals with life in all its sinuous windings, and that the nature of that First Cause must necessarily be only good, we can by logical deduction evolve a doctrine that must of necessity be universal in its application.

It is sometimes thought that man should not attempt to find out the nature of God, because He is so far above and beyond comprehension of the finite that such attempts are sacrilegious folly. Yet when carefully analyzed it is found that the one aim and end of man's existence is to find God. The source of life is the great mystery which has commanded the closest attention and study of men in all ages, and as that source must be the Infinite, it is thus ever inviting man to comprehend it.

The Bible says, "No man hath seen God at any time," and our physical scientists all agree that primordial life, or First

Cause, is invisible or spiritual, exhibiting itself as an intelligent force. Hence, as corollary to the statement that God, or First Cause, is *good*, we also assert that He is Spirit.

Having established a basis grounded in irrefutable truth, from which deductions may be drawn in an infinite number of directions, the next very natural question that presents itself is, "What good can come to man from a study of God?"

It requires no deep thinking to perceive that as God is the source of all *good* and all *life*, in no other direction can man find that for which his heart longs. Yet so material are the concepts of men that the foregoing question is frequently asked. The intellect also questions whether or not the finite can ever comprehend the Infinite, and consequently doubts the usefulness of such study. The facts are that the only good that has come to this world has been through the study of God, notwithstanding that the preponderance of that study has been of a nature to preclude the discovery of God or His mode of manifestation. People have been taught that God is a personal being who rules the universe much after the manner of an arbitrary monarch. This erroneous and contracted teaching has led to a belittlement of God in the concepts of men and they have imaged a man-god, and have also formed a "graven image" of God, who is Spirit.

The true concept of God is that He is the intelligent Principle of the universe, and, like all principles, totally impartial in His expressions. This is the concept of God which has come to us in this awakening age, but it is not new; the wise old sages of the Orient tell us that their ancestors thousands of years ago, in secret temples dedicated to the study of God, or the Primal Cause of all, found that in certain stages of high understanding, the result of systematic training, they came into such harmonious relations with this Primal Principle, or First Cause, that they were endowed with causing power themselves. They did not seek God for the sake of the power over things which might thereby accrue to them, but that they might have wisdom and understanding of the good. They found that by thinking right thoughts and living unselfishly, they awakened new faculties within themselves. They sought the good, or God, and in harmony with the law by which like attracts like, the good, or God, sought them. They found that when they came into right relations with the good, they had apparently supernatural powers. They discovered what Jesus Christ called "the kingdom of God within," and all things were thereby added unto them. They caused, so tradition and certain records say, rain or sunshine, heat or cold, and produced at will all the fruits and flowers of the field. These records state that they could also fly through the air, having acquired an understanding of that which lies back of gravity. They, in short, controlled all the so-called forces of nature by the word or thought, and proved conclusively that we become like that which we study. They studied Cause and became masters of the world of effects.

They found that by coming into interior relations with the invisible Cause, they were moved by it to give expression both in thought and speech to certain words, and that when those words were so expressed by them, wonderful transformations took place in their surroundings. The conditions which they had always assumed to be impossible of variation from what are known as the laws of nature, were in the twinkling of an eye set at naught. They had always believed that sickness, decay, and death were part of an immutable law; yet they found that certain words, which are in harmony with the pivotal Truth that First Cause, or God, is Spirit and All-Good, heal the sick, make happy the sorrowful and fill the coffers of the poor.

They thus found that this invisible Principle is pure intelligence, and that it expresses itself *only* in the words or thoughts that produce happy results. They also found that the

words which work such wonders in transforming their surroundings, always represent those qualities which by deductive reasoning they found can only originate in a Being or
Principle of goodness. Thus they not only knew God as All-
Good through the intuitive faculty, but they proved Him so
by demonstrating that He responds *only* to those attributes
that are representative of the good. Hence these words they
called *words of Truth* or *Reality*. On the other hand they found
that certain other words or thoughts that do not correspond
to or harmonize with the attributes of a primal cause of good,
produce conditions of inharmony. Under their expression
people become sick, sorrowful, and generally unhappy.

Through spiritual illumination, by comparison, logical deduction, and practical demonstration, they definitely arrived
at words of Truth and their opposites, or words of error.
They knew that the words of Truth must proceed from the
cause to which they correspond and consequently must be
the Real; and that, as they could find no tenable point of origin for the opposites or words of error, they necessarily classified them as the unreal, the nothings, the dropping away
from the one Principle of the Universe.

They arranged and classified their words of *Reality* and *unreality* as the electrician of our day classifies the positive and
the negative poles of electrical action. In the realm of mind,
the effect of the expressed words of Truth is fully as forcible
as is the positive pole of the battery in the realm of electricity. The effect of words is an exact science, and it can be
demonstrated as such by all who will study it assiduously. It
is the science of life, and upon its understanding hinges the
happiness or unhappiness of man's existence. It is not a science whose laws were discovered and arbitrarily classified by
those metaphysicians of the past. On the contrary, it is universal in its unfoldment and application. Every man works
in its laboratory every day of his life, and is using its princi-

ples with every thought he thinks and every word he speaks; he uses the law whether he knows it or not. Hence no one should be ignorant of the effects which the manipulation of these hidden forces produce in the character and surroundings of each child of earth.

This is the science of the higher metaphysics. Not the metaphysics of a certain school of these latter days of whom Carpenter and Lewis are representatives, who claim that mind is a product of the brain as bile is of the liver. That these metaphysicians are strictly on the mortal plane, is clearly evidenced in the vague and irreconcilable literature which their hazy theories have produced. Pure Christianity is a spiritual doctrine, and it does not permit a material interpretation of its character. In its purity it is *one* with the underlying cause of all that *is,* and it admits of no differences among those who understand it. The modes of teaching it may vary, as do the characteristics of each teacher; but all its teachers must necessarily present the same Truth, though their words and illustrations may differ. So each individual needs but to be given the key in order to unlock for himself the entire metaphysical plan of the universe.

The Principle of Being is not only *All-Good,* but it is *All-Intelligence.* It is the fount of your intelligence, and when you study it you will find yourself becoming one with the principle of all wisdom. Thus to be one with the principle of All-Intelligence is to *know,* and when you *know* you will find yourself so broad in judgment and understanding that you will have charity for all who differ from you in religion, metaphysics, or even politics.

This system of metaphysics is but another name for universal Truth, and it consequently covers the therapeutic, ethical, and religious departments of life.

Metaphysical therapeutics treats of healing by an understanding of the reality of things. It does not in its exact meaning teach how to heal diseases by the power of thought; it teaches how, by the power of thought, false conceptions may be eradicated and the Divine Reality brought into manifestation, showing forth in health and harmony. This department attracts the majority of people, because of the great need of healing.

Ethics in the curriculum of metaphysics shows the student how the moral world may be reformed. It teaches him how he may be wise and happy by holding in mind certain thoughts that will bring about these conditions. It shows him how he may attain his ideal ends in reforming society. It shows him how a dull, stupid, or ignorant mind may be quickened morally and brightened intellectually by the power of right thinking.

The religion of metaphysics includes all these and adds to them a certain and sure knowledge of man's immortality and divine relation. The religion of metaphysics is its crowning principle—it is this department that places it in the category of science, and there is no other religious doctrine before the western world today which can claim and demonstrate that it is based on scientific principle. This religion is a science—the science of life—and it will so demonstrate itself to the student, both logically and practically. When you understand it in its religious aspect you know your true relation to the Creator, and just what that relation must lead to. You get a revelation of your status as a living soul that is impregnable in its logic, and you are brought into such close relation with the Divine Cause that you know intuitively that you are not of the flesh but of God.

But it is in its therapeutic department that man is most interested. He has one or more of the many thousand ills that the mortal is heir to, and he seeks help. He has sought in vain for a panacea among the physicians, and as a last resort flies to metaphysics. For this reason the primary course in this line of study deals largely with the cure of bodily ills. In its higher aspects it translates the body into spiritual ideas, and proves itself by regulating every department of life. Nothing is too small or insignificant for its uplifting presence. It is not a theory of life; it is life itself, and it is the harmonious manifestation of life. Those who have honestly studied it and applied its rules in their daily work, will tell you that it has made them over physically, mentally, and morally. They will tell you that they are better men and women; that life has new zest for them, and that they can now do good and help others where before they were powerless.

Yet they will also tell you that they were not able to make this science fit into their old theories and incoherent vagaries in matters religious and ethical. They will tell you that its very simplicity stood in the way of their quick acquirement of its power. They had listened all their lives to learned and ponderous disquisitions of professors upon the body and mind, man's relation to his Maker, etc., and had long ago decided that only the very learned could ever hope to fathom the depths of wisdom necessary to comprehend even a very little of the subject. They will also tell you that from childhood they have listened to flowery sermons by learned ministers about God and man's duty to God. In all these, the subjects were so weighted with the ponderous appearance of wisdom that they failed to connect them with simple, everyday life. But here we have a presentation of the deep things of God so simple and easy that the wise and mighty of this age pass it by as a religious vagary. In this connection, let us remember the words of Jesus, "Except ye . . . become as little children, ye shall not enter into the kingdom of heaven."

For many hundreds of years the church has been in more or less of a wrangle over points of doctrine, notwithstanding [the fact that] Jesus Christ left no doctrinal precedents to quarrel about. He is not recorded as ever having written a line except upon one occasion, and that was in the sand. His was peculiarly a religion of works, and when the disciples of John the Baptist came to inquire as to his divinity, he told them to tell John what they saw: "The blind receive their sight, and the lame walk, the lepers are cleansed, and the deaf hear, the dead are raised up, and the poor have the gospel preached to them."

Jesus knew that words without works are dead, and his whole life and teaching had for object and aim the demonstration in actual, everyday life of a religion based upon Truth. The established churches in that day, as in this, had through formalism and materialism, lost the power to demonstrate the Truth in the affairs of the people, and Jesus Christ, as he said, came to restore the law. So today this doctrine of Christ comes again to restore the law of Pure Logic.

The problem of life is getting into more and more of a tangle among those who depend upon the material. There is much running to and fro upon the earth by the seekers for satisfaction, yet no satisfaction is found.

Where will you find a person who will admit that he has peace of mind, health of body, and a knowledge of Truth? The rich admit that their possessions bring increased cares and great mental disquietude. The poor long to be rich, not knowing that happiness cannot be bought with money. The learned are not satisfied with their acquirements because when they just begin to get wisdom their bodies fail them and they die. So it goes among the denizens of this discontented world of matter. Many lose faith in things ever being better and commit suicide, thinking thus to be free from their trouble, but the great majority live on, hoping that the next world will give them the desires of their hearts. Poor sufferers! They are trusting an indefinite future to bring them what may be had right now for the taking.

The feature of happiness here and now is the beautiful part of Jesus' teaching. He did not defer health nor salvation to a world to come after death; he taught that both are attainable wherever we are. He taught that the kingdom of heaven is within you, and he proved by his works that it could be made to show forth in the bodies and minds of those who follow the way he pointed out. But the wise and mighty of his day did not get the benefits of his doctrine that the poor and humble did. They despised to listen to the statements of the poor carpenter's son. They had been instructed by the learned scribes and were expert in explaining the Scriptures exactly as they had been explained by their ancestors, generation after generation. It is true that they could not heal as did Jesus, yet they scorned his interpretation of this sacred law because it was not in accordance with that of their preceptors, notwithstanding [that] the interpretation of Jesus was demonstrated through him to be correct.

Jesus said, "Except ye . . . become as little children, ye shall not enter into the kingdom of heaven." No greater Truth was ever uttered. He found it true in his day when he presented his simple doctrine to the Pharisees and Sadducees, and it is again found true in this day when that same simple doctrine is revived. Only those who solve all the problems of life by its help get the true understanding of this beautiful philosophy, and they must, for the time at least, put aside all the lofty learning with which the world has endowed them. "The wisdom of this world is foolishness with God," and if you would get Truth in its purity you must listen to its statements with the unprejudiced mind of the child. All about you are potencies and powers of which you do not dream. Your philosophy has not grasped the faintest concept of the wonderful, undiscovered country that lies right within your reach, yet unseen and unknown to the mortal senses because of their narrow range. You live, move, and have your being in a realm Elysian, yet you but now and then catch faint glimpses of its rare beauty in your high moments of spiritual illumination. This realm is not of matter but of Mind. It encompasses you on every side and you contact its invisible glories, but know them not. A false education has shut you away from God's beautiful creations and, like the prodigal son, you tarry in a far country. Do you say this is idealism? The illusions of imagination? Here again do you betray the mental congealing which hereditary prejudices and race education have produced. Did not that subtle fluid, electricity, exist in the invisible before it was brought into manifestation? Does not the modern analytical chemist tell us that our planetary atmosphere carries in solution all the elements that go to make up this visible world? These same chemists are now extracting from the invisible atmosphere the exact essences that give flavor to the peach, apple, and other fruits. The essences so produced are not imitation flavoring extracts; they are the identical chemical ingredients that form the fruits that grow in our orchards. It is rash for any man to assert that anything is impossible, for, as was said by Arago, "Outside the realm of pure mathematics there is no such word as impossible."

A new era has dawned. The old is passing away. The Christ, or Truth, has come in the clouds of heaven. The end of the rule of the beast, physical strength, has come. "He that leadeth into captivity shall go into captivity: he that killeth with the sword must be killed with the sword." This is the sure outworking of the dominating methods of brute strength, the "beast" of Revelation. The World War was a terrible example of its last struggle for existence in national dominance. In the advent of this new dispensation the heavens are rolled up as a scroll, and in that process is revealed the long hidden realm of causes. Invisible forces are always the most powerful, and the dynamics of mind control the universe. In mind originates all that is, and by its actions all things are moved. It is the Alpha and Omega, the beginning and the end. When man understands the laws of mind he has solved the mysteries of the universe, and then the sphinx no longer hides her secret from him.

This is the realm in which centers the doctrine of Practical Christianity. This philosophy deals exclusively with Spirit-Mind as the origin and causing power of all that appears. It recognizes no cause outside of mind, and consequently does not waste any time in examining or discussing effects as seen in the material universe.

All sin, sickness, trouble, war, poverty, disease, and death originate in the mind; they can be permanently healed only by regulating that point of departure. Every thought registers itself with unerring accuracy in the body. You are a walking picture, flashed by the camera of your mind into visible manifestation.

Christ made this the basis of his teaching. He knew that disease is the result of sin, or a falling short of perfection. He said, "Sin no more, lest a worse thing come unto thee." His whole life's work, as recorded in the New Testament, was to show people how to get rid of their sins in order that they might have health and freedom for the mental burdens under which they struggled. The New Testament is a sealed book to one who has no knowledge of these laws of mind. It is a secret manual, and reads like an ordinary narrative unless one has the key that unlocks its hidden meaning. Practical Christianity gives that key, and he who knows all the principles of its philosophy can enter the holy of holies of the Bible; he can penetrate the mysteries of the Scriptures of all peoples.

We call this doctrine Practical Christianity because Jesus Christ gave a fuller demonstration of the principles upon which it is based than any other teacher of whom we have a record. He showed that religion is a hollow mockery unless it demonstrates, here and now, freedom from the ills of the flesh. He said that the evidences of a Christian and the signs that follow and bear witness to his belief or understanding, are healing the sick, cleansing from sin, raising from death, and preaching the Word. Through his teachings and those of his disciples, Christians were made in large numbers from among the people of Judea; these demonstrated that the promised signs do follow conversion to the true doctrine. He said he was led by the Spirit of Truth, and that his words are life to those who receive them. He also said that whatever should be asked in his name (the Divine Spirit of Truth) should be granted, and that he would be with those who believe on him, always, even unto the end of the world.

There was no limit as to time, place, or personality in these promises. Those who claim that the works of healing which he and his followers did were limited to the disciples and those in the church during that particular spiritual outpouring, must see that they have no Scriptural authority whatever for such conclusions.

Practical Christianity explains fully that Jesus of Nazareth in all his teachings referred to a universal Principle which was common to all men who would live in harmony with Divine Law, or the "Father in heaven." By a righteous, pure life, Jesus became one with that Principle of Goodness or the "Father that dwelleth in me," and he said that all men could do the same; he also said that even greater works than he did would be done by those who follow after him in faith.

In reviving in this age the pure doctrine of Jesus Christ, we find that he was not the only one who advocated salvation from sin, sickness, and death, by right thinking, but that his methods are paralleled by the avatars and teachers of nearly every nation of which history reports.

Hence we are safe in claiming that we have an exact science in this doctrine; that it is susceptible of universal demonstration, and that when applied with the same faithfulness that man gives to his daily affairs, it will do all that is claimed for it.

This science has always been known to the spiritually wise; the prophets of all ages have been witnesses to its efficacy, and to them we owe what are known as the sacred books and Scriptures of all peoples. When sounded to their depths with the mind of understanding, it is found that all Scriptures agree in fundamental points, although their transcribers were widely separated and ignorant of each other's existence, and at the time of transcription beyond the probability of personal intercourse.

These facts prove conclusively that in Truth there is but one Mind; that the one Mind is universal; that Truth is not the property of any particular race or chosen people, but is given freely to all who open their understanding to that one Divine Mind, from which the only real wisdom, life, and love, ever come.

Jesus Christ understood this universality of Truth and that the prophets were its avenues of expression; hence he advised a study of the Scriptures. He declared that he came to fulfill or again explain the law, and not to destroy it. Thus, in teaching this science of the Christ, we find our corroborative testimony in the sacred Scriptures, because there is transcribed a preponderance of Truth. The perpetuity of these sacred writings proves this, for had the error therein outweighed the Truth, they would have sunk into oblivion with the secular histories of the many nations of the past. Although glittering with the Oriental imagery of a race of idealists, the Hebrew Bible is a full exposition of that doctrine which we call Practical Christianity.

It must not be understood that this science is based upon any external authority in the way of the teaching of books or persons. The Science of Christ is based alone on the Truth of Being, and needs no authority outside of the Divine Principle in man to prove its case. It is the inherent Truth that wells up spontaneously in the soul of every man and woman in the universe, when pure reason is allowed full sway.

This is the problem of life, and it is not reasonable to suppose that a just and impartial Creator would manifest Himself to one particular nation or man, or that He would make either of them the specific custodian of His Word, thereby excluding a part of his creations. This would not only show a partial God but an unjust God. No, the God we worship is a universal principle, the one Principle of Life, and by or through it comes all the life and intelligence we have. That which is not God-Intelligence and God-Life is no intelligence and no life, but mere seeming.

This God-Principle is not far off in some distant heaven which you can enjoy only by dying; it is the loving Father, right here in reach of the humblest man that walks the earth. You, and each of you, are working your life problem according to the rules of God-Principle, or you are deviating therefrom and suffering the results of error in consequence. It is your privilege to know how to come into harmony with universal Mind and thereby discover to yourself your real inheritance as a child of Spirit. Man is Spirit. The Bibles of all races declare it; every true philosopher and seer since the dawn of history reiterates it, and universal man knows it intuitively. And as Spirit, man knows that he must have originated in a cause which is Spirit, as "like must produce like," and Jesus said, "God is Spirit."

But we need not go to Scripture or the opinion of any man to prove this, for all about is the evidence that the cause for all that is, is invisible—is Spirit. Our physical scientists say that matter in its last analysis eludes their grasp in neurons of force.

Then the nature of this spiritual cause next presents itself. Is it good or evil? No one with an understanding mind has ever said that God, or First Cause, could be anything but Good, and no other quality or attribute is ever for an instant entertained as belonging to the Divine Mind. Therefore it follows in strict logic that there can be nothing caused but good, if the cause itself is good and nothing but good. No other conclusion can possibly be reached, and in all the schools of theology the premise of a good First Cause is admitted. Blinded by sense appearances, man has let his reason be overridden; in his folly he has declared that certain things exist which are not in harmony with *Spirit* and *good*. He has been influenced by the shifting character of matter, and has been disappointed at every turn; yet he has allowed his senses to delude him into the belief that appearances are real. He has witnessed the unstable and deceptive character of sense consciousness, the lack of harmony in its manifestations, the varying states of antagonism which it shows in its relations, and its generally unreliable nature; nevertheless, in the face of all these, and with that ever-present internal monitor that tells him that First Cause, or God, is Spirit and all harmony, he humbly bows to what his senses tell him is the inevitable. Through them he sees, smells, tastes, and feels, and he listens to their varying testimonies, instead of to the clear logic of pure reason.

But in the study of Truth you are not under any circumstances to listen to the testimony of your external senses. You are placed in the clear light of logic and reason, and are expected to draw all of your conclusions from that standpoint. From the premise of Spirit alone you shall evolve the world of reality in which you live, and you can demonstrate to your full satisfaction that you have been deluded all these years in believing that which is not true. You shall prove that all cause is in Spirit, that you are Spirit and can make the world in which you live conform to that which you know by clear reason to be true.

The one Life-Intelligence is your life-intelligence, and when you let it freely flow up into your consciousness, you know that it is good. As there can be but one cause for all that is, and as that Cause is All-Good, you have a pivotal center from which you can draw conclusions that will settle definitely all the debatable questions of existence.

This Infinite Cause, or Divine Principle, is All-Good, and there is nothing but it in the universe. Hence, it must be all Life, Love, Truth, Intelligence. There can of necessity be nothing else in existence but this one Principle, consequently it must be omnipotent, omniscient, and omnipresent. It is the *All* of existence, and there can be nothing real outside of it or separate from it or in any way apart from it, in nature or character of any description. It is Spirit, and all of its manifestations must be spiritual. It is Life, and all of its manifestations must express life and nothing but life. It is Love, and all of its manifestations must express love and *only* love. It is Intelligence, and all of its manifestations must express intelligence and nothing but intelligence. It is Truth, and its manifestations must express Truth *only*. It is Good, and its manifestations must be *all* good. It is All—fills all; there can be no other, *and there is no other.* "Above all, and through you all, and in you all."

These basic statements are the foundation stones of all the religions of the world; they are the intuitive promptings of every unbiased mind, and all the deep philosophers of the past and present so postulate the Causing Power of the universe.

We hold with mankind universally that these predications of the nature and character of God, or First Cause, are correct. Our postulates as to the character of God are also those of the Christian church, and upon these points we agree. But to avoid entangling ourselves in a maze of illogical and inconsistent sequences, we are careful to draw our conclusions as to God's manifestations, so that they shall harmonize with the qualities which all the world predicate as exclusively His.

We do not say God is Good and there is nothing beside Him, yet evil exists; nor that God is Spirit and fills full the universe, yet matter also exists; nor that God is Love and Divine Love *only* pulsates to the ends of Being, yet hate exists; nor that God is Life and all life, yet death holds sway over a part of His dominion; nor that God is Truth, yet error is a potent principle; nor that God is all Intelligence, yet ignorance benumbs man. *No,* we refuse to let the evidences of sense belie the lofty reason. We hold to the basic statements; we formulate them along lines of harmonious sequence and reach our conclusions regardless of the seeming [appearances]—the phenomenal universe.

These conditions which appear to the senses as existing in opposition to the clear reason of the higher Self, and which are opposed to what reason tells us are the attributes of God, are but the illusions of those senses. That only is true and permanent which corresponds to a cause which is all-good, all-powerful, all-intelligent, and everywhere present. A proper application of this doctrine by mankind will demonstrate its Truth.

God is Good—there is no evil!

God is Spirit—there is no matter!

God is Life—there is no death!

God is Intelligence—there is no ignorance!

God is Strength—there is no weakness!

God is Health—there is no sickness!

Chapter 3

FAITH PRECIPITATIONS (1946)

W HEN ASKED what electricity is, an eminent scientist replied that he had often thought of it as an adjunct to faith, judging from the way it acted in the electrical field.

This linking of faith and electricity seems at first glance fantastic, but when we compare it with what takes place when certain substances in solution and electricity are brought in conjunction, there seems a confirmation of Scripture authority. "Now faith is the substance of *things* hoped for." (A.V.)

For example, certain metals in solution in acid are precipitated by electricity. Science says that everything on this earth was once in electronic elements in space, and that there are many more of the same kind of aggregations awaiting manifestation. It is the electrical units of the sun that gather from earth and ether the vitamins found in vegetables. In a similar way the electrons of man's brain are stirred to action by faith, and acting concurrently with the spiritual ethers, they hasten nature to produce quickly what ordinarily requires months of seedtime and harvest.

In the time of Elisha, the widow, so distressed with debt

that she had even mortgaged to slavery her two children, appealed to the prophet, who said, "What hast thou in the house?" She said, "Thy handmaid hath not anything in the house, save a pot of oil." He told her to borrow all the empty vessels her neighbors had and then to go into the house and shut the door, and pour the oil in the pot into all those vessels; which she did until they were all full. She then paid her debts and had plenty left.

Jesus fed four thousand persons at one time and five thousand at another by the same means. He also precipitated the elements of wholeness many times and healed the multitude. He required co-operation in faith by those He healed in order thus to complete the electrical circuit.

Speedy answers to prayer have always been experienced, and always will be, when the right conditions are established between the mind of the one who prays and the surrounding spiritual atmosphere, which is closely allied to an electrical field. The power to perform what seems to be miracles has been relegated to some God-selected one; but now we are inquiring into the law, since God is no respecter of persons, and we find that the fulfillment of the law rests with man or a group of men, when they quicken by faith the spiritual forces latent within them.

The reason that some prayers are not answered is lack of proper adjustment of the human mind to the omnipresent creative spiritual life.

Jesus was the most successful demonstrator of prayer of whom we have any record, and He urged persistence in prayer. If at first you don't succeed, try, try again. Like Lincoln, Jesus loved to tell stories to illustrate His point, and to emphasize the value of persistence in prayer. He told of a woman who demanded justice of a certain judge and importuned him until in sheer desperation he granted her request.

Every Christian healer has had experiences where persistent prayer saved his patient. If he had merely said one prayer, as if giving a prescription for the Lord to fill, he would fall far short of demonstrating the law. Elijah prayed persistently until the little cloud appeared, or as we should say, he had a "realization"; then manifestation followed.

The Bible is treasured as the word of God because it records so many of these apparent miracles but the fact is that all over this land enough demonstrations of the supermind are taking place every day to fill many books of the size of the Bible. Some of them go on record and people read about them, but these are few compared with the multitude that are happening. All of which goes to prove that there is a restorative law that, if taken advantage of, would heal the world of all its ills.

Many of the old-school faith healers object to the scientific explanation of the healing process. They have believed in a personal God and that all superworld forces are brought about by His personal intervention. However it is much more satisfying to our logical minds to know that God is the law and that the Spirit that we have thought of as a projection is in fact God in His own spiritual identity. This is the teaching of Jesus, and our men of science are proving it to be true. And understanding of this all-accessible Truth is making seers, prophets, and mighty men of God out of pygmies. On every hand men of mediocre ability are becoming world leaders through exploiting the supermind qualities that they have merely glimpsed as existing within them.

These ephemeral Caesars have gained a meager inkling of disciplined mind's dominion and are using it to control the negative mass thought, and through the hypnotic force of words they are evolving chaos and dark night the world over.

When men accept and understand Jesus' teaching about the mastery of the spiritual man, all the evils that arise from these upstart saviors will disappear. But now in the night of mind's eclipse

"We petty men
 Walk under his huge legs and peep about
 To find ourselves dishonorable graves."

Then the question arises, If this Supermind ability is in
every man, why is it not more widely understood and used?

There are several answers to this pertinent question, the
most plausible being the lack of human initiative. Men prefer to let others do their thinking for them. This is especially
true in matters religious. The race thought has been so sat-
urated with the belief that spiritual revelation must come
through some authorized channel that the man without an
ecclesiastical degree is timid about expressing an opinion
about God or man's spiritual nature.

Jesus broke this hypnotic spell when without ecclesiastical authority He claimed to be the Son of God.

We should remember that Jesus included as sons of God
all those who, as He said, are "my sheep," that is, follow Him.
He quoted Psalm 82, in which it is written,

"I said, Ye are gods,
And all of you sons of the Most High."

The church elders and the people cried, "Crucify him!"
Jesus taught great truths, which were grasped by but a few
open-minded followers, and they formed a new church.
They in turn, after doing mighty works for hundreds of years,
built an ecclesiastical hierarchy from which the common
people were excluded. The Church Fathers gathered and selected certain religious manuscripts and compiled the Bible,
which they proclaimed to be the very word of God, to be
read and interpreted by those only having the authority of
the church.

Here again we see positive thought submitting to negative
thought, thereby keeping the world in darkness for ages.

As Luther started the Protestant Reformation so we are
now at the beginning of another reformation, in which the

freedom and power of man spiritually will not only be taught but demonstrated. The Supermind demonstrations that mark this modern religious reformation seem so at variance with nature that they are still looked upon as miracles, notwithstanding the fact that logic and science shout from the housetops the universality of law.

Those who study the spiritual import of Jesus' teaching have revealed to them a mental technique for which no adequate language has yet been invented.

The Jews demanded of Jesus that He tell them plainly, and His reply was that the works would testify that He was the Son of God and that He and the Father were one. We who have experienced Spirit baptism freely testify to the dynamic thrill that ripples through the nerves for days and months and is often repeated in silent meditation for years after the first outpour. Thus revelation, observation, and actual experience prove that man develops spirituality according to a divine pattern, called in Genesis *the image and likeness of God.* The natural man in the physical world is merely the beginning of the formation of the man planned by creative Mind. When the natural man finishes his unfoldment he enters the next cycle, that of the Christ man illustrated by Jesus. In our schools the student is expected to get his education in a certain number of years. So in the divine school we are limited to the cycle that is spoken of as the "end of the age." The human cycle for this earth is billions of years in length, and we are just now beginning the cycle of the divine man, which will be of equal length. Jesus was the first man or fruit of the earth's first cycle. He opened the way for all those who aspire to the attainment of immortality. To the present time the followers of Jesus have been told by spiritual leaders that He taught the immortality of the soul only. But now it is revealed that He immortalized His body and said, "Follow me." It was man's sins that brought death to his body, and his redemption must include the healing of the body. When the mind or soul is healed of its sins the body will respond. "Your body is a temple of the Holy Spirit, which is in you, which ye have from God."

So we find as we study and apply the doctrine of Jesus that our body must be included. Faith in the omnipresent pure substance precipitates that substance in body and we are transformed.

Proofs may be found in profusion that the divine law of body restoration is in action in a large way right here in our midst. Our literature teems with testimonials of persons who have been healed, and they can be found and will give personal proof that they are indebted to God for renewed health, strength, prosperity, and happiness. Thus it is not necessary to strengthen your faith by reading about the work of God in ages past; you can personally consult your next-door neighbor, who can doubtless tell you of marvels fully as great as any recorded in the Bible.

The majority of cases that come to us belong to the class of the discouraged woman told of in Luke 8:43, "who had spent all her living upon physicians, and could not be healed." Doctors have pronounced them incurable, and as a last resort they try God. The hardest part of the work in their healing is to get out of their mind the verdict of the doctor that their case is incurable. We have discovered that there are no incurables, that with God all things are possible. Any experienced metaphysical healer will tell you that he has been the instrument through which all the popular diseases have been healed.

Some of the stories told by patients are beyond human credence; for example, the restoration of the eyes of a man from whom they had been removed, and the growth of the nose of a woman who had lost it by disease. These are very rare but well authenticated in metaphysical circles. I am not prepared to give the names of these cases, but I can testify to my own healing of tuberculosis of the hip. When a boy of ten I was taken with what was at first diagnosed as rheumatism, but developed into a very serious case of hip disease. I was in bed over a year, and from that time an invalid in constant pain for twenty-five years, or until I began the application of the divine law. Two very large tubercular abscesses developed at the head of the hip bone, which the doctors said would finally drain away my life. But I managed to get about on crutches, with a four-inch cork-and-steel extension on the right leg. The hip bone was out of the socket and stiff. The leg shriveled and ceased to grow. The whole right side became involved; my right ear was deaf and my right eye weak. From hip to knee the flesh was a glassy adhesion with but little sensation.

When I began applying the spiritual treatment there was for a long time slight response in the leg, but I felt better, and I found that I began to hear with the right ear. Then gradually I noticed that I had more feeling in the leg. Then as the years went by the ossified joint began to get limber, and the shrunken flesh filled out until the right leg was almost equal to the other. Then I discarded the cork-and-steel extension and wore an ordinary shoe with a double heal about an inch in height. Now the leg is almost as large as the other, the muscles are restored, and although the hip bone is not yet in the socket, I am certain that it soon will be and that I shall be made perfectly whole.

I am giving minute details of my healing because it would be considered a medical impossibility and a miracle from a religious standpoint. However I have watched the restoration year after year as I applied the power of thought, and I know it is under divine law. So I am satisfied that here is proof of a law that the mind builds the body, and can restore it.

My application of the divine law in restoring health to a

limb has also resulted in a regeneration of my whole body. Although ninety-two years of age, I am being rejuvenated and my whole organism is going through a transformation that can only end in body perpetuity. In the face of human experience this of course seems a preposterous claim, but all the signs of feebleness and advancing years are disappearing from face and form, and I can arrive at no other conclusion than that I am fulfilling the promise of the Bible "So *that* thy youth is renewed like the eagle."

Chapter 4

UNITY OF RELIGION AND SCIENCE (1933)

M<small>Y AIM IS</small> to prove that science, in developing the unseen forces of the ether, is merely revealing the mechanical side of that realm which Jesus called the "kingdom of the heavens."

That science and religion have not worked in unity is borne out by history. Religion functions in the realm of ideas and science in the realm of facts. By facts we mean anything that may be proved by material tests. Christianity has been very jealous of its revelations and has assumed that they are far more valuable than the discoveries of science. When Saint Augustine proclaimed that "nothing is to be accepted save on the authority of the Scriptures," a wall of ecclesiastical authority inclosed Christianity, and the pages of church history testify to the entrenchment within that inclosure of millions of followers of Jesus. There could be no new revelations from God; the slogan of religious authorities was "Where the Scriptures speak, we speak; where they are silent, we are silent." Then followed the persecution even to death of anyone who dared to discover anything that seemed to conflict with the accepted interpretations of the Bible. The horrors of the Inquisition are almost unspeakable.

But the proved facts of scientific research and discovery have bit by bit broken down the wall of narrow dogmatic assumptions reared by Christianity, and we are finding that we have, like the Pharisees of Jesus' time, been making the dead letter of Scripture revelation take the place of the living Christ. Jesus was a demonstration of the fact of God's existence and power in this world, and when charged by the ecclesiastical congress with breaking their law He thundered, "Ye search the scriptures, because ye think that in them ye have eternal life; and these are they which bear witness of me; and ye will not come to me, that ye may have life."

Jesus taught that the scientific realities of God were capable of expression here in this world. He taught that man within himself had God capacity and power. Jesus was crucified because He claimed to be the Son of God. Yet the Scriptures, which the Pharisees worshiped, had this bold proclamation, which Jesus quoted to them from Psalm 82:

"I said, Ye are gods,
And all of you sons of the Most High."

Jesus differed from other men in that He proved by His works that He was the Son of God, while the average man is still striving to attain that excellency. Jesus attributed His marvelous demonstrations to His acquaintance with a realm that He called "the kingdom of the heavens," also "the kingdom of God." He said that this kingdom was very near to us and might be made manifest in us.

The reports by His followers of what He taught clearly point to two subjects that He loved to discourse upon. The first was the Son of God, that He was the Son of God, and that we might all become as He was and demonstrate our dominion by following Him in the regeneration. "And Jesus said unto them, Verily I say unto you, that ye who have followed me, in the regeneration when the Son of man shall sit on the throne of his glory, ye also shall sit upon twelve thrones, judging the twelve tribes of Israel." But Jesus did not promise the regenerate man divinity alone, He described in many parables and figures an environment, a kingdom in which regenerate man was to live eternally. He called it the kingdom of the heavens, not the kingdom of *heaven*, a place, as given in the King James Version of the Scriptures.

Jesus loved to talk about this kingdom of the heavens, and He compared it or said it was "like unto" this and that in many parables and mind pictures. This kingdom of the heavens was not, according to Jesus, a place to which the good go after death; it was a state to be attained by all who seek immortality, and its essential elements were right at hand, to be grasped and retained by the faithful. "The kingdom of God is come nigh unto you" was the proclamation.

There has been much speculation as to the source of Jesus' marvelous powers and many theories as to how He attained them. They have been classed as miracles, beyond the ken of scientific research. But the word "miracle" and the meaning attached to it are not found in the original text. Jesus did "signs" and "mighty works," but there is no claim in the Scriptures that He did anything outside law. Mighty works are being done by modern science that in past ages would have been classed as miracles.

To perform its miracles modern science draws upon the kingdom of the heavens. It tells us that out of this kingdom come light, heat, power, color, sound, electricity, magnetism, life, and substance; in fact, that everything that exists in this universe came out of this invisible, omnipresent kingdom of the heavens, the luminiferous ether. They tell us that in their discoveries they have mere touched the hem of the garment of a kingdom that, by further discoveries along the same line, will revolutionize our whole civilization.

Science says that a single drop of water contains energy equivalent to a year's continuous supply of 200 horsepower—enough to run several motor cars. If you suddenly freed the energy that is in a lump of sugar, it would be enough to blow up the city of London. Jesus said, "Seek ye first his kingdom, and his righteousness; and all these things shall be added unto you"; which epitomizes these discoveries of science, and more.

We should remember that this kingdom of the heavens is interpenetrating. The ultra-violet ray of science, the X ray, the cosmic ray are within our body. They are the protons and electrons of the atoms of which our body is formed.

Dr. George W. Crile, eminent surgeon and scientist, says that our bodies are composed of *"twenty-eight trillion* electric cells. Every one of these twenty-eight trillion cells is a tiny wet battery, with negative and positive poles. . . . Emotions—love, hate, fear, jealousy, are but stimulating processes, *loosing* currents of electricity through certain paths."

Man does not destroy his body "with his intellect; he worries, fears, hates, and is jealous with his organs." Jesus said, "For out of the heart comes forth evil thoughts . . . these are the things which defile the man."

Dr. Crile continues:

"If he [man] can learn to harness the hidden electricity of Niagara, can he not learn to control, to some degree at least, the electric battery in his own body?" Jesus, referring to His body, said, "I have power to lay it down, and I have power to take it again."

Jesus taught that this kingdom of the heavens is the potential home of the inhabitants of earth. He said, "It is your Father's good pleasure to give you the kingdom." He pointed to faith in it as a mind seed that develops capacity in man and builds a structure that enables man to become a citizen of that kingdom. Faith as a grain of mustard seed will make man's mind strong, wise, and divinely efficient.

This kingdom of God, which is so near to us, is not an abstract ether, as science has intimated, but according to Jesus and other great spiritual masters, it is inhabited by entities of intelligence and power far beyond our earthly comprehension. This kingdom of the heavens is not new to the wise men of the Orient. They have for ages taught its existence, and adepts among them have explored it and entered into it long before the time of Jesus. By the mystics of India this kingdom is variously named, but all designations point to it as the source of tremendous power for good or ill to man.

It may be literally true, as Pythagoras taught, that this universe is God performing a mighty symphony of creation, with the suns and planets merely musical notes on the staff of nature.

Another almost unbelievable marvel that our scientists anticipate is a phonograph record that will reproduce the voice of the speaker without mechanical means; that whole pages of our daily papers will record the voices of the speakers, and that those who read will hear every word without any appliance, other than the mechanism of this marvelous kingdom of the heavens, the luminiferous ether.

Jesus said that the seed planted in the soil represented the word of God. He also said that the kingdom of the heavens is like a field in which man, the sower, sowed his words, and that they brought forth some thirtyfold, and some a hundredfold. He also said that we should be held accountable for our lightest word: "By thy words thou shalt be justified, and by thy words thou shalt be condemned."

Whoever reads the words of Jesus with spiritual understanding, or even the imagination of a modern scientist, must conclude that He understood the properties of the ether and gave power to it even beyond the most vivid imaginings of any scientist.

To the superbly tuned mind and brain of Jesus the ether was a soil so eager with vibrant life that it would take only a few seed thoughts of supply, represented by the little lad's five loaves and two fishes, and at the word of a master like Jesus, they would increase enough to feed five thousand, besides women and children.

As we examine the marvelous inventions of science, and compare them with the so-called miracles of Elijah, Elisha, and Jesus, we find that they all are working in the same great field, the kingdom of the heavens, the universal cosmic ether.

Science is also proving by experimentation that living cells have within them the elements of continuous life, and scientists are at a loss to know why man's body should ever die, if it were properly fed and cleansed. Herbert Spencer came to the same conclusion theoretically. He said in substance that if man understood the issues of life in his body and was cast in a right environment he would overcome death. He said that "the theory of science would abolish the practice of both by substituting a perfect organism functioning in a perfect environment, into which death, having no correspondence with it could not enter. Then there would be eternal existence and perfect knowledge."

This was accomplished by Jesus, and through His understanding of how to release the protons and electrons concealed in the atoms and cells of His body, He overcame death. He said, "And this is life eternal, that they should know thee the only true God, and him whom thou didst send, *even* Jesus Christ."

We thus see that both science and religion agree that eternal life depends on a harmonious environment combined with an understanding of that creative mind from which such an environment is derived.

In order to follow Jesus in the regeneration, we must become better acquainted with our soul and how it functions in and through the body.

The human soul is a form of what our modern scientists have named the ether of space. The soul is the intermediate between the spirit and the body. Soul may be compared to the radio ether that carries sound radiations that a receiving set converts into words. For aught we know, the radio ether is a living, breathing, intelligent entity, like the entity man, who uses it to transmit his intelligence. As the mind of man uses his soul to transmit his intelligence to his body, so God, the universal mind, uses that same soul force to transmit His ideas to man. So we find that physical science is discovering the unity of all things, visible and invisible.

They tell us that light, heat, and energy, and even matter are fast being merged into one primal force, which is radiation, and that this radiation fills all space. Formerly, science taught that space was empty, and matter the only reality. Now we are taught by science that matter is empty, and space the only reality. Thus we see that science is fast approaching the truths intuitively accepted by the spiritual-minded of every age, everywhere, and that God speaks to man out of the omnipresent heavens or ethers. It was not from some distant planet that Jesus talked to Paul, but out of the light; a light that blinded Paul and those that were with him, as they journeyed toward Damascus. The author of Acts in his testimony says: "Suddenly there shone round about him a light out of heaven: and he fell upon the earth, and heard a voice saying unto him, Saul, Saul, why persecutest thou me? . . . and when his eyes were opened, he saw nothing; and they led him by the hand, and brought him into Damascus."

This light that shone upon Paul from the heavens was so bright that it blinded him, as persons are often blinded by a flash of lightning. This proves that all light is of like character. Space is filled with vibrations of light, and light is the vehicle of intelligence: so it is a logical and demonstrable fact that space is vibrant with life and intelligence. God is wisdom, God is light, God is love. God is thus everywhere present as Spirit and there is no absence of that one and only all-knowing life and light. Thus "God is all, and there is none beside Him."

Right here let us say that Jesus did not teach that our body in its present material density is eternal, but that life is eternal. He taught and demonstrated, in the resurrection of His body, that the electronic energy in the cells forming the body could be released and synchronized with its source, the luminiferous ether (which He called the kingdom of the heavens), and that through this transformation the body would attain immortality. Paul wrote, "For this corruptible must put on incorruption, and this mortal must put on immortality. . . ."

The space-filling ether is the mother of all life and intelligence. It may be conceived as the tremulous waters of life in which all things live as fishes in the sea. It is radiant with ideas. Its creations are ideas, and those ideas in their turn form infinite combinations from the original fount of ideas. These formed ideas crystallize into suns, planets, systems, and a universe of sentient beings at the head of which is man.

Thus the ether radiates intelligence and man, its most intelligent offspring, may cup the ear of his mind to the ether and catch its messages, as the plainsman lays his ear to the earth and hears the vibrations of the tread of animals far beyond his sight. The omnipresent ether is the throne of God, from which radiations of intelligence, love, and power continually flow to every living creature. As those who seek the same things are attracted to one another, so those who seek to know God open their inner intelligence to the radiations of the everywhere present ether.

The Scriptures are replete with accounts of those in every walk of life who have been guided by dreams and visions, but never in the history of the race has Jehovah used this means of directly intervening in the personal lives of those who seek to follow His law so often as in our day. Men and women and even children, all over the world, testify to having received in dreams and visions messages from a source higher than that of earth. This avenue of contact between God and His sons is becoming so common that we see the fulfillment of Joel's prophecy:

"And it shall come to pass afterward, that I will pour out my Spirit upon all flesh; and your sons and your daughters shall prophesy, your old men shall dream dreams, your young men shall see visions."

There is urgent need of this direct instruction by Jehovah of the spiritual-minded. Our theological schools have lost the direct inspiration of Spirit through looking to the past for it instead of the present. The study of history is futile unless it can be made alive with present parallels. It does not benefit me to read that the Lord talked to the prophets of old unless I see the possibility of that same Spirit of omnipresence talking to prophets of today.

Science freely admits that it has not found all the potentialities that exist in the ether. It has released a few of the mechanical forces, but the great unknown intelligence—God—is still beyond its ken. But those who "tune in" to this kingdom of God with soul and body will effect a complete unity between the mechanical energies of the ether and the intelligent forces of Spirit. Then will be fulfilled the vision of John: "And I saw a new heaven and a new earth: for the first heaven and the first earth are passed away; and the sea is no more. And I saw the holy city, new Jerusalem, coming down out of heaven from God, made ready as a bride adorned for her husband. And I heard a great voice out of the throne saying, Behold, the tabernacle of God is with men, and he shall dwell with them, and they shall be his peoples, and God himself shall be with them, and be their God."

Part Two
METAPHYSICAL THEOLOGY: THE NATURE OF GOD

METAPHYSICAL THEOLOGY: THE NATURE OF GOD

ETAPHYSICS is the study of "first principles," the search for the nature of Being, for the meaning and nature of fundamental concepts such as Cause, Substance, Reality, and Law. These and other concepts are the basis of metaphysical theology. Metaphysics was called "divine science" and "theology" by Aristotle,[1] and ever since metaphysicians have been concerned with questions about God as First Cause and Ultimate Being. Fillmore's theology is part of that strand of Western thought, but he also attempts to synthesize that rational tradition with the equally venerable tradition of biblical theology. In addition, Fillmore attempts to tie in ideas from science and the mystical tradition. Always essential to his theological concerns is how the abstract concepts of metaphysics can be used for the practical concerns of everyday living.

"The True Character of Being" is the first chapter from Fillmore's first book, *Christian Healing* (1909). The title tips off the metaphysical concern in this chapter: "What is the nature of being?" Fillmore first lays out some of his epistemological principles for "spiritual science," before entering into discussion of being. He emphasizes the importance of intuition and holding to logical deduction. But note that he makes no attempt to rationally prove the existence and goodness of God, rather he takes those propositions as givens. He also assumes that God is Spirit and that Spirit is synonymous with Mind; these points are central to his metaphysical theology. He had been praying, meditating, and doing spiritual healing work for almost twenty years before he wrote this chapter, so his experience of God was sufficient proof for him, if not for his readers. He suggests to his readers that they not judge by appearances, but hold true ideas about God in mind and spend time daily in prayer and meditation. In that way, they, too, can experience God for themselves.

Fillmore does not seek to rationally deduce the nature of God, but rather takes it that humanity's basic ideas about God are true and that holding these ideas in mind will demonstrate God's nature in our experience. Instead of trying to deduce that God is First Cause, Fillmore suggests, in effect, that we assume God is First Cause and do our reasoning from that proposition. This is a reasonable strategy, since the classic argument for a First Cause is invalid.

The classic argument, derived from Aristotle, is that everything must have a cause, but there cannot be a chain of causes without a beginning, so there must be a First Cause. The problem with this argument is that the second premise contradicts the first premise. If *everything* has a cause, then there cannot be anything without a cause, so there could not be an uncaused first cause. Fillmore himself, perhaps somewhat unconsciously, alludes to the fallacy of the "first cause" argument in the chapter "God Presence" (included in this section) when he writes: "Who made you? Who made me? Who made the earth, the moon, and the sun? God. *Then who made God?*"

In "The True Character of Being," Fillmore claims that through understanding of First Cause and opening our thoughts to divine ideas "men have acquired the ability to raise dead bodies." This is clearly an enthusiastic overstatement of the facts. Fillmore loved to make spectacular claims for the possibilities he saw in "spiritual science." Having witnessed and experienced healings, he extrapolated to as yet unrealized powers and accomplishments. Fillmore may well have known of cases in which people who were apparently dead, "came back to life" while receiving prayer. If he did know of such cases, he does not specify them here. However, before dismissing such claims as pure fabrications, we ought to pause and consider the reports of "near-death experiences" in our own times. In books like *Life After Life* by Dr. Raymond Moody, there are reports of people declared clinically dead who have come back to life. Probably many of them had people praying for them. The conjunction of the events (a) people praying and (b) recovery of vital signs does not prove that (a) caused (b). Nevertheless, people who have faith in God and prayer often connect prayer to positive events in precisely such a casual manner. Perhaps all we can say is that some things are a matter of faith rather than of proof.

In "Reform Your God Thought" (from *Talks on Truth*, 1926), Fillmore expands on his ideas about the nature of God by incorporating a few ideas from mysticism. First, he emphasizes the mystical idea of God as the Silence. The idea that God is experienced in a deep state of meditation characterized by silence has a long and venerable history. The Gnostics of the early Christian era emphasized the Silence, and statements of some of the early "Church Fathers" seem to allude to the silence of God.[2] The concept of the Silence remained in the teachings of Christian mystics, if not in Church dogma, throughout the centuries until it was highlighted and brought into popular consciousness by George Fox and the Quakers. The Silence is also a theme of Eastern mysticism, especially in Taoism.

Second, Fillmore speaks of God as "your higher Self . . . in constant waiting upon you." The idea of God as higher Self has not been a standard way of speaking about God in the Christian tradition. However, God as Self is characteristic of Hindu mysticism, with which Fillmore had some familiarity. Interestingly, New Thought founder P. P. Quimby frequently referred to God as the True Self, even though Quimby does not seem to have been familiar with Eastern thought.

Third, Fillmore suggests relating to God in an informal, childlike way, as if God were an intimate and nearby friend. That attitude toward God is found in the lives of some of the saints of the Church as well as occasionally among Sufi and Hindu sages. While most of Fillmore's writings have the tone and concerns of a philosophical or introspective mystic, the passages in this chapter referring to the informal approach to God reveal Fillmore's more personal, devotional mystical side.

In the next chapter, "Spiritual Substance—the Fundamental Basis of the Universe" (from *Prosperity,* 1936), Fillmore expounds on the three main themes of his teachings on prosperity: (1) What is the nature of substance? This is a fundamental question for both science and metaphysics; (2) How can we access substance? This is an attempt to apply metaphysical theory to the everyday challenge of provision; and (3) What is the ideal form and possibility for human economy? This is a speculative question regarding the larger issue of economic justice and prosperity in human society.

Fillmore weaves the three themes together in this chapter in a very loosely structured way. At times this looseness may be disconcerting to the reader, so it is helpful to note what Fillmore's main ideas are expressed in a more linear way.

Regarding the nature of substance, Filllmore maintains, as

always, that Divine Mind and divine ideas are the "one and only reality." However, he goes beyond that basic concept to holding that the new concepts of physics reveal the dynamics of spiritual substance. Physics conceives of tremendous potential energy in space and in atomic particles, which are no longer thought of as the indivisible building blocks of the universe but rather as susceptible themselves to conversion to waves of energy. Fillmore compares this concept of vast energy potential all around us to Jesus' teaching on the kingdom of the heavens. If the analogy is not immediately apparent to the reader, consider Jesus' "expansion parables," in which he compares the kingdom of God to leaven expanding in bread, or a tiny mustard seed growing like a weed into a large shrub. The release of tremendous energy from infinitesimal subatomic particles is indeed analogous to the tremendous expansive properties of leaven or yeast or tiny weed seeds. Fillmore maintains that the basic difference between the potential energy of physicists and the spiritual substance of the Christian metaphysician is that the metaphysician recognizes the attribute of responsive intelligence in this substance. Hence the metaphysician conceives of the energy of the universe as "mind energy" rather than material energy. And if there is no matter in the sense of "indivisible particles," then it makes just as much sense to think of the substance as "God-Energy" as it does to think of it as "matter."

How then can we access this spiritual substance? If it has responsive intelligence, then theoretically it could be accessed, at least in part, through mental activities. This is of course exactly what Fillmore maintains, so he suggests ways to use the mind to tap into spiritual substance. He proposes believing and speaking thoughts of abundance related to the omnipresent, unlimited substance. In this, Fillmore follows Jesus' proclamation of believing and speaking from your belief. Fillmore also advises forming a covenant with God. Charles and his wife Myrtle themselves wrote out a covenant with God; so we can be sure that the Fillmores were being very literal in their recommendation of forming written covenants.

Unlike other New Thought teachers of prosperity, Fillmore did not focus purely on the idea of personal success through "positive thinking," for he recognized that personal prosperity is related to collective human prosperity. He emphasized the importance of giving liberally to receive abundantly and the importance of overcoming greed. Unlike more secular economic theorists, Fillmore did not hold to an idea of distribution of finite resources to expanding populations, for he believed in unlimited spiritual resources available to all through our connection with Spirit.

One might well ask, "If supply is unlimited and available to each individual through mind, what difference does it make if we hoard our supply or give liberally to the common good?" For Fillmore, the importance of overcoming greed and giving was not related to a belief in limited resources and problems of scarcity and distribution. Rather, he held that there are spiritual laws related to the idea of divine love which require us to give generously for both spiritual growth and personal prosperity. In other words, he held that true prosperity inherently involves our relationship to God as well as to the rest of humanity. His speculations about ideal economy and the possibility of drawing directly on Spirit for our supply are rooted in his views on metaphysics and the nature of the Good.

"God Presence" (from *Jesus Christ Heals,* 1939), expresses Fillmore's awareness of both the immanence and transcendence of God. Fillmore maintained that God can be known and experienced as immanent, yet God is indescribable and "other" than what we experience in the world and so has a transcendent aspect. "It is true that all power comes from God, but it does not follow that the character of the thing we term power is the same in the unexpressed [God] as in the expressed [the world]."

The chapter begins with an affirmation of the presence of God as the Holy Spirit, working in human consciousness and manifestation, Fillmore's term for the world of experience. He then discusses the human intuition of God's reality that drives us to seek knowledge of God. Fillmore recognizes that our language cannot express the unlimited nature of God, but that we can nevertheless experience and express God. For Fillmore, language can both point to the reality of God and mislead us regarding the nature of God. So for example, while it is true that God is power, "if by power we mean force, energy, action, oppression, then we should say that God has no power, that God is powerless; because His power is not like the so-called power that is represented by these human activities."

Fillmore juxtaposes affirmations such as *God is substance* with disclaimers such as "but if we mean by this that God is matter, a thing of time, space, condition, we should say that God is substanceless." He makes startling claims such as "God is Mind. . . . Mind . . . does not exist but inheres in all that is" and "God is not loving. God is love, the great heart of the universe and of man." This is the strategy of mystics, who attempt to shake our minds loose of limiting conceptions of God, the unlimited. But Fillmore's mysticism is ever rooted in his metaphysical pragmatism; in speaking of a way to commune with Spirit, he says, "If there is not in your consciousness a demonstration that Mind has a language on its own silent plane and that it can manifest itself in your mind, body, and affairs, then you can go back to your old convictions." That sentence is typical of Fillmore's pragmatic approach in which the student is told not to accept anything on the basis of someone else's authority, but to judge teachings according to their practical fruits. In keeping with that pragmatism, Fillmore closes the chapter with a "healing drill."

Chapter 5

THE TRUE CHARACTER OF BEING (1909)

"THERE IS a spirit in man, and the breath of the Almighty giveth them understanding." The science that is here set forth is founded upon Spirit. It does not always conform to intellectual standards, but it is, nevertheless, scientific. The facts of Spirit are of a spiritual character and, when understood in their right relation, they are orderly. Orderliness is law, and is the test of true science.

The lawful truths of Spirit are more scientific than the constantly shifting opinions based on intellectual standards. The only real science is the science of Spirit. It never changes. It is universally accepted by all who are in Spirit, but one must be "in the Spirit" before one can understand this science of Spirit. The Mind of Spirit must become active in those who would grasp the orderly science of Being that these lessons proclaim.

It is not absolutely necessary that the spiritual part of man's nature be active at the beginning of his study of this science. The primal object of the lessons is to quicken the spiritual realm of consciousness and to bring about the "breath of the Almighty" that gives understanding.

So let it be understood that we are teaching the science of Spirit, and that those who are receptive to the teaching will be inspired to spiritual consciousness. It is not difficult to accomplish, this receiving the "breath" or inspiration of Spirit. We all are inspired by Spirit, in certain states of consciousness. Understanding of the laws governing the realm of Spirit will make it possible to attain this consciousness and to receive this inspiration whenever requirements are met.

The starting point in spiritual realization is a right understanding of that One designated as the Almighty. It is strictly logical and scientific to assume that man comes forth from this One, who is named variously, but who, all agree, is the origin of everything. Since man is the offspring of the Almighty, he must have the character of his Parent. If the earthly child resembles its parents, how much more should the heavenly child resemble its Parent. The Truth that God is the Father of man does away with the oft proclaimed presumption that it is impossible for the finite to understand the Infinite. God must be in His universe as everywhere intelligent power; otherwise, it would fall to pieces. God is in the universe as its constant "breath" or inspiration; hence it is only necessary to find the point of contact in order to understand the One in whom we all "live, and move, and have our being."

A sense of logic is a fundamental constituent of man's being, and all minds acquiesce in statements of logical sequence. We all see the relation and unity of cause and effect, mentally stated, but, because the realm of forms does not always carry out our premise, we fall away from the true standard and try to convince ourselves that our logic is, somehow, defective. The one important thing that the student of spiritual science must learn is to trust the logic of the mind. If appearances are out of harmony with your mental premise, do not let them unseat your logic. "Judge not according to appearance, but judge righteous judgment." You would not take the mixed figures of a child working a problem in mathematics as an example of the trueness of the principle; nor could you detect an error in the problem unless you were somewhat familiar with the rules of mathematics. Mental propositions are the standards and governing principles in all sciences developed by man. In the science of creation the same rule holds good. You may rest in the assurance that the principles that you mentally perceive as true of God are inviolate, and that, if there seems to be error in their outworking, it is because of some misapplication on the part of the demonstrator. By holding to the principle and insisting upon its accuracy, you open the way to a fuller understanding of it; you will also be shown the cause of the errors in the demonstration.

Then, if you have been in confusion mentally through contemplation of a world both good and evil, and have, in consequence, got into skeptical ways, the only true remedy is to stand by the pure reason of your spiritual perception and let it clear up the proposition for you. Dismiss all prejudices based upon the mixed perception; make your mind receptive to the clearer understanding that will surely appear when you have taken sides with Spirit, when you look to Spirit alone for the outworking of the problem.

This is not blind belief; it is, in the superconsciousness, an acquiescence in the logic of Being. The superconsciousness is man's only sure guide in the mazes of the creative process. By trusting to the infallibility of this guide, man opens himself to the inspiration of the Almighty. Spirituality may be cultivated by, and the deep things of God may be revealed to, anyone who will mentally proclaim and affirm the logical perception of the goodness and the Truth of Being.

The central proposition in the inspiration of Spirit is that God, or primal Cause, is good. It does not make any great difference what you name this primal Cause; the important consideration is a right concept of its character. The Hindu calls it Brahma, a being of such stupendous proportions that man shrinks into nothingness in contemplating it. Although this greatness of absolute Being is true, there is also another point of view—the smallness of that same Being as evidenced in the presence of its life in the most insignificant creations. So, in order to get at the very heart of Being, it is necessary to realize that it is manifesting in the least as well as in the greatest, and that, in the bringing forth of a universe, not one idea could be taken away without unbalancing the whole. This brings us to fuller realization of our importance in the universe and to the necessity of finding our right place. It also puts us into very close touch with the Father of all, the one omnipresent Intelligence pervading everything.

The Father within you, so lovingly and familiarly revealed by Jesus, is not at a distance, far away in a place called "heaven." His abode is in the spiritual realms that underlie all creative forces. As Jesus realized and taught, "the kingdom of God is within you." Spirit is the seat of power; its abode is on the invisible side of man's nature.

This revelation of God immanent in the universe was clearly set forth by Paul: "over all, and through all, and in all." The inspired ministers of all times have proclaimed the same.

The Power that creates and sustains the universe includes in its activity the creating and the sustaining of man. The desire for a fuller understanding of this Power has awakened a great inquiry into the character of the all-pervading One. On every hand men are earnestly seeking to know about God, seeking to come into harmonious relation with Him. Some are succeeding, while others seem to make but little progress. The diversity of results obtained is caused by the variety of ways of approaching the one Mind—for such God is. In mind is the key to the whole situation, and when man clearly discerns the science of mind, he will solve easily all the mysteries of creation.

The dictionary definitions of *mind* and *spirit* are nearly identical; with this analogy realized, we much more easily get in touch with God. If *spirit* and *mind* are synonymous, we readily perceive that there is no great mystery about spiritual things, that they are not far removed from our daily thoughts and experiences. "Ye are a temple of God, and . . . the Spirit of God dwelleth in you," simply means that God dwells in us as our mind dwells in our body. Thus we see that God creates and moves creation through the power of mind. The vehicles of mind are thoughts, and it is through our mind in thought action that we shall find God and do His will.

There are mental laws that investigators are discovering, observing, and tabulating as never before in the world's history. Man has the ability to discern and understand the various factors entering into the creative processes of mind, and he is, through the study of mental laws, perceiving and accepting the science of ideas, thoughts, and words. But those who investigate nature and her laws from the intellectual and physical viewpoint fall short of complete understanding, because they fail to trace back to the causing Mind the multitudinous symbols that make up the visible universe. The material forms that we see about us are the chalk marks of a mighty problem being outworked by the one Mind. To comprehend that problem and to catch a slight glimpse of its meaning, we must grasp the ideas that the chalk marks represent; this is what we mean by studying Mind back of nature. Man is mind and he is capable of comprehending the plan and the detailed ideas of the supreme Mind.

Divine ideas are man's inheritance; they are pregnant with all possibility, because ideas are the foundation and cause of all that man desires. With this understanding as a foundation, we easily perceive how "all . . . mine are thine." All the ideas contained in the one Father-Mind are at the mental command of its offspring. Get behind a thing into the mental realm where it exists as an inexhaustible idea, and you can draw upon it perpetually and never deplete the source.

With this understanding of the potentiality of primal Cause, we find it a simple matter to work the problem of life—the key to the situation being *ideas.* Thus life in expression is activity; in Being it is an idea of activity. To make life appear on the visible plane, we have but to open our mind and our thoughts to the divine idea of life and activity, and lo, all visibility is obedient to us. It is through this understanding, and its cultivation in various degrees, that men have acquired the ability to raise dead bodies. Jesus understood this realm of supreme ideas, or, as He termed it, "the kingdom of God . . . within you." When he raised Lazarus He invoked this power. When Martha talked about a future resurrection, He said, "I am the resurrection, and the life: he that believeth on me, though he die, yet shall he live." One who identifies his whole mind with omnipresent Mind becomes so much at one with it that he can overcome death.

The real of the universe is held in the mind of Being as ideas of life, love, substance, intelligence, Truth, and so forth. These ideas may be combined in a multitude of ways, producing infinite variety in the realm of forms. There is a right combination, which constitutes the divine order, the kingdom of heaven on earth. This right relation of ideas and the science of right thought is practical Christianity.

The student in the science of Being should start all his investigations and mental activities from the One Mind foundation. If you are skeptical about the existence of God, or if you are an abstract believer in God without having had any experience or conscious mental awakening that has given you proof, you should be very industrious in prayer, affirmation, and invocation. Remember, God is not a king who can force His presence upon you whether you will or not, but an omnipresent Mind enfolding and interpenetrating all things.

There are goodness everlasting and joy beyond expression in a perfect union between your mind and this perfect Mind. The point of contact is a willingness and a seeking on your part. "Seek, and ye shall find; knock, and it shall be opened unto you."

This question naturally presents itself: If we are offspring of Divine Mind, why are we not naturally conscious of its presence? The answer to this is: In using the privilege of our inheritance—the power to make ideas visible as things—we have created a realm that separates us in consciousness from the Father-Mind. This is the teaching of Jesus in the parable of the prodigal son. When we are weary of the sense consciousness, we have only to turn our face (intelligence) toward our Father's house; there we shall meet a loving welcome.

The understanding that God is not in a distant heaven, nor located in any way geographically, gives us a feeling of nearness to and unity with the parent Mind. This intercommunion of the man consciousness with the omnipresent spiritual force of the universe was beautifully exemplified by Jesus. God was closer to Him than hands or feet. He referred all things to this loving Father, who was in constant communion and cooperation with the Son; yet there was, even in His case, the independent personal consciousness that beset Him when He sought to be free from mortal limitations. So we should not be discouraged or cast down if we do not quickly find the kingdom of God within us. Jesus spent whole nights in prayer; we should not be weary with a few moments each day. A daily half hour of meditation will open up the mind to a consciousness of the inner One and will reveal many things that are hidden from the natural man.

The fact is, Truth cannot be imparted—it must be individually experienced. The presence of Divine Mind in the soul cannot be told in words; it can be hinted at and referred to in parable and likened to this or to that, but it can never be described as it is. The ability of the individual mind to combine the ideas of Divine Mind in a consciousness of its own makes each of us the "only begotten Son," a particular and special creation. No two individuals in all the universe are exactly alike, because there is always diversity in the ideas appropriated by each individual from Divine Mind.

The Truth is, then:

That God is Principle, Law, Being, Mind, Spirit, All-Good, omnipotent, omniscient, omnipresent, unchangeable, Creator, Father, Cause, and Source of all that is;

That God is individually formed in consciousness in each of us, and is known to us as "Father" when we recognize Him within us as our Creator, as our mind, as our life, as our very being;

That mind has ideas and that ideas have expression; that all manifestation in our world is the result of the ideas that we are holding in mind and are expressing;

That to bring forth or to manifest the harmony of Divine Mind, or the "kingdom of heaven," all our ideas must be one with divine ideas, and must be expressed in the divine order of Divine Mind.

Chapter 6

REFORM YOUR
GOD THOUGHT (1926)

THIS IS DISTINCTLY the age of reforms. Never before have there been such widespread and persistent efforts by both men and women to right the wrongs of religion, society, and politics. From the hearts and the souls of millions goes up the cry, "Set us free from our burdens!" Every imaginable scheme of release is proposed, and each advocate of a panacea for the people's ills stoutly affirms his to be the only remedy that has virtue. It is observed that the majority of these reformers are clamorous that laws be enacted to force their theories upon the people. In this they are following the same methods to cure the ills of the body politic that they have followed in curing the body physical, and the results will surely be of like impotency.

Laws, whether natural or artificial, are but the evidence of an unseen power. They are simply effects, and effects have no power in themselves. When man looks to them for help in any condition of inharmony, he is departing from a universally recognized principle of sequence. God, Spirit, or Mind— whatever you choose to name it—is the supreme dictator, and thought is its only mode of manifestation. Mind generates thought perpetually; all the harmonious and permanent affairs of men, and the innumerable systems of the infinite cosmos, are moved in majestic measures by its steady flow.

All power has its birth in the silence. There is no exception to this rule in all the evidence of life. Noise is the dying vibration of a spent force. All the clatter of visibility, from the harangue of the ward politician to the thunder's roar, is but evidence of exhausted power. As well try to control the lightning's flash by wrapping the thunder about it, as attempt to regulate mind by statutory enactments.

All reforms must begin with their cause. Their cause is mind, and mind does all its work in the realm of silence, which in reality is the only realm where sound and power go hand in hand. The visible outer world, with all its social, religious, and political laws, customs, and ceremonies, is but the flimsy screen upon which mind throws its incongruous opinions. God's thought is love, the inherent potentiality of the God man, which knows neither persons nor things, mine nor thine, but a universal brotherhood in which perfect equity and justice reign in joint supremacy. All philosophers and sages have recognized this silent cause, this perpetual outflow from center to circumference. Emerson says of Plato: "He was born to behold the self-evolving power of Spirit, endless generator of new ends; a power which is the key at once to the centrality and the evanescence of things." Jesus Christ said: "The kingdom of God is within you." "Seek ye first his kingdom, and his righteousness; and all these things shall be added unto you." Elijah found God, not in the whirlwind, or the earthquake, or the fire, but in the "still small voice."

All men who have moved the world to better things have received their inspiration from the Spirit within and have always looked to it for instruction. God is not a person who has set creation in motion and gone away and left it to run down like a clock. God is Spirit, infinite Mind, the immanent force and intelligence everywhere manifest in nature. God is the silent voice that speaks into visibility all the life there is. This power builds with hands deft beyond the comprehension of man and keeps going, with all its intricate machinery, universe upon universe, one within another, yet never conflicting. All its building is from center to circumference. The evidence for this runs from the molecule and the atom of the physicist to the mighty swing of a universe of planets around their central sun.

Every act of man has its origin in thought, which is expressed into the phenomenal world from a mental center that is but a point of radiation for an energy that lies back of it. That point of radiation is the conscious *I*, which in its correct relation is one with Cause, and has at its command all the powers potential in Cause. The conscious *I* can look in two directions—to the outer world where the thoughts that rise within it give sensation and feeling, which ultimate in a moving panorama of visibility; or to the world within, whence all its life, power, and intelligence are derived. When the *I* looks wholly within, it loses all sense of the external; it is then as the Hindu yogi sitting under his banyan tree with his eyes riveted on the point of his nose, denying his very [physical] existence until his body is paralyzed [loses sensation]. When it looks wholly without, upon sensation and feeling, it loses its bearings in the maze of its own thought creations. Then it builds up a belief of separateness from, and independence of, a causing power. Man sees only form, and makes his God a personal being located in a city of dimensions. This belief of separateness leads to ignorance, because all intelligence is derived from the one Divine Mind, and when the soul thinks itself something alone, it cuts itself off in consciousness from the fount of inspiration. Believing himself separate from his source, man loses sight of the divine harmony. He is like a musical note standing alone, looking upon other notes but having no definite place upon the great staff of nature, the grand symphony of life.

Life is a problem solvable by a principle whose essence is intelligence, which the wise man always consults. The ignorant and headstrong trusts to his intellect alone to carry him through, and he is always in a labyrinth of errors.

A belief prevails that God is somewhat inaccessible; that He can be approached only through certain religious ordinances; that is, a man must profess religion, pray in a formal way, and attend church in order to know God. But these are mere opinions that have been taught and accepted by those who perceive the letter instead of the spirit. For if God is Spirit, the principle of intelligence and life, everywhere present at all times, He must be just as accessible as a principle of mathematics and fully as free from formalism. When a mathematician finds that his answer to a problem is not correct, he consults the principle and works out the correct solution. He knows that all mathematical problems inhere in mathematical principles and that only through them can they be worked correctly. If he persistently ignored principles and blundered around in a jungle of experiments, he would be attempting to get up "some other way," and he would prove himself a "thief and a robber," for there is but one way. Jehovah God, infinite Mind in expression, is the way, and this Mind is always within reach of every man, woman, and child.

It is not necessary to go in state to God. If you had a friend at your elbow at all times who could answer your every question and who loved to serve you, you certainly would not feel it necessary to go down on your knees to him or ask a favor with fear and trembling.

God is your higher Self and is in constant waiting upon you. He loves to serve, and will attend faithfully to the most minute details of your daily life. If you are a man of the world, ask Him to help you to success in any line that you may choose, and He will show you what true success is. Use Him every hour of the day. If you are in doubt about a business move, no matter how trivial, close your eyes for an instant and ask the silent one within yourself what to do, just as you would send a mental message to one whom you know and who could catch your thought. The answer may not come instantly; it may come when you least think of it, and you will find yourself moved to do just the right thing. Never be formal with God. He cares no more for forms and ceremonies than do the principles of mathematics for fine figures or elaborate blackboards.

You cannot use God too often. He loves to be used, and the more you use Him the more easily you use Him and the more pleasant His help becomes. If you want a dress, a car, a house, or if you are thinking of driving a sharp bargain with your neighbor, going on a journey, giving a friend a present, running for office, or reforming a nation, ask God for guidance, in a moment of silent soul desire.

Nothing is too wicked or unholy to ask God about. In my early experience in the study of Christian metaphysics, I was told that through the power of Divine Mind I could have anything I desired. I had a lot I wanted to sell and I asked God to dispose of it to a certain man who I thought needed it. That night I dreamed that I was a bandit holding up my customer. The dream showed me that I was asking God to do what was not right and I thereby gained a lesson. A saloonkeeper came to me for health treatments and was helped. He said: "I also need treatments for prosperity, but of course you could not prosper a man in my business." I replied: "Certainly. God will help you to prosper. 'If ye shall ask anything of the Father, he will give it you in my name' does not exclude saloonkeepers." So we treated the man for prosperity.

He afterward reported that he was out of the saloon business, and had found prosperity in other lines of work.

If you are doing things that are considered wicked, you will find swift safety in asking God first, then acting or refraining, as you are moved. Some people act as if they thought that they could hide themselves from the one omnipresent intelligence, but this is the conclusion of thoughtlessness. God knows everything you do, and you might just as well have His advice. God does not want you to reverence Him with fear. God certainly never can get your confidence if you constantly stand in quaking fear of Him. He will do you a favor just as quickly if you ask in a jolly, laughing way as He would if you made your request in a long, melancholy prayer. God is natural, and He loves the freedom of the little child. When you find yourself in His kingdom it will be "as a little child."

God's kingdom of love and unity is now being set up in the earth. His hand will guide the only ship that will ever sail into the Arcadian port, and the contented, peaceful, and happy people that throng its decks will sing with one voice: "Glory to God in the highest."

Chapter 7

SPIRITUAL SUBSTANCE— THE FUNDAMENTAL BASIS OF THE UNIVERSE (1936)

DIVINE MIND is the one and only reality. When we incorporate the ideas that form this Mind into our mind and persevere in those ideas, a mighty strength wells up within us. Then we have a foundation for the spiritual body, the body not made with hands, eternal in the heavens. When the spiritual body is established in consciousness, its strength and power is transmitted to the visible body and to all the things that we touch in the world about us.

Spiritual discernment reveals that we are now in the dawn of a new era, that the old methods of supply and support are fast passing away, and that new methods are waiting to be brought forth. In the coming commerce man will not be a slave to money. Humanity's daily needs will be met in ways that are not now thought practical. We shall serve for the joy of serving, and prosperity will flow to us and through us in streams of plenty. The supply and support that love and zeal will set in motion are not as yet largely used by man, but those who have tested their providing power are loud in their praise.

The dynamic power of the supermind in man has been sporadically displayed by men and women of every nation. It is usually connected with some religious rite in which mystery and priestly authority prevail. The so-called "common herd" are kept in darkness with respect to the source of the superhuman power of occult adepts and holy men. But we have seen a "great light" in the discovery by physical scientists that the atom conceals electronic energies whose mathematical arrangement determines the character of all the fundamental elements of nature. This discovery has disrupted the science based on the old mechanical atomic theory, but has also given Christian metaphysicians a new understanding of the dynamics back of Spirit.

Science now postulates space rather than matter as the source of life. It says that the very air is alive with dynamic forces that await man's grasp and utilization and that these invisible, omnipresent energies possess potentialities far beyond our most exalted conception. What we have been taught about the glories of heaven pales into insignificance compared with the glories of the radiant rays—popularly referred to as the "ether." We are told by science that we have utilized very meagerly this mighty ocean of ether in producing from it the light and power of electricity. The seemingly tremendous force generated by the whirl of our dynamos is but a weak dribble from a universe of energy. The invisible waves that carry radio programs everywhere are but a mere hint of an intelligent power that penetrates and permeates every germ of life, visible and invisible. Scientific minds the world over have been tremendously moved by these revolutionary discoveries, and they have not found language adequate to explain their magnitude. Although a number of books have been written by scientists, setting forth guardedly the far-reaching effects that will inevitably follow man's appropriation of the easily accessible ether, none has dared to tell the whole story. The fact is that the greatest discovery of all ages is that of physical science that all things apparently have their source in the invisible, intangible ether. What Jesus taught so profoundly in symbols about the riches of the kingdom of the heavens has now been proved true.

According to the Greek, the language in which the New Testament has come down to us, Jesus did not use the word *heaven* but the word *heavens* in His teachings. He was not telling us of the glories of some faraway place called "heaven" but was revealing the properties of the "heavens" all around us, called both "space" and "ether" by physicists. He taught not only its dynamic but also its intelligent character, and said that the entity that rules it is within man: "The kingdom of God is within you." He not only described this kingdom of the heavens in numerous parables but made its attainment by man the greatest object of human existence. He not only set this as man's goal but attained it Himself, thereby demonstrating that His teaching is practical as well as true.

The scientists tell us that the ether is charged with electricity, magnetism, light rays, X rays, cosmic rays, and other dynamic radiations; that it is the source of all life, light, heat, energy, gravitation, attraction, repulsion; in short, that it is the interpenetrating essence of everything that exists on the earth. In other words, science gives to the ether all the attractions of heaven without directly saying so. Jesus epitomized the subject when He told His followers that it was the kingdom from which God clothed and fed all His children. "Seek ye first his kingdom, and his righteousness; and all these things shall be added unto you." Science says that the electrical particles that break into light in our earth's atmosphere are also a source of all substance and matter. Jesus said that He was [embodied] the substance and bread that came from the heavens. When will our civilization begin really to appropriate and use this mighty ocean of substance and life spiritually as well as physically?

This inexhaustible mind substance is available at all times and in all places to those who have learned to lay hold of it in consciousness. The simplest, shortest, and most direct way of doing this was explained when Jesus said, "Whosoever . . . shall not doubt in his heart, but shall believe that what he saith cometh to pass, he shall have it." When we know that certain potent ideas exist in the invisible mind expressions, named by science both "ether" and "space" and that we have been provided with the mind to lay hold of them, it is easy to put the law into action through thought and word and deed.

> "There is a tide in the affairs of men,
> Which, taken at the flood, leads on to fortune,"

said Shakespeare. That flood tide awaits us in the cosmic spaces, the paradise of God.

The spiritual substance from which comes all visible wealth is never depleted. It is right with you all the time and responds to your faith in it and your demands on it. It is not affected by our ignorant talk of hard times, though we are affected because our thoughts and words govern our demonstration. The unfailing resource is always ready to give. It has no choice in the matter; it must give, for that is its nature. Pour your living words of faith into the omnipresent substance, and you will be prospered though all the banks in the world close their doors. Turn the great energy of your thinking toward "plenty" ideas, and you will have plenty regardless of what men about you are saying or doing.

God is substance, but if by this statement we mean that God is matter, a thing of time or condition, then we should say that God is substanceless. God is not confined to that form of substance which we term matter. God is the intangible essence of that which man has formed into and named matter. Matter is a mental limitation of that divine substance whose vital and inherent character is manifest in all life expression.

God substance may be conceived as God energy, or Spirit light, and "God said, let there be light, and there was light." This is in harmony with the conclusions of some of the most advanced physicists. Sir James Jeans says, in *The Mysterious Universe*, "The tendency of modern physics is to resolve the whole material universe into waves, and nothing but waves. These waves are of two kinds: bottled-up waves, which we call matter, and unbottled waves, which we call radiation, or light. The process of annihilation of matter is merely unbottling imprisoned wave energy, and setting it free to travel through space."

Spirit is not matter. Spirit is not person. In order to perceive the essence of Being we must drop from our mind all thought that God is in any way circumscribed or has any of the limitations that we associate with things or persons having form or shape. "Thou shall not make unto thee a graven image, nor any likeness of *any thing* that is in heaven above, or that is in the earth beneath."

God is substance, not matter, because matter is formed, while God is the formless. God substance lies back of matter and form. It is the basis of all form yet does not enter into any form as a finality. Substance cannot be seen, touched, tasted, or smelled, yet it is more substantial than matter, for it is the only substantiality in the universe. Its nature is to "*sub*-stand" or "stand under" or behind matter as its support and only reality.

Job says, "The Almighty shall be thy defence, and thou shalt have plenty of silver." This refers to universal substance, for silver and gold are manifestations of an everywhere present substance and are used as symbols for it. Lew

Wallace, in *Ben-Hur*, refers to the kingdom as "beaten gold." You have doubtless in your own experience caught sight of this everywhere present substance in your silence, when it seemed like golden snowflakes falling all about you. This was the first manifestation from the overflow of the universal substance in your consciousness.

Substance is first given form in the mind, and as it becomes manifest it goes through a threefold activity. In laying hold of substance in the mind and bringing it into manifestation, we play a most important part. We do it according to our decree. "Thou shalt decree a thing, and it shall be established unto thee." We are always decreeing, sometimes consciously, often unconsciously, and with every thought and word we are increasing or diminishing the threefold activity of substance. The resulting manifestation conforms to our thought, "As he thinketh within himself, so is he."

There is no scarcity of the air you breathe. There is plenty of air, all you will ever need, but if you close your lungs and refuse to breathe, you will not get it and may suffocate for lack of air. When you recognize the presence of abundance of air and open your lungs to breathe it deeply, you get a larger inspiration. This is exactly what you should do with your mind in regard to substance. There is an all-sufficiency of all things, just as there is an all-sufficiency of air. The only lack is our own lack of appropriation. We must seek the kingdom of God and appropriate it aright before things will be added to us in fullness.

There is a kingdom of abundance of all things, and it may be found by those who seek it and are willing to comply with its laws. Jesus said that it is hard for a rich man to enter into the kingdom of heaven. This does not mean that it is hard because of his wealth, for the poor man gets in no faster and no easier. It is not money but the thoughts men hold about money, its source, its ownership, and its use, that keep them out of the kingdom. Men's thoughts about money are like their thoughts about all possessions; they believe that things coming out of the earth are theirs to claim and control as individual property, and may be hoarded away and depended on, regardless of how much other men may be in need of them. The same belief is prevalent among both rich and poor, and even if the two classes were suddenly to change places, the inequalities of wealth would not be remedied. Only a fundamental change in the thoughts of wealth could do that.

Before there is any fundamental social or economic change men must begin to understand their relationship to God and to one another as common heirs to the universal resource that is sufficient for all. They must give up some of their erroneous ideas about their "rights." They must learn that they cannot possess and lock up that which belongs to God without themselves suffering the effects of that sequestration. The poor man is not the greatest sufferer in this concentration of wealth, for he has not concentrated his faith in material things and chained his soul to them. Those who are rich in the things of this world are by their dependence on those things binding themselves to material things and are in material darkness.

Every thought of personal possession must be dropped out of mind before men can come into the realization of the invisible supply. They cannot possess money, houses, or land selfishly, because they cannot possess the universal ideas for which these symbols stand. No man can possess any idea as his own permanently. He may possess its material symbol for a little time on the plane of phenomena, but it is such riches that "moth and rust consume, and where thieves break through and steal."

Men possess as valuables their education, trade, ability, or intellectual talent. Ministers of the gospel possess scholarship or eloquence, and take pride in these spiritual possessions. Yet even these are burdens that must be unloaded before they may enter the kingdom of the heavens. The saint who is puffed up with his saintly goodness must unload his vanity before he gets in. Whoever is ambitious to do good, to excel his fellow men in righteousness, must lose his ambition and desire before he beholds the face of the all-providing Father.

The realm of causes may be compared to steam in a glass boiler. If the glass is clear one may look right at it and see nothing at all. Yet when an escape valve is touched the steam rushes out, condenses and becomes visible. But in this process it has also lost its power. Substance exists in a realm of ideas and is powerful when handled by one who is familiar with its characteristics. The ignorant open the valves of the mind and let ideas flow out into a realm with which they have nothing in common. The powerful ideas of substance are condensed into thoughts of time and space, which ignorance conceives as being necessary to their fruition. Thus their power is lost, and a weary round of seedtime and harvest is inaugurated to fulfill the demands of the world.

It is the mind that believes in personal possessions that limits the full idea. God's world is a world of results that sequentially follow demands. It is in this kingdom that man finds his true home. Labor has ceased for him who has found this inner kingdom. Divine supply is brought forth without laborious struggle: to desire is to have fulfillment.

This is the second step in demonstration for the one who has fully dedicated himself to the divine guidance. He immediately enters into easier experiences and more happiness than the world affords, when he covenants to follow only the good. There is an advanced degree along the same line of initiation into the mysteries of the divine. Before this step may be taken, a deeper and more thorough mental cleansing must be undergone. A higher set of faculties is then awakened within the body, and new avenues of expression are opened for the powers of the Spirit, not only in the body but also in the affairs of the individual. As he proceeds to exercise these faculties he may find some of them clogged by the crystals of dead thought that some selfish ideas have deposited, which makes him go through a fresh cleansing. If he is obedient to the Spirit and willing to follow without cavil or protest, the way is easy for him. If however he questions and argues, as did Job, he will meet many obstructions and his journey will be long and tedious.

Again, he who seeks the kingdom of substance for the sake of the loaves and fishes he may get out of it will surely be disappointed in the end. He may get the loaves and fishes, that is quite possible; but if there remains in his soul any desire to use them for selfish ends, the ultimate result will be disastrous.

Many people are seeking the aid of Spirit to heal them of their physical ills. They have no desire for the higher life, but having found their lusts and passions curtailed by physical infirmities, they want these erased in order that they may continue in their fleshly way. It is the experience of all who have dealt with Spirit that it is a vigorous bodily stimulant. It restores the vitality of the body until it is even more sensitive to pleasure or pain than it was before the spiritual quickening. This supersensitiveness makes it more susceptible and liable to more rapid waste if further indulgence is gratified. That is why those who receive spiritual treatment should be fully instructed in the Truth of Being. They should be shown that the indulgence of bodily passions is a sin against their success in every walk of life and especially in the way of finances and prosperity. If substance is dissipated, every kind of lack begins to be felt. Retribution always follows the indulgence of appetite and passion for mere sensation. Both sinners and saints suffer in this valley of folly. The alternative is to dedicate yourself to the Father's business. Make a definite and detailed covenant with the Father, lay your desires, appetites, and passions at His feet and agree to use all your substance in the most exalted way. Then you are seeking the kingdom, and all things else shall be added unto you.

We want to make this substance that faith has brought to our mind enduring and abiding, so that we do not lose it when banks fail or men talk of "hard times." We must have in our finances a consciousness of the permanency of the omnipresent substance as it abides in us. Some wealthy families succeed in holding their wealth while others dissipate it in one generation because they do not have the consciousness of abiding substance. For many of us there is either a feast or a famine in the matter of money and we need the abiding consciousness. There is no reason why we should not have a continuous even flow of substance both in income and outgo. If we have freely received we must also freely give and keep substance going, confident in our understanding that our supply is unlimited and that it is always right at hand in the omnipresent Mind of God.

In this understanding we can stand "the slings and arrows of outrageous fortune," depressions, losses, and financial failures and still see God as abundant substance waiting to come into manifestation. That is what Paul meant by taking up "the whole armor of God that ye may be able to withstand in the evil day." The substance that has in the past been manifest in our affairs is still here. It is the same substance and it cannot be taken away. Even though there seems to be material lack, there is plenty of substance for all. We are standing in the very midst of it. Like the fish we might ask, "Where is the water?" when we live and move and have our being in it. It is in the water, in the air everywhere, abounding, glorious spiritual substance. Take that thought and hold it. Refuse to be shaken from your spiritual stand in the very midst of God's prosperity and plenty, and supply will begin to come forth from the ether and plenty will become more and more manifest in your affairs.

Jesus was so charged with spiritual substance that when the woman touched His garment the healing virtue went out from it and she was healed. There were thousands of people in the crowd, but only the woman who had faith in that substance got it. It was already established in her consciousness, and she knew that her needs would be met if she could make the contact. In this there is a lesson for us. We know that strength is manifest everywhere, for we see it in the mechanical world. A great locomotive starts from the depot, moving slowly at first, but when it gains momentum it speeds down the track like a streak. Thus it is with spiritual strength. Beginning sometimes with a very small thought, it takes on momentum and eventually becomes a powerful idea. Every one of us can strengthen his hold on the thought of divine substance until it becomes a powerful idea, filling the consciousness and manifesting itself as plenty in all our affairs.

As you lay hold of substance with your mind, make it permanent and enduring. Realize your oneness with it. You are unified with the one living substance, which is God, your all-sufficiency. From this substance you were created; in it you live and move and have your being; by it you are fed and prospered.

The spiritual substance is steadfast and immovable, enduring. It does not fluctuate with market reports. It does not decrease in "hard times" nor increase in "good times." It cannot be hoarded away to cause a deficiency in supply and a higher price. It cannot be exhausted in doles to meet the needs of privation. It is ever the same, constant, abundant, freely circulating and available.

The spiritual substance is a living thing, not an inanimate accumulation of bread that does not satisfy hunger nor water that fails to quench thirst. It is living bread and living water, and he that feeds on God's substance shall never hunger and never thirst. The substance is an abiding thing, not a bank deposit that can be withdrawn nor a fortune that can be lost. It is an unfailing principle that is as sure in its workings as the laws of mathematics. Man can no more be separated from his supply of substance than life can be separated from its source. As God permeates the universe and life permeates every cell of the body, so does substance flow freely through man, free from all limit or qualification.

In the new era that is even now at its dawn we shall have a spirit of prosperity. This principle of the universal substance will be known and acted on, and there will be no place for lack. Supply will be more equalized. There will not be millions of bushels of wheat stored in musty warehouses while people go hungry. There will be no overproduction or underconsumption or other inequalities of supply, for God's substance will be recognized and used by all people. Men will not pile up fortunes one day and lose them the next, for they will no longer fear the integrity of their neighbors nor try to keep their neighbor's share from him.

Is this an impractical utopia? The answer depends on you. Just as soon as you individually recognize the omnipresent substance and put your faith in it, you can look for others around you to do the same. "A little leaven leaveneth the whole lump," and even one life that bears witness to the truth of the prosperity law will quicken the consciousness of the whole community.

Whoever you are and whatever your immediate need, you can demonstrate the law. If your thoughts are confused, become still and know. Be still and know that you are one with the substance and with the law of its manifestation. Say with conviction: *I am strong, immovable Spirit substance.*

This will open the door of your mind to an inflow of

substance-filled ideas. As they come, use them freely. Do not hesitate or doubt that they will bring results. They are God's ideas given to you in answer to your prayer and in order to supply your needs. They are substance, intelligent, loving, eager to manifest themselves to meet your need.

God is the source of a mighty stream of substance, and you are a tributary of that stream, a channel of expression. Blessing the substance increases its flow. If your money supply is low or your purse seems empty, take it in your hands and bless it. See it filled with the living substance ready to become manifest. As you prepare your meals bless the food with the thought of spiritual substance. When you dress, bless your garments and realize that you are being constantly clothed with God's substance. Do not center your thought on yourself, your interests, your gains or losses, but realize the universal nature of substance. The more conscious you become of the presence of the living substance the more it will manifest itself for you and the richer will be the common good of all.

Do not take anyone's word for it, but try the law for yourself. The other fellow's realization of substance will not guarantee your supply. You must become conscious of it for yourself. Identify yourself with substance until you make it yours; it will change your finances, destroy your fears, stop your worries, and you will soon begin to rejoice in the ever-present bounty of God.

Be still and turn within to the great source. See with the eye of faith that the whole world is filled with substance. See it falling all about you as snowflakes of gold and silver and affirm with assurance:

Jesus Christ is now here raising me to His consciousness of the omnipresent, all-providing God substance, and my prosperity is assured.

I have unbounded faith in the all-present spiritual substance increasing and multiplying at my word.

Chapter 8

GOD PRESENCE (1939)

*J*AM NOW *in the presence of pure Being and immersed in the Holy Spirit of life, love, and wisdom.*

I acknowledge Thy presence and power, O blessed Spirit. In Thy divine wisdom now erase my mortal limitations, and from Thy pure substance of love bring into manifestation my world, according to Thy perfect law.

Man knows intuitively that he is God's supreme creation and that dominion and power are his, though he does not understand fully. The I AM of him ever recognizes the one divine source from which he sprang, and he turns to it endeavoring to fathom its wonderful secrets. Even children grope after the truths of Being.

No man knows the beginning of the query, *Who, what, and where is God?* It is dropped from the lips of the little child when he first begins to lisp the name of father and of mother, and it is repeated throughout the years.

Who made you? Who made me? Who made the earth, the moon, and the sun? God.

Then who made God?

Thus back to the cause beyond the cause ever runs the questioning mind of man. He would understand the omnipresence that caused him to be.

Does an answer ever come to these questionings? Does

man ever receive satisfactory returns from this mental delving in the unfathomable? Each man and each woman must answer individually; for only the Mind of God can know God. If you have found God in your own mind you have found the source of health, of freedom, and of the wisdom that answers all questions.

Language is the limitation of mind; therefore do not expect the unlimited to leap forth into full expression through the limited.

Words never express that which God is. To the inner ear of the mind awakened to its depths words may carry the impulses of divine energy and health that make it conscious of what God is, but in their formulations such words can never bind the unbindable.

So let us remember that by describing God with words in our human way we are but stating in the lisping syllables of the child that which in its maturity the mind still only faintly grasps. Yet man may know God and become the vehicle and expression of God, the unlimited fount of life, health, light, and love.

God is the health of His people.

Man recognizes that health is fundamental in Being and that health is his own divine birthright. It is the orderly state of existence, but man must learn to use the knowledge of this Truth to sustain the consciousness of health.

Health is from the Anglo-Saxon word meaning "whole," "hale," "well." The one who uses the word really implies that he has an understanding of the law of the perfect harmony of Being. Health is the normal condition of man and of all creation. We find that there is an omnipresent principle of health pervading all living things. Health, real health, is from within and does not have to be manufactured in the without. Health is the very essence of Being. It is as universal and enduring as God.

Being is the consciousness of the one Presence and the one Power, of the one intelligence, and man stands in the Godhead as *I will*. When man perceives his place in the great scheme of creation and recognizes his I AM power, he declares, "I discern that I will be that which I will to be."

Man is the vessel of God and expresses God. But there is a mighty difference between the inanimate marble, chiseled by the sculptor into a prancing steed, and the living, breathing horse consciously willing to be guided by the master's rein.

So there is a wide gap between the intelligence that moves to an appointed end under the impulse of divine energy and that which knows the thoughts and desires of Divine Mind and cooperates with it in bringing about the ends of a perfect and healthy creation.

"No longer do I call you servants; for the servant knoweth not what his Lord doeth; but I have called you friends; for all things that I have heard from my Father I have made known unto you."

It must be true that there is in man a capacity for knowing God consciously and communing with Him. This alone insures health and joy and satisfaction. It is unthinkable that the Creator could cause anything to be that is so inferior to Himself as to remove it beyond the pale of fellowship with Him.

It is our exalted ideas of God and our little ideas of ourselves that built the mental wall that separates us from Him. We have been taught that God is a mighty monarch with certain domineering characteristics, who wills us to be sick or healthy; that He is of such majesty that man cannot conceive of Him.

Even in metaphysical concepts of God the impression left us is of a Creator great in power, wisdom, and love. In one sense this is true, but the standard by which man compares and judges these qualities in his mind determines his concept of God.

If I say that God is the almighty power of the universe and have in mind power as we see it expressed in physical energy and force, I have not set up the right standard of comparison. It is true that all power comes from God, but it does not follow that the character of the thing we term power is the same in the unexpressed as in the expressed.

God is power; man is powerful. God is that indescribable reservoir of stored-up energy that manifests no potency whatever until set in motion through the consciousness of man yet possesses an inexhaustible capacity that is beyond words to express. When that power is manifested by man it becomes conditioned. It is described as powerful, more powerful, most powerful, and it has its various degrees of expansion, pressure, velocity, force, and the like.

This power is used by men to oppress one another, and there has come to be a belief that God is power in the sense of great oppressing capacity. It is an ancient belief that He can and does exercise His power in punishing His creations, pouring out upon them His vengeance.

But this is not the character of divine power. If by power we mean force, energy, action, oppression, then we should say that God has no power, that God is powerless; because His power is not like the so-called power that is represented by these human activities.

God is wisdom—intelligence—but if we mean by this that God is "intelligent," that His knowledge consists of the judgments and inferences that are made in a universe of things, then we should say that God is nonintelligent.

God is substance; but if we mean by this that God is matter, a thing of time, space, condition, we should say that God is substanceless.

God is love; but if we mean by this that God is the love

that loves a particular child better than all children, or that loves some particular father or mother better than all fathers and mothers, or that loves one person better than some other person, or that has a chosen people whom He loves better than some other people who are not chosen, then we should say that God is unloving.

God does not exercise power. God is that all-present and all quiet powerlessness from which man "generates" that which he calls power.

God does not manifest intelligence. God is that unobtrusive knowing in everyone which, when acknowledged, flashes forth into intelligence.

God is not matter nor confined in any way to the idea of substance termed matter. God is that intangible essence which man has "formed" and called matter. Thus matter is a limitation of the divine substance whose vital and inherent character is above all else limitless.

God is not loving. God is love, the great heart of the universe and of man, from which is drawn forth all feeling, sympathy, emotion, and all that goes to make up the joys of existence.

Yet God does not love anybody or anything. God is the love in everybody and everything. God is love; man becomes loving by permitting that which God is to find expression in word and act.

The point to be clearly established is that God exercises none of His attributes except through the inner consciousness of the universe and man.

God is the "still small voice" in every soul that heals and blesses and uplifts, and it is only through the soul that He is made manifest as perfect wholeness.

Drop from your mind the idea that God is a being of majesty and power in the sense that you now interpret majesty and power.

Drop from your mind the belief that God is in any way separated from you, that He occupies form or space outside of you, or that He can be manifested to you in any way except through your own consciousness.

We look at the universe with its myriad forms and stupendous evidences of wisdom and power and we say: All this must be the work of one mighty in strength and understanding; I should stand in awe of such a one and realize my own insignificance in His presence. Yet when we behold the towering oak with its wide-spreading branches, we say it grew from a tiny acorn. A little stream of life and intelligence flowed into that small seed and gradually formed the giant tree. It was not created in the sense that it was made full-orbed by a single fiat of will, but it grew from the tiny slip into the towering tree through the inherent potentialities of the little seed, the acorn.

So God is in us the little seed through which is brought forth the strong, healthy Christ man.

That "still small voice" at the center of our being does not command what we shall be or what we shall do or not do. It is so gentle and still in its work that in the hurly-burly of life we overlook it entirely. We look out and beholding the largeness of the world of things, we begin to cast about for a god corresponding in character with this world.

But we do not find such a god on the outside. We must drop the complex and find the simplicity of "the most simple One" before we can know God. We must become as a little child.

Jesus said, "God is Spirit," not "a Spirit," as in the King James Version. According to Webster, the word *spirit* means life or living substance considered independently of corporeal existence; an intelligence conceived of apart from any physical organization or embodiment; vital essence, force, or energy as distinct from matter; the intelligent, immaterial, and immortal part of man; the spirit, in distinction from the body in which it resides.

Paul says, "In him we live, and move, and have our being." If we accept Scripture as our source of information there can be no higher authority than that of Jesus and Paul. They say that God is Spirit.

Spirit is not matter, and Spirit is not person. In order to perceive the essence of Being we must drop from mind the idea that God is circumscribed in any way or has any of the limitations usually ascribed to persons, things, or anything having form or shape. "Thou shalt not make unto thee a graven image, nor any likeness *of any thing* that is in heaven above, or that is in the earth beneath."

God is life. Life is a principle that is made manifest in the living. Life cannot be analyzed by the senses. It is beyond their grasp, hence it must be cognized by Spirit.

God is substance; but this does not mean matter, because matter is formed while God is the formless. This substance which God is lies back of all matter and all forms. It is that which is the basis of all form yet enters not into any form as finality. It cannot be seen, tasted, or touched. Yet it is the only "substantial" substance in the universe.

God is Love: that from which all loving springs.

God is Truth: the eternal verity of the universe and man.

God is Mind. Here we touch the connecting link between God and man. The essential being of God as principle cannot be comprehended by any of the senses or faculties, but the mind of man is limitless, and through it he may come in touch with divine Principle.

It is the study of mind that reveals God. God may be inferentially known by studying the creations that spring from Him, but to speak to God face to face and mouth to mouth, to know Him as a child knows his father, man must come consciously into the place in mind that is common to both man and God.

Men have sought to find God by studying nature, but they have always fallen short. This seeking to know God by analyzing things made is especially noticeable in this age. Materialistic science has sought to know the cause of things by dissecting them. By this mode they have come to say: We must admit that there is a cause, but we have not found it; so we assume that God is unknowable.

To know God as health one must take up the study of the healthy mind and make it and not physical appearance the basis of every calculation. To study mind and its ideas as health is a departure so unusual that the world, both religious and secular, looks upon it as somehow impracticable. The man who lives in his senses cannot comprehend how anything can be got out of the study of something apparently so intangible.

The man of affairs cannot see what mind or its study has to do with matters pertaining to his department of life, and the religionist who worships God in forms and ceremonies makes no connection between the study of mind and finding out the real nature of God.

> "Behold, I go forward, but he is not *there;*
> And backward, but I cannot perceive him;
> On the left hand, when he doth work, but I cannot
>   behold him;
> He hideth himself on the right hand, that I cannot see
>   him."

Thus ever cries the man who looks for God in the external; for health from an outside source.

In mathematics the unit enters into every problem; and in existence mind is common to all, above and below, within and without. The secret of existence will never be disclosed before man takes up and masters the science of his own mind.

Man's consciousness is formed of mind and its ideas, and these determine whether he is healthy or sick. Thus to know the mysteries of his own being he must study mind and its laws.

Many people in every age have come into partial consciousness of God in their souls and have communed with Him in that inner sanctuary until their faces shone with heavenly light; yet the mysteries of creative law were not revealed to them, because they did not get an understanding of its key, which is mind.

Mind is the common meeting ground of God and man, and only through its study and the observation of all the conditions and factors that enter into its operation can we come into the realization of God as abiding health and sustenance.

God is mind; and we cannot describe God with human language, so we cannot describe mind. To describe is to limit, to circumscribe. To describe mind is to limit it to the meanings of sense. In our talk about mind we are thus forced to leave the plane of things formed and enter the realm of pure knowing.

We can only say: I am mind; I know. God is Mind; He knows. Thus knowing is the language I use in my intercourse with God.

If you ask me about the language I use in communicating with God, I am not able to tell you; because you are talking from the standpoint of using words to convey ideas, while in the language of God ideas in their original purity are the vehicles of communication.

But ideas are the original and natural agents of communication; and everyone is in possession of this easy way of speaking to God and man. Thus we may learn to use this divine and only true way consciously if we will but recognize it and use it on the plane of mind.

But we must recognize it. This is the one truth that we have to reveal to you: How to recognize this divine language in your own consciousness and how through recognition to bring it forth into visibility. It is a truth however that we cannot reveal to you by a series of eloquent essays on the majesty, power, and wisdom of God and on the everlasting joy that follows when you have found Him; but only by showing you in the simplest way how to come into conscious relations with the source of omnipresent wisdom, life, and love, by taking with you in the silent inner realms the first steps in the language of the soul.

Compared with audible language, communion in mind can be said to be without sound. It is the "still small voice," the voice that is not a voice, the voice using words that are not words. Yet its language is more definite and certain than that of words and sounds, because it has none of their limitations. Words and sounds are attempts to convey a description of emotions and feelings, while by the language of mind emotions and feelings are conveyed direct. But again you must transcend what you understand as emotion and feeling in order to interpret the language of God. This is not hard. It is your natural language, and you need only return to your pristine state of purity to achieve it entirely.

You are mind. Your consciousness is formed of thoughts. Thoughts form barriers about the thinker, and when contended for as true they are impregnable to other thoughts. So you are compassed about with thought barriers, the result of your heredity, your education, and your own thinking. Likewise your degree of health is determined by your thoughts, past and present.

These thoughts may be true or false, depending on your understanding and use of divine law. You must open the walls of your mental house by a willingness to receive and weigh these thoughts in the balance of good judgment and to drop out of your mind everything except the one idea:

I want to know Truth, I am willing to learn. I want to express radiant health.

If there is not in your consciousness a demonstration that mind has a language on its own silent plane and that it can manifest itself in your mind, body, and affairs, then you can go back to your old convictions.

The fundamental basis and starting point of practical Christianity is that God is principle. By principle is meant definite, exact, and unchangeable rules of action. That the word *principle* is used by materialistic schools of thought to describe what they term the "blind forces of nature" is no reason why it should convey to our minds the idea of an unloving and unfeeling God. It is used because it best describes the unchangeableness that is an inherent law of Being.

From the teaching that the Deity is a person we have come to believe that God is changeable; that He gets angry with His people and condemns them; that some are chosen or favored above others; that in His sight good and evil are verities, and that He defends the one and deplores the other. We must relieve our minds or these ideas of a personal God ruling over us in an arbitrary, manlike manner.

God is Mind. Mind evolves ideas. These ideas are evolved in an orderly way. The laws of mind are just as exact and undeviating as the laws of mathematics or music. To recognize this is the starting point in finding God.

God loves spiritual man, and that love is expressed according to exact law. It is not emotional or variable, nor is there any taint of partiality in it. You are primarily a spiritual being, the expression of God's perfection, the receptacle of His love; and when you think and act in the consciousness of perfection and love, you cannot help being open to the influx of God's love and to the fulfillment of His divine purpose. This is the exact and undeviating law that inheres in the principle that God is.

God is wisdom; and wisdom is made manifest in an orderly manner through your consciousness.

God is substance—unchangeable incorruptible, imperishable—to the spiritual mind and body of man.

This substance of mind—faith—does not happen to be here today and there tomorrow, but it is moved upon by ideas which are as unchanging as Spirit.

In Spirit you never had a beginning, and your I AM will never have an ending. The world never had a beginning and will never have an ending. All things that are always were and always will be, yesterday, today, and forever the same.

But things formed have a beginning and may have an ending.

But God does not form things. God calls from the depths of His own being the ideas that are already there, and they move forth and clothe themselves with the habiliments of time and circumstance in man's consciousness. We must have firmly fixed in our understanding the verity that we shall have to square all the acts of life.

God is never absent from His creations, and His creations are never absent from their habiliments; hence wherever you see the evidences of life, there you may know that God is.

If you are manifesting health, that health has a source that is perpetually giving itself forth. A perpetual giving forth implies a perpetual presence.

There is no absence or separation in God. His omnipresence is your omnipresence, because there can be no absence in Mind. If God were for one instant separated from His creations, they would immediately fall into dissolution. But absence in Mind is unthinkable. Mind is far removed from the realm where time and distance prevail. Mind is without metes or bounds; it is within all metes and bounds; it does not exist but inheres in all that is. Hence in Spirit and in Truth you can never for one instant be separated from the life activity of God even though you may not externally feel or know of His presence.

God lives in you, and you depend on Him for every breath you draw. The understanding you have, be it ever so meager, is from Him, and you could not think a thought or speak a word or make a movement were He not in it. Your body is the soil in which God's life is planted. Your mind is the light for which He supplies the oil. "I am the light of the world," said Jesus. "Ye are the light of the world."

Intelligence is the light of the world. "Let your light shine." How? By increasing the supply of oil, by increasing your consciousness of life, and by learning how to draw upon the omnipresent God for every need.

A good healing drill is to deny the mental cause first, then the physical appearance. The mental condition should first be healed. Then the secondary state, which it has produced in the body, must be wiped out and the perfect state affirmed.

Deny:

I deny that I inherit any belief that in any way limits me in health, virtue, intelligence, or power to do good.

Those with whom I associate can no longer make me believe that I am a poor worm of the dust. The race belief that "nature dominates man" no longer holds me in bondage, and I am now free from every belief that might in any way interfere with my perfect expression of health, wealth, peace, prosperity, and perfect satisfaction in every department of life.

By my all-powerful word, in the sight and presence of almighty God, I now unformulate and destroy every foolish and ignorant assumption that might impede my march to perfection. My word is the measure of my power. I have spoken, and it shall be so.

Affirm:

I am unlimited in my power, and I have increasing health, strength, life, love, wisdom, boldness, freedom, charity, and meekness, now and forever.

I am now in harmony with the Father, and stronger than any mortal law. I know my birthright in pure Being, and I boldly assert my perfect freedom. In this knowledge I am enduring, pure, peaceful, and happy.

I am dignified and definite, yet meek and lowly, in all that I think and do.

I am one with and I now fully manifest vigorous life, wisdom, and spiritual understanding.

I am one with and I now fully manifest love, charity, justice, kindness, and generosity.

I am one with and I now fully manifest infinite goodness and mercy.

Peace floweth like a river through my mind, and I thank Thee, O God, that I am one with Thee!

Part Three
METAPHYSICAL CHRISTOLOGY: DIVINE HUMANITY

METAPHYSICAL CHRISTOLOGY: DIVINE HUMANITY

C HRISTOLOGY is the branch of Christian theology that involves thinking about the person, nature, and mission of Jesus Christ. Charles Fillmore had a very rich Christology which contained many points in common with traditional Christology as well as interpretations and speculations which went beyond previous Church doctrines.

One early Christian doctrine and area of theological speculation was the concept of the Word ("Logos" in Greek). The Logos doctrine is rooted in a Greek philosophical idea about the rationality of the universe, the rationality of Divine Mind that gives order to the cosmos. Christians adopted this idea and claimed that Jesus incarnated the Logos, that Jesus was the Word made flesh. Early Christian theologians like Justin Martyr (2nd Century) argued that the Logos was in everyone and those who lived according to it, before and after Christ, were true Christians.[1]

Charles Fillmore revived and developed this early view. Unity students generally express a great interest in religious ideas outside of mainstream Christianity, partly because of the beliefs that God is in all people and that all religions express something of the Mind of God. The chapter "Being's Perfect Idea" (from *Christian Healing*) focuses on the Logos concept and its practical implications for wholeness and enlightenment. Fillmore's essential view of the true nature of humanity is found in the passage: "Every man asks the question at some time, 'What am I?' God answers: 'Spiritually you are My idea of Myself as I see Myself in the ideal; physically you are the law of My Mind executing that idea.'"

Fillmore's emphasis throughout his writings, and especially when dealing with Christology, is on the deification of the human. That idea is prevalent also in Eastern Orthodox mysticism,[2] but not in Roman Catholic and Protestant teachings. Fillmore's Christology also emphasizes Jesus Christ as the great teacher and exemplification of deification—the process of full union with the divine. Hence Fillmore emphasizes the words, actions, and life of Jesus as central to practical Christianity.

In Fillmore's later writings, he also develops the idea of Jesus Christ's role as redeemer. Fillmore's idea of Jesus as Lord and Savior is in agreement with other Christian denominations, but Fillmore's speculations as to the metaphysical meaning of the Crucifixion, Resurrection, and Ascension diverge from other Christian doctrines.

"Jesus Christ's Atonement" (from *Talks on Truth*) explores the doctrines of the "Fall of Humanity," the meaning of the Atonement, Jesus Christ's nature as both man and God, and what it means to follow Jesus and keep his words. A few points to note in this chapter are these: (1) the "fall" was from the divine dimension into the world as we know it, which consists of our own "crystalized thought" emanations; (2) Jesus Christ's atonement took place "not through His death on the cross, but through His overcoming death" and his breaking "through the crystallized thought strata"; (3) the son of God, the Christ, is the true identity of all humans, but Jesus realized and demonstrated this Truth: "He was more than man, as we understand the appellation in its everyday use, because there came into His manhood a factor to which most men are strangers . . . the Christ consciousness. The unfoldment of this consciousness by Jesus made Him God incarnate"; (4) keeping the words of Jesus is to take his words and contemplate them, believe in them, and obey them.

"I Am the Way, and the Truth, and the Life" (from *Jesus Christ Heals*) focuses on the power of words and especially the power of the name "Jesus Christ." Fillmore uses a biblical argument that the world was made by the creative word of God, that we are the incarnate word of God, and that therefore "our words bring forth whatever we put into them." He further argues that the most powerful words are those connected with and descriptive of the Deity. That is why Unity emphasizes Jesus Christ and the powerful name of Jesus Christ used in affirmative prayer and meditation. Fillmore maintains that Jesus was "the greatest of all exponents of the impersonal I AM," by which he means that Jesus identified with the sacred name of God in the Hebrew tradition (Yahweh/Jehovah, translated as "I Am" in Exodus 3) to such an extent that Jesus revealed the nature of God incarnate, the real "spiritual man."

This chapter also reveals Fillmore's soteriology (how are we saved?) in relation to Jesus Christ, his name, and true communion. According to Fillmore, Jesus Christ, through his thought and word, transformed his physical body into a spiritual body that exists in the "ethers" and which is shared with us when we pray and meditate in the name of Jesus. We thereby appropriate his body and blood, his substance and life, for the transformation of our own physical bodies into eternal spiritual bodies. The "appropriation . . . of His life and substance is the very foundation of salvation through Jesus Christ." This is a speculative, esoteric, and controversial doctrine that is not universally accepted within the Unity movement. On the other hand, there is no reason to doubt that this doctrine of salvation was central to Fillmore's theology and practice. It is a theory that is consistent with Fillmore's metaphysics and Bible interpretation and is just plausible enough to merit consideration. Taken metaphorically, the theory suggests that to the degree we have an accurate idea of the character of Jesus Christ and take his teachings to heart, we appropriate his consciousness and thereby his life and substance.

"All the Way" (from *Keep a True Lent* and first published in *Unity* magazine in January 1937) is interesting as a concise description of Fillmore's fully developed Christology and soteriology. It repeats basic points referred to in "Jesus Christ's Atonement" and "I Am the Way, and the Truth, and the Life," but also adds the interesting feature of Fillmore's imaginative speculation that Jesus evolved in a previous universe. What I refer to as "speculation" seems so to me; no doubt Fillmore considered his ideas to be revelations from Spirit.

Chapter 9

BEING'S PERFECT IDEA (1909)

HE FOUNDATION of our religion is Spirit, and there must be a science of Truth. The science of Truth is God thinking out creation. God is the original Mind in which all real ideas exist. The one original Mind creates by thought. This is stated in the 1st chapter of John:

"In the beginning was the Word [Logos—thought-word], and the Word was with God, and the Word was God. The same was in the beginning with God. All things were made through him; and without him was not anything made that hath been made."

Eadies's Biblical Cyclopedia says: "The term *Logos* means thought expressed, either as an idea in mind or as vocal speech."

An understanding of the Logos reveals to us the law under which all things are brought forth—the law of mind action. Creation takes place through the operation of the Logos. God is *thinking* the universe into manifestation right now. Even He cannot create without law. The law of the divine creation is the order and harmony of perfect thought.

God-Mind expresses its thoughts so perfectly that there is

no occasion for change, hence all prayers and supplications for the change of God's will to conform to human desires are futile. God does not change His mind, or trim His thought, to meet the conflicting opinions of mankind. Understanding the perfection of God thoughts, man must conform to them; so conforming, he will discover that there is never necessity for any change of the will of God in regard to human affairs.

A key to God-Mind is with everyone—it is the action of the individual mind. Man is created in the "image" and "like-ness" of God; man is therefore a phase of God-Mind, and his mind must act like the original Mind. Study your own mind, and through it you will find God-Mind. In no other way can you get a complete understanding of yourself, of the universe, and of the law under which it is being brought forth. When you see the Creator thinking out His universe, as the mathematician thinks out his problem, you will understand the necessity for the very apparent effort that nature makes to express itself; you will also understand why the impulse for higher things keeps welling up within your soul. God-Mind is living, acting thoughts. God-Mind is thinking in you; it is pushing your mind to grasp true ideas and carry them into expression.

It is therefore true, in logic and in inspiration, that man and the universe are within God-Mind as living, acting thoughts. God-Mind is giving itself to its creations, and those creations thus are evolving an independence that has the power to cooperate with, or to oppose, the original God will. It is then of vital importance to study the mind and under-stand its laws, because the starting point of every form in the universe is an idea.

Every man asks the question at some time, "What am I?" God answers: "Spiritually you are My idea of Myself as I see Myself in the ideal; physically you are the law of My Mind executing that idea." "Great is the mystery of godliness," said Paul. A little learning is a dangerous thing in the study of Being. To separate oneself from the whole and then attempt to find out the great mystery is like dissecting inanimate flesh to find the source of life.

If you would know the mystery of Being, see yourself in Being. Know yourself as an integral idea in Divine Mind, and all other ideas will recognize you as their fellow worker. Throw yourself out of the Holy Trinity, and you become an onlooker. Throw yourself into the Trinity, and you become its avenue of expression. The Trinity is known commonly as Father, Son, and Holy Spirit; metaphysically it is known as mind, idea, expression. These three are one. Each sees itself as including the other two, yet in creation separate. Jesus, the type man, placed Himself in the Godhead, and said: "He that hath seen me hath seen the Father." But, recognizing the supremacy of spiritual Principle, which He was demonstrating, He said: "The Father is greater than I."

Reducing the Trinity to simple numbers takes away much of its mystery. When we say that there is one Being with three attitudes of mind, we have stated in plain terms all that is involved in the intricate theological doctrine of the Trinity. The priesthood has always found it profitable to make complex that which is simple. When religion becomes an industry it has its trade secrets, and to the uninitiated they seem very great. Modern investigation of the character of the mind is taking away all the mysteries of Egyptian, Hindu, Hebrew, and many other religious and mystical systems of the past. Advocates of these systems are attempting to perpetuate their so-called secret knowledge through the occult societies springing up on every side in our day, but they meet with indifferent success. The modern Truth seeker takes very little on trust. Unless the claimant to occult lore can demonstrate his power in the world of affairs, people are suspicious of him. . . .

The Mind of God is Spirit, soul, body; that is, mind, idea, expression. The mind of man is Spirit, soul, body—not separate from God-Mind, but existing in it and making it manifest in an identity peculiar to the individual. Every man is building into his consciousness the three departments of God-Mind, and his success in the process is evidenced by the harmony, in his consciousness, of Spirit, soul, and body. If he is all body, he is but one-third expressed. If to body he has added soul, he is two-thirds man, and if to these two he is adding Spirit, he is on the way to the perfect manhood that God designed. Man has neither Spirit, soul, nor body of his own—he has identity only. He can say, "I." He uses God Spirit, God soul, and God body, as his "I" elects. If he uses them with the idea that they belong to him, he develops selfishness, which limits his capacity and dwarfs his product.

In his right relation, man is the inlet and the outlet of an everywhere-present life, substance, and intelligence. When his "I" recognizes this fact and adjusts itself to the invisible expressions of the one Mind, man's mind becomes harmonious; his life, vigorous and perpetual; his body, healthy. It is imperative that the individual understand this relation in order to grow naturally. It must not only be understood as an abstract proposition, but it is necessary that he blend his life consciously with God life, his intelligence with God intelligence, and his body with the "Lord's body." Conscious identification must prevail in the whole man before he can be in right relation. This involves not only a recognition of the universal intelligence, life, and substance, but also their various combinations in man's consciousness. These combinations are, in the individual world, dependent for perfect expression upon man's recognition of and his loyalty to his origin—God-Mind. Man is in God-Mind as a perfect idea. God-Mind is constantly trying to express in every man its perfect idea, the real and only man.

The perfect-man idea in God-Mind is known under various names in the many religious systems. The Krishna of the Hindu is the same as the Messiah of the Hebrews. All the great religions of the world are founded upon spiritual science, but not all of that science is understood by their followers. The Hebrews had been told again and again, by the spiritually wise, that a Messiah, or Christ man, would be born in their midst, but when He came they did not recognize Him, because of their lack of understanding. They understood only the letter of their religion. A similar lack of understanding prevails generally today. The Christ man, or perfect idea of God-Mind, is now being expressed and demonstrated by men and women as never before in the history of the race. Those who claim to be followers of the true religion should beware of putting the perfect-man idea out of their synagogues as the Jews put out Jesus Christ. The ancient Pharisees asked Jesus: "By what authority doest thou these things?" Modern Pharisees are repeating the same question. The substance of Jesus' answer was: "By their fruits ye shall know them." (Read Matthew 21:23-46.)

This perfect-idea-of-God man is your true Self. God-Mind is, under the law of thought, constantly seeking to release its perfection in you. It is your Spirit, and when you ask for its guidance and place yourself, by prayer and affirmation, in mental touch with it, there is a great increase in its manifestation in your life. It has back of it all the powers of Being, and there is nothing that it cannot do if you give it full sway and make your thought strong enough to express the great forces that it is seeking to express in you.

A most important part of the law of mind action is the fact of thought-unity. It is absolutely necessary to understand the nature of this fact before one can demonstrate the power of the superconscious mind. Among our associates, we like and are attracted to those who understand and sympathize with our thoughts. The same law holds good in Divine Mind—its thoughts are drawn to and find expression in the minds of those who raise themselves to its thought standard. This means that we must think of ourselves as God thinks of us, in order to appreciate and to receive His thoughts and to bring forth the fruits. If you think of yourself as anything less than the perfect child of the perfect Parent, you lower the thought standard of your mind and cut off the influx of thought from Divine Mind. Jesus referred to this law when He said: "Ye therefore shall be perfect, as your heavenly Father is perfect."

When we go forth in the understanding of man's perfect nature, we find a new state of consciousness forming in us; we think and do many things not according to the established custom, and the old consciousness rises up and asks: "By what authority?" We have so long looked for man-made authority in religious matters that we feel that we are treading on dangerous ground if we dare to think beyond prescribed doctrines. Right here we should appeal to the supreme reason of Spirit and proclaim what we perceive as the highest Truth, regardless of precedent or tradition, mental ignorance or physical limitation: I AM is the "image of God," the "only begotten Son" (the expressed, or *pressed out*, Mind) of the Most High. This is our true estate, and we shall never realize it until we enter into it in *mind*, because there it is, and nowhere else.

Only through the superconscious mind can we behold and commune with God. "No man hath seen God at any time; the only begotten Son, who is in the bosom of the Father, he hath declared *him*." It is taught that Jesus was exclusively the "only begotten Son," but He Himself said: "Is it not written in your law, I said, Ye are gods?" He proclaimed the unity of all men in the Father. "I am the light of the world." "Ye are the light of the world." Paul says, "As many as are led by the Spirit of God, these are sons of God." We are "heirs of God, and joint-heirs with Christ."

In this matter of sonship is one important point that we should not overlook; that point is the difference between those who perceive their sonship as a possibility, and those who have demonstrated it in their lives. "Ye must be born anew," was the proclamation of Jesus. The first birth is the human—the self-consciousness of man as an intellectual and physical being; the second birth, the being "born anew," is the transformation and translation of the human to a higher plane of consciousness as the son of God.

The second birth is that in which we "put on Christ." It is a process of mental adjustment and body transmutation that takes place right here on earth. "Have this mind in you, which was also in Christ Jesus," is an epitome of a mental and physical change that may require years to work out. But all men must go through this change before they can enter into eternal life and be as Jesus Christ is.

This being "born anew," or "born from above," is not a miraculous change that takes place in man; it is the establishment in his consciousness of that which has always existed as the perfect-man idea in Divine Mind. God created man in His "image" and "likeness." God being Spirit, the man that He creates is spiritual. It follows as a logical sequence that man, on the positive, formative, creative side of his nature, is the direct emanation of his Maker; that he is just like his Maker; that he is endowed with creative power, and that his very being is involved in God-Mind which he is releasing by his creative thought. It is to this spiritual man that the Father says: "All things that are mine are thine."

Understanding of the status of all men in Divine Mind gives us a new light upon the life of Jesus of Nazareth and makes plain many of His seemingly mysterious statements. This spiritual consciousness, or Christ Mind, was quickened in Him, and through it He realized His relation to First Cause. When asked to show the Father, whom He constantly talked to as if He were personally present, He said, "He that hath seen me hath seen the Father." His personality had been merged into the universal. The mind of Being and the thought of Being were joined, and there was no consciousness of separation or apartness.

Everything about man presages the higher man. Foremost of these prophesies is the almost universal desire for the freedom that spiritual life promises, freedom from material limitations. The immortal perception spurs man on to invent mechanical devices that will carry him above limitations. For example, he flies by means external. In his spiritual nature he is provided with the ability to overcome gravity; when this power is developed, it will be common to see men and women passing to and fro in the air, without wings or mechanical appliances of any description.

The human organism has a world of latent energies waiting to be brought into manifestation. Distributed throughout the body are many nerve centers whose offices are as yet but vaguely understood. In the New Testament, which is a work on spiritual physiology, these centers are referred to as "cities" and "rooms." The "upper room" is the very top of the head. Jesus was in this "upper room" of His mind when Nicodemus came to see Him "by night"—meaning the ignorance of sense consciousness. It was in this "upper room" that the followers of Jesus prayed until the Holy Spirit came upon them. The superconsciousness, or Christ Mind, finds its first entrance into the natural mind through this higher brain center. By thought, speech, and deed this Christ Mind is brought into manifestation. The new birth is symbolically described in the history of Jesus.

"Verily I say unto you, that many prophets and righteous men desired to see the things which ye see, and saw them not; and to hear the things which ye hear, and heard them not."

Statements for the Realization of the Son of God

1. *I am the son of God, and the Spirit of the Most High dwells in me.*
2. *I am the only begotten son, dwelling in the bosom of the Father.*
3. *I am the lord of my mind, and the ruler of all its thought people.*
4. *I am the Christ of God.*
5. *Through Christ I have dominion over my every thought and word.*
6. *I am the beloved son in whom the Father is well pleased.*
7. *Of a truth I am the son of God.*
8. *All that the Father has is mine.*
9. *He that hath seen me hath seen the Father.*
10. *I and my Father are one.*
11. *My highest ideal is a perfect man.*
12. *My next highest ideal is that I am that perfect man.*
13. *I am the image and likeness of God, in whom is my perfection.*
14. *It is written in the law of the Lord, "Ye are gods, and . . . sons of the Most High."*
15. *These are written, that ye may believe that Jesus is the Christ, the Son of God; and that believing ye may have life in his name.*

Chapter 10

JESUS CHRIST'S ATONEMENT (1926)

THERE MAY be found, in the traditions of nearly all peoples, reference to a time when man was in a state of consciousness very much superior to that which he now manifests. In the Hebrew Scriptures that superior plane is symbolically described as the Edenic state, and the departure from that place in the divine economy is called the "fall of man." Of late years we have been taught in the new metaphysics that there never was a "fall of man"; that man never fell; that his creation was spiritual, and that he is just as spiritual today as he ever was, or ever will be. Of man as an idea in Divine Mind, this is true; but that there is not a harmonious manifestation of that idea clearly indicates that there has somewhere been a lapse in man's evolution.

When by study of himself as "mind" and finding his place in Being man gets away from the sense consciousness, he rises into a mental atmosphere where he sees the relation of ideas in divine order. This perception can be attained by anyone who will detach his thinking ego from the world of phenomena and let his free ego float out into the universe of causes. It has been attained by thousands in every age, and their testimony is worthy of careful consideration.

When man touches in mind this plane of causes, he sees that the discords of humanity, in body and affairs, are the direct result of disorder in his relation to creation. He sees that there has been, through man's power of free thought, a most vital and far-reaching departure from the divine idea of his being.

Man cannot thwart the divine plan, but by virtue of his own creative or formative power he can turn his part of the work in that plan out of its true course and impede the consummation of it. This has been done, and we exist today in a state of lapse, so far as our relation to God and the orderly movement of His idea of creation are concerned. So we have to admit that the "fall of man" is in a measure true. When we understand this "fall" we shall perceive more fully why certain conditions that prevail are so incongruous in a world where a good and perfect God is supposed to rule.

Material science says that evolution is the order of nature and that all the silent records of earth, as left by departed races, testify to a steady rise of man from lower to higher conditions.

A large number of metaphysical writers and teachers have fallen into this line of thought and have assumed that the records of man's evolution, as found in archaeological and geological research, bear testimony to his mind evolution, and that the experiences through which he has passed are in the divine order of creation. We must accept this, reconcile it, or expunge it.

We accept the testimony, but we say that it is but the evolution of man out of a lapse from divine order in creation, and that it is no part of the original divine plan, any more than a fall into a muddy swamp would be a necessary part of a journey to a beautiful city. Man is the son of a God whose methods are harmonious in bringing forth His ideas. Man is His idea—a self-conscious entity, having in embryo all the faculties and powers of that from which it came forth. In following the orderly path of its unfoldment this man idea is in conscious mental communication with its source, and knows what to do and what not to do in bringing forth creation. "And Jehovah God commanded the man, saying, Of every tree of the garden thou mayest freely eat; but of the tree of the knowledge of good and evil, thou shalt not eat of it: for in the day that thou eatest thereof thou shalt surely die."

The Garden of Eden or Paradise of God is in the ether, and we see that the "fall of man" antedated the formation of this planet as we behold it geologically. Jesus recognized this when He said: "And now, Father, glorify thou me with thine own self with the glory which I had with thee before the world was."

We are by birth a spiritual race, and we should never have known matter or material conditions if we had followed the leadings of our higher consciousness.

It is the recognition of this higher consciousness and the reorganization of our place in Being that we are seeking. We are emerging from the darkness of Egyptian bondage—we see the Promised Land, and we want to know the shortest way to it. That way is the Jesus Christ way. The demonstration of Jesus relates Him to us in a metaphysical sense, because it is only by a study of states of consciousness formed by thought that it can be understood.

We have been taught by the church that Jesus died for us—as an atonement for our sins. By human sense this belief has been materialized into a flesh-and-blood process, in which the death of the body on the cross played the important part. Herein has the sense consciousness led the church astray. That spiritual things must be spiritually discerned seems to have escaped the notice of the church in forming its scheme of atonement. At the root of the church's teaching is Truth; Jesus of Nazareth played an important part in opening the way for every one of us into the Father's kingdom. However, that way was not through His death on the cross, but through His overcoming death. "I am the resurrection, and the life."

To comprehend the atonement requires a deeper insight into creative processes than the average man and the average woman have attained; not because they lack the ability to understand, but because they have submerged their thinking power in a grosser thought stratum. So only those who study Being from the standpoint of pure mind can ever understand the atonement and the part that Jesus played in opening the way for humanity into the glory that was potentially theirs before the world was formed.

We who have studied these creative processes through thought action know how states of consciousness are formed and how persistent a certain mental state is after it has once crystallized. The man ego seems to lose its identity in its own formations, and forgets for the time all its past experiences and powers. We see this in certain social states among the people. No matter how miserable and degraded their state, people get so accustomed to it that they do not aspire to anything higher. Reformers of the criminal classes in our large cities tell us that their most difficult problem is to awaken in these people a desire for better things. They are attached to their habits of thought and living, and they do not want to be reformed. The same is true in the history of efforts to civilize the savage races. Just when they are about to reach the place where they will see the desirability of a better way of living, they suddenly fall back into the old life, and are satisfied. The tendency of thought emanation is to crystallize about the form that it has made and, in spite of the struggles of the man ego, to hold to it.

We can readily see how a whole race might be caught in

the meshes of its own thought emanations and, through this drowsy ignorance of the man ego, remain there throughout eternity, unless a break were made in the structure and the light of a higher way let in. This is exactly what has happened to our race. In our journey back to the Father's house we became lost in our own thought emanations, and Jesus Christ broke through the crystallized thought strata and opened the way for all those who will follow Him.

By so doing He made a connection between our state of consciousness and the more interior one of the Father—He united them—made them a unit—*one*, hence the at-one-ment or atonement through Him. He became the way by which all who accept Him may "pass over" to the new consciousness. That which died upon the cross was the consciousness of all mortal beliefs that hold us in bondage—such as sin, evil, sickness, fleshly lusts, and death—which He overcame. "I have overcome the world." Jesus' "overcoming" made a great rent in the sense consciousness, and opened a way by which all who desire may demonstrate easily and quickly.

But in order to receive the benefit of Jesus' work it is necessary for everyone to go to the place where He made the rent in the race beliefs. If you were held in the meshes of a great spider web, and someone made a hole through which you could pass, you would go where the hole was and would pass out that way. The same rule holds good of this breach that Jesus made in the limitations of sense that hold the race in bondage—we have to go where He is, mentally and spiritually. "I go to prepare a place for you." So we see that the church is not so far wrong in its call to "follow Jesus." The error lies in the belief that He was the *only* begotten Son of God, and that He overcame for us, and that by simply *believing* on Him we are saved.

In believing Him to be the *only* begotten Son of God, we have confounded His higher consciousness or Christ consciousness, which is the only begotten Son of God, with His lower or Jesus consciousness. He recognized His identity in God as the Christ, the Son of God; He also recognized His consciousness of self, the son of man. So each of us is a son of God. We shall come into conscious recognition of the Christ mind, effecting the junction between our mind and God's mind just as soon as we let go of the limitations of mortal sense. God has but one Son, the Christ, the one ideal man. This divine conjunction was accomplished by Jesus, and the Christ shone out through His mortal self and illumined it, until it lost its personality and disappeared into divine individuality.

By believing that Jesus was more divine than other men, the church has assumed that He had certain privileges that the Father does not extend to all; that in a superhuman way He made good all our shortcomings; that we are saved from suffering for our acts by simply believing on Him and accepting Him, in a perfunctory way, as our Saviour. Paul is responsible for a good share of this throwing of the whole burden upon the blood of Jesus—doubtless the result of an old mental tendency carried over from his Hebrew idea of the blood sacrifices of the priesthood. In order to show the parallel in the life of Jesus, Paul preached to the Jews that He was the great once-for-all blood sacrifice and that no other blood sacrifice would ever become necessary.

But Jesus went further than this. He said: "Come, follow me." "Keep my sayings." He meant: Do as I do. I have overcome; now by following in my footsteps you shall overcome.

We all recognize the advantage of thought cooperation. It is much easier to hold ourselves in the true consciousness when we are associated with those who think as we do. It was the work of Jesus to establish in our race consciousness a spiritual center with which everyone might become associated mentally, regardless of geographical location. He said to His disciples, "I go to prepare a place for you. . . . that where I am, *there* ye may be also." That place is a state of consciousness right here in our midst, and we can at any time connect ourselves with it by centering our mind on Jesus and silently asking His help in our demonstrations. It is not the prayer of a "worm of the dust" to a god, but of one who is on the way asking the guidance of one who has passed over the same road, and who knows all the hard places and how to get through them.

This in one sense is the relation of Jesus to each of us, and so far as our present demonstration is concerned, it is the most important relation. The road that we are traveling from the mortal plane of consciousness to the spiritual plane is beset with many obstructions, and we need the assistance of one stronger than any of those who now dwell in flesh bodies. He who is still in the perception of the earthly is not always a safe guide, because he sees in a limited way. We want one who sees wholly in Spirit, and such a one we find in Jesus Christ.

He has not left us or gone to some faraway heaven, but He may be reached by the humblest of us in a moment's time, if we really aspire in soul for His companionship and help.

This is a simple statement of the relation that Jesus of Nazareth bears to us. Yet He was more than Jesus of Nazareth, more than any other man who ever lived on the earth. He was more than man, as we understand the appellation in its everyday use, because there came into His manhood a factor to which most men are strangers. This factor was the Christ consciousness. The unfoldment of this consciousness by Jesus made Him God incarnate, because Christ is the mind of God individualized, and whoever so loses his personality as to be swallowed up in God becomes Christ Jesus, or God man.

We cannot separate Jesus Christ from God, or tell where man leaves off and God begins in Him. To say that Jesus Christ was a man as we are men is not true, because He had dropped that personal consciousness by which we separate ourselves into men and women. He was consciously one with the absolute principle of Being. He had no consciousness separate from that Being, He *was* that Being to all intents and purposes.

Yet He attained no more than is expected of every one of us. "That they may be one, even as we *are*" was His prayer.

It is all accomplished through the externalization of the Christ consciousness, which is omnipresent and ever ready to manifest itself through us as it did through Jesus.

This principle has been perceived by the spiritually wise in every age, but they have not known how to externalize it and to make it an abiding state of consciousness. Jesus accomplished this and His method is worthy of our adoption, because, so far as we know, it is the only method that has been successful. It is set forth in the New Testament and whoever adopts the life of purity and love and power there exemplified in the experiences of Jesus of Nazareth will in due course attain the place that He attained.

The way to do this is the way Jesus did it. He acknowledged Himself to be the Son of God. The attainment of the Christ consciousness calls for nothing less on our part than a definite recognition of ourselves as sons of God right here and now, regardless of appearances to the contrary. We know that we are sons of God—then why not acknowledge it and proceed to take possession of our God right? That is what Jesus did in the face of most adverse conditions. Conditions today are not so stolidly material as they were in Jesus' time. People now know more about themselves and their relation to God. They are familiar with thought processes and how an idea held in mind will make itself manifest in the body and in affairs; hence they take up this problem of spiritual realization under favorable conditions. It must work out just as surely as a mathematical problem, because it is under immutable law. The factors are all in our possession and the rule that was demonstrated in one striking instance is before us. By following that rule and doing day by day the work that comes to us, we shall surely put on Christ as fully and completely as did Jesus of Nazareth.

The process of Jesus' evolving from sense to soul was first a recognition of His spiritual selfhood and a constant affirmation of its supremacy and power. Jesus loved to make the highest statements: "I and the Father are one." "All authority hath been given unto me in heaven and on earth." He made these statements before the resurrection, so we know that He was not fully conscious of their reality. But by the power of His word He brought about the realization.

Next in the process was that constant cleansing of the consciousness through denial, or fasting. He prayed much alone, and fasted. He was being tempted on every side, within and without, and was always overcoming. He daily put out of His mind all the ideas that bind men to the world. He recognized that the kingdom of the spiritual man is not of this world—that it is a world that transcends this and controls it; therefore He was not attached in any way to the things of sense. Personal self, the Devil, told Him to turn stones into bread, but He did not yield to this temptation to use His God-given power for material gain. Personal sense took Him upon ambition's high place and showed Him what He might have in the fame of the world if He would worship personal sense, but He refused to lower His standard. He was using spiritual power and He was true to its character; He did not mix it with matter or with material ways.

When Jesus said, "The words that I have spoken unto you are spirit, and are life," He touched the inner Christ word which created all things, and we know that His words were vivified from that center with a life essence and moving power that will demonstrate the truth of His statement.

These words have rung through the souls of men and set them afire with God's Spirit, throughout the ages. This is because they are spiritual words. Within them are the seeds of a divine life and they grow in the minds of all who give them place, just as a beautiful flower or a great tree grows from the seed germ planted in the ground.

Jesus recognized that the consciousness of man was submerged in the things of sense; that it could not perceive Truth in the abstract, and that it must, under these conditions, be stirred into activity by some stimulating force dropped into it from without. Hence He sent forth His powerful words of Truth to the thirsty souls, and said to them, "Keep my saying."

To keep a saying is to revolve it in mind—to go over it in all its aspects, to believe it as a truth, to treasure it as a saving balm in time of need, and above all to obey the law that it sets forth.

People in all ages have known about the saving power of words and have used them to the best of their understanding. The Hebrews bound upon their foreheads and wrists parchments with words of Scripture written upon them. The Hindus, Japanese, Chinese, and the people of nearly all other known nations have their various ways of applying the sacred words to the modification of their ills, and the invocation of the invisible powers to aid them in both their material and spiritual needs.

Although these methods are faulty in that they use the letter of the word, instead of its spirit, they are useful to us as indicators of the universal belief in the power of the sacred word.

We know that words express ideas, and to get at their substantial part we must move into the realm of ideas. Ideas are in the mind and we must go there if we want to get the force of our words. The Hebrew phylacteries and the lamas' [Buddhist] prayer wheels are suggestive of the wordy prayers of the Christian; but their use is not keeping the sayings of Jesus, nor reaping the inner substance of the mystical word. This can be done only by those who believe in the omnipresent Spirit of God and in faith keep in mind the words that express His goodness, wisdom, and power.

Jesus more fully voiced this nearness of God to man than any of the prophets, and His words are correspondingly vivified with inner fire and life. He said that those who kept His sayings should even escape death, so potent was the life energy attached to them.

This is a startling promise, but when we understand that it was not the personal man, Jesus, making it, but the Father speaking through Him, we know that it was not an idle one; for He said, speaking to His disciples, "The word which ye hear is not mine, but the Father's who sent me."

This is the reason why these words of Jesus endure, and why more and more they are attracting the attention of men.

Whoever takes these words into his mind should consecrate himself to the Truth that they represent. That Truth is not the doctrine of any church, nor the creed of any sect— not even Christianity. That Truth is written in the inner sanctuary of every soul, and all know it without external formulas. It is the intuitive perception of what is right in the sight of God. It is the Truth and justice that every man recognizes as the foundation of true living.

Whoever consecrates himself to follow this inner monitor and live up to its promptings, regardless of social or commercial customs, consecrates himself to do God's will. He is fitted to take the words of Jesus and make them his own.

It is no idle experiment, this keeping in the mind the words of Jesus. It is a very momentous undertaking, and may mark the most important period in the life of an individual. There must be sincerity and earnestness and right motive, and withal a determination to understand the spiritual import.

This requires attention, time, and patience in the application of the mind to solving the deeper meanings of the sayings that we are urged to keep.

People deal with sacred words in a way that is too superficial to bring results. They juggle with words. They toss them into the air with a heavenly tone or an oratorical ring and count it as compliance with divine requirements. This is but another form of the prayer wheel and the phylactery. It is the lip service that Jesus condemned because its object is to be "seen of men."

To keep the sayings of Jesus means much more than this. It has peculiar significance for the inner life. Only after the inner life is awakened is the true sense of the spiritual word understood. But the sincere keeper of Jesus' sayings will by his devotions awaken the inner spirit, and the Lord will come to him and minister to his call, as lovingly as a father to a beloved son.

Jesus tells us that His words are Spirit, and then tells us to keep them. How can one keep a thing of which he knows nothing? How can one keep the words and sayings of Jesus unless he gets them into his consciousness and grasps them with his mind, his spirit?

Surely there is no other way to keep His sayings. Those who are doing so from any other standpoint are missing the mark. They may be honest, and they may be good, sincere people, living what the world calls pure Christian lives, but they will not get the fruits of Jesus' words unless they comply with His requirements.

Unless you perceive that there is something more in the doctrine of Jesus than keeping up a worldly moral standard as preparation for salvation after death, you will fall far short of being a real Christian.

Jesus did not depreciate moral living, but neither did He promise that it fulfilled the law of God. Very negative people are frequently trusty and moral. But that does not make them Christians after the Jesus Christ plan. His Christianity had a living God in it—a God that lived in Him and spoke through Him. It was a religion of fire and water—life as well as purity. Men are to be alive—not merely exist half dead for a few years and then go out with a splutter, like a tallow dip. Jesus Christ's men are to be electric lights that glow with a perpetual current from the one omnipresent Energy. The connection with that current is to be made through the mind by setting up sympathetic vibrations.

The mind moves upon ideas; ideas are made visible through words. Hence holding right words in the mind will set the mind going at a rate proportioned to the dynamic power of the idea back of those words. A word with a lazy idea back of it will not stimulate the mind. The word must represent swift, strong, spiritual ideas in order to infuse the white energy of God into the mind. This is the kind of word in which Jesus reveled. He delighted in making great and mighty claims for His God, Himself, His words, and for all men: "I and the Father are one." "All authority hath been given unto me in heaven and on earth." "The Father is greater than I." "Is it not written in your law, I said, Ye are gods?" "The works that I do shall ye do also; and greater." These were some of the claims with which He stimulated His mind. And He produced the results—His words were fulfilled.

Many who for years have been students of the science of Christ and have a clear, intelligent perception of its truths are yet outside the kingdom of Spirit. They anxiously ask: "Why do I not realize the presence of Spirit?"

Have you kept the sayings of Jesus? Have you said to yourself in silence and aloud until the very ethers vibrated with its Truth, "I and the Father are one"?

Have you opened the pores of your mind, by mentally repeating the one solvent of crystallized conditions, "I in them, and thou in me"?

This means mental discipline day after day and night after night, until the inertia of the mind is overcome and the way is opened for the descent of Spirit.

The personal consciousness is like a house with all the doors and windows barred. The doors and the windows of the mind are concrete ideas, and they swing open when the right word is spoken to them. Jesus voiced a whole volume of right words. If you will take up His sayings and make them yours, they will open all the doors of your mind, the light will come in, and you will in due time be able to step forth.

Another cannot do this for you. You really do not want him to do it, though you may think it would be nice if some master of spiritual ideas would help you to his understanding.

But this is a childish dream of the moment. You want to be yourself, and you can be yourself only by living your own life and finding its issues at the Fountainhead. If it were possible for one to reveal Truth to another [without this self-discipline], we should find heaven cornered by cunning manipulators of mind and its glories stored up in warehouses waiting a higher market.

Let us be thankful that God is no respecter of persons, that Truth cannot be revealed by one mortal to another. God is a special, personal Father to every one of His children, and from no other source can they get Truth.

Jesus, who has clearly revealed the Father in His consciousness, may tell all men how it came about. He may point the way. He may say, "I am the way, and the truth, and the life," but there is always a condition attached to its realization: One must exercise faith, keep His sayings, and follow Him. Summed up, it means that by adopting His methods one will find the same place in the Father that He found.

"If a man love me, he will keep my word: and my Father will love him, and we will come unto him, and make our abode with him."

Chapter 11

"I AM THE WAY, AND THE TRUTH, AND THE LIFE" (1939)

ᴊEHOVAH Gᴏᴅ *restores me to health and wholeness.* Words are quickened by those who speak them and they pick up and carry the ideas of the speaker, weak or strong, ignorant or wise, good or ill. Thus words descriptive of deity have been personalized in the thought stuff of the race and those who invoke them in prayer and meditation are given a spiritual impetus far beyond what they would receive from common words. It is a fact that the name Jehovah came to be held in such reverence by the rabbis that they never spoke the word aloud. Jesus said that His words were so charged with Spirit and life that they would endure longer even than heaven and earth.

Next to Spirit the word of Spirit is the most powerful thing in existence. The author of the Book of Hebrews says "that the worlds have been framed by the word of God." We read in Genesis that "God said" and it came to pass. And God said, "Let us make man in our own image, after our likeness." Thus we see that man is the incarnate word of God, and it logically follows that our words bring forth whatever we put into them. Study the 1st chapter of John. Jesus said that a man will be held accountable for his lightest word.

Spiritually classified, the Jehovah of the Old Testament is identical with the Christ in the New. One who heals by the power of the word should become familiar with the inner meaning of all the words and use those that appeal to him as possessing the greatest healing potency. Jesus promised that He would unite with the Holy Spirit in helping those who called upon Him. Unity healers have found that this promise is fulfilled when they concentrate in prayer and positive affirmation on the presence of the Holy Spirit and Jesus Christ. A new and strong contact is felt with spiritual life, as if it were a mighty battery, when the name *Jehovah God* or *Jehovah-rapha* ("the Lord that healeth thee") is spoken silently and audibly; then the ethers quicken with the name and shower spiritual life on both patient and healer. The word *Jehovah* or *Yahweh* is charged with spiritual power far above and beyond any other word in human language.

I am raised to perfection in mind and body by the healing power of Jesus Christ.

Quite a few Truth students ask why we emphasize Jesus Christ so strongly in our writings and statements of Truth. Spiritual psychology proves that the name of a great character carries his mind potency and that wherever his name is repeated silently or audibly his attributes become manifest. Jesus Christ knew this and commanded His disciples to go forth in His name. The marvelous works they did prove that they exercised power far beyond anything warranted by their education or previous ability, power springing directly from Spirit.

Every thinker who studies the life and teachings of Jesus readily admits that He attained an understanding of spiritual things far beyond that of any other man that ever lived. His mind touched heights far beyond those of other advanced searchers for Truth. As we unfold spiritually we see more and more that Jesus understood the finer shades of metaphysical reasoning and related His mind and body to both ideas and their manifestation.

Jesus demonstrated that He understood the healing power stored up in the body, which He said is released through faith. "Thy faith hath made thee whole." Jesus identified Himself and His name with the sacred name of the Hebrew dispensation, Jehovah, and added another link to that long chain of names and events that brought forth the perfect man ideated by God-Mind, Jesus Christ.

As a directive head is essential in any army, militant or spiritual, so in every forward movement of the human family there must be a leader. The leader is chosen because of his ability as a demonstrator of the principles adopted by the group he represents. The religious principles taught and demonstrated by Jesus were not originated by Him, nor did He claim them as a "discovery." He said that Moses wrote of Him, and He often quoted Moses, but with an interpretation quite different from that of the popular religious leaders. He told them that they studied the Scriptures expecting through them to attain eternal life when the only way to attain that life was through Him [Christ], and they would not come to Him. Right here Jesus emphasized the spiritual man, the I AM in man, as the only way by which man can enter the kingdom of God.

Jesus was undoubtedly the greatest of all exponents of the impersonal I AM, which is revealed to man when he opens up the supermind within his own soul. Jesus Christ's real name is Jehovah, I AM. The personal man Jesus is merely the veil or mask worn by the spiritual man Christ or Jehovah. We are all, in our personality, wearing the mask that conceals the real, the spiritual, I AM. Jesus shattered that mask and revealed the spiritual man. He also taught the way by which we may all do what He did and thus fulfill the destiny implanted in us by the parent Mind.

There are many distractions to keep us from finding the one door into the inner kingdom and many voices calling to us that they will show us the easy way, but Jesus Christ is the only one that appeals to those who are grounded in principle.

Any declaration man may make in which the name *Jesus Christ* is used reverently will contact the spiritual ether in which the Christ I AM lives and will open the mind and body to the inflow of spiritual healing rays. These healing rays are very much superior to the ultraviolet rays that come from the sun or our best medical appliances, because they minister to the mind as well as the body.

Thy vitalizing energy floods my whole being, and I am healed.

The most inclusive name for Being is Jehovah God. Jehovah represents the individual I AM and God (Elohim) the universal Principle. When man thinks or says "I am" he is potentially giving freedom to the seed ideas that contains in its spiritual capacity all of Being. The natural man in his narrowed mental comprehension barely touches the seed ideas that expand in the Christ man to infinite power. The more we dwell upon and expand our I AM the greater looms its originating capacity before us. When Jesus proclaimed, "Before Abraham was born, I am," He realized that the I AM preceded all manifestation, however great, and was capable of infinite expression.

The proposition that the seemingly insignificant individual I AM contains infinite creative capacity appears absurd to the thoughtless, but we have numerous examples of extraordinary capacity for expansion in the little seeds that bring forth gigantic trees. The Scriptures plainly teach that men may become gods. Adam was expelled from the Garden of Eden because Jehovah realized that he might appropriate eternal life and live forever in his ignorance.

When man realizes that "death and life are in the power of the tongue" and begins to use his "I am" statements wisely, he has the key that unlocks the secret chambers of existence in heaven and earth.

The Christ substance (body) and the Christ life (blood) are accessible at all times and in all places to the one who awakens his soul to spiritual omnipresence. The table of the Lord is spread everywhere for those who believe on Him as Spirit and in their Spirit affirmation eat of His body and blood. The appropriation by His followers of His life and substance is the very foundation of salvation through Jesus Christ. The mere acceptance intellectually of the teaching that we are saved by the blood of the Lord Jesus and the partaking of the bread and wine in a perfunctory manner will save neither mind nor body. The only thing that will do it is the understanding that Jesus raised His body life and substance out of the race consciousness into Spirit consciousness and that with our minds poised in that consciousness we can lay hold of the Spirit elements that will save us to the uttermost.

Nearly everyone needs both mind and body healing, and those who give faithful attention to the law as it operates in man are rewarded by demonstrations of healing. Jesus healed "all manner of disease," the same Jesus has broadcast that healing Spirit to the uttermost ends of the earth, and today all who will may be made whole.

The Christ life quickens and heals me.

Although millions have testified that they have felt the quickening life of Christ, other millions doubt if such a thing as the Christ life exists.

The unseen forces have always been an enigma to the masses, and even those who are expecting the unseen to spring forth suddenly into some marvelous manifestation do not recognize it when it comes to pass. It is said that when Marconi demonstrated to a group of scientists in Paris the power of radio waves, they doubted his claims and sought in various ways to discover the concealed wires, which they were sure were being used. So every unseen force man uses has had to prove its existence by some visible manifestation that can be mechanically demonstrated. But are there unseen forces that cannot be mechanically demonstrated? The answer is that all unseen forces can be mechanically demonstrated and that they are being demonstrated every day the world over, but scientists have not yet recognized as mechanical all the devices through which man brings unseen forces into manifestation; for example, his own brain and the radio. These with many other unseen forces come under the head of mechanism.

Brain cells are the only material things that will transmit mind, and man has never yet been able to invent so fine a piece of mechanism outside his own organism. But brains are mechanical, and man does build and use them in expressing his intelligence.

The fact is that each of us builds a brain especially designed and fitted for our individual use and for no one else's. All attempts to turn our brains over to others in hypnosis or mediumship will prove abortive in the end.

In radio terms your brain cells correspond to the tubes in a combined broadcasting and receiving set, and you have tuned them to certain wave lengths and turned on the power. If you have not been informed of your innate ability to turn on or off the mind waves, you are functioning in the established race programs of personality: what your ancestors have thought, what other people think, and what little thought you can conjure up yourself. Unless your mind has been quickened by the light of spiritual understanding, you are living in a little three-dimensional world whose beginning and end is sin or a falling short of the divine ideal.

"If a man keep my word, he shall never see death."

"I am the resurrection, and the life."

Jesus stressed the power of words, especially His words. In the parable of the sower He said, "When anyone heareth the word of the kingdom." Here He referred to the Logos, the creative Word, which framed the worlds, according to John. The creative Word or Logos is also identified as Holy Spirit, which is carrying forward the ideas of God as they unfold in the manifest universe.

As the Word of God, the Logos, is creating in the universe (body of God) so man's word is creating in his universe (man's body). That is why Jesus said that we should be judged by our words. We are creating a little universe in which the cells of the body correspond to the planets of the solar system. "And I say unto you, that every idle word that men shall speak, they shall give account thereof in the day of judgment."

The "day of judgment" to us is any day that we get the fruit in body and affairs of some thought or word that we have expressed.

The creative power of man's word is in proportion to his understanding of God-Mind and his unity with its law. The creative power of most men does not get beyond their own body consciousness, because they know very little about Spirit and their relation to its laws. The better we realize our spiritual relationship to creative Mind and conform our thoughts and words to its laws the greater is the power of our words. Jesus "tuned in" to Divine Mind until that Mind reinforced His mind and raised it to superhuman capacity. It was in one of His moments of mental exaltation that He declared, "The words that I have spoken unto you are spirit, and are life."

We have thought that we were to be saved by Jesus' making personal petitions and sacrifices for us, but now we see that we are to be saved by using the creative principles that He developed in Himself, and that He is ever ready to cooperate with us in developing in ourselves by observing the law as He observed it. "I in them, and thou in me, that they may be perfected into one."

Thus we see that when Jesus said, "If a man keep my word, he shall never see death," He meant that we should realize the life-giving properties of the creative words of God as He had realized them, that we should have no consciousness of death.

I have new life in Christ and I am healed.

To attain this realization of the word of life we must create currents of life in our bodies as Jesus did in His. Of all man's possessions the most valuable is life. "For what shall a man be profited, if he shall gain the whole world, and forfeit his life? or what shall a man give in exchange for his life?"

When Jesus uttered these words He was explaining to His disciples that He was about to pass through a transformation in which He would give up His physical life, though He would continue His manifestation in a spiritual life. They did not understand Him, and Peter "began to rebuke him." Jesus told them they did not understand the things of God "but the things of men." Up to this day the passing over of the natural life into the spiritual life is not fully understood by Christians. It is almost universally interpreted as something that takes place after the death of the body, while in fact it is a transformation of the issues of life while the body is intact. Paul said, "I die daily." So Jesus could not have appeared after His crucifixion in the same body if He had not daily given up the physical life and daily put on the Christ life. It is a step-by-step or cell-by-cell transformation.

What did Jesus mean when He said, "If a man keep my

word, he shall never see death"? Did He mean death of the soul? There is nothing in His teaching to warrant such a conclusion. He meant that we shall escape physical death if we identify ourselves with the creative Word in Him, the Logos.

Then to understand the new life in Christ we must give attention to that mystical Word or Logos, because in it are wrapped the principles that, planted in our minds, will spring into new life in mind and body.

Eternal life and strength are here, and I am made whole through Jesus Christ.

Among the seven sacred names given to Jehovah by the Hebrew priesthood is *Jehovah-shammah,* meaning "Jehovah is there." Jehovah is the name of the ever-living I AM. When the mystic desired to commune with the omnipresent life he did not speak the name aloud but silently intoned, "Jehovah-shammah!" This pervasion of his I AM with the ever-living I AM harmonized the spiritual man with his source, and the individual was merged with the universal.

A certain mystery has always accompanied the use of the sacred name, and the priesthood gained their ascendancy over the people by performing marvelous works through the silent and audible intoning of words charged with thoughts of spiritual power.

However a priest must undergo discipline to acquire mastery of the elemental forces that function in mind and body. A cursory reading of Exodus conveys the idea that for forty years Moses was a shepherd, tending the flocks of his father-in-law Jethro, priest of Midian. But his mastery of nature, as evidenced by his works in Egypt, plainly shows that he understood the control of matter by mind better than did the magicians of Egypt, although he was versed in their magic.

The followers of Jesus did marvelous works in His name, but that name was also used by those who were not His immediate disciples, and they succeeded in casting out demons so well that John complained about it. Jesus said, "Forbid *him* not: for he that is not against you is for you." So we find that a person's name identifies him with his character. If that character is mighty in spirituality and power, he who invokes it in his prayers is automatically raised into a like sphere of power and what he says comes to pass. "And whatsoever ye shall ask in my name, that will I do, that the Father may be glorified in the Son."

Salvation through Jesus Christ is not accomplished by looking forward to freedom but by realizing that we are now free through His freeing power, which we are using to cut the bonds with which our thoughts have bound us. Then we have only to establish ourselves in real life and strength by understanding that these attributes of Being are omnipresent and that our affirmations of that presence, will cause us to become conscious that we do now and here live, move, and have our being in eternal life and strength.

In the name and by the power and authority of Jesus Christ I am made every whit whole.

Man gives a name—that is, "character"—to every idea that comes into consciousness, and whatever he conceives a thing to be, that it becomes to him. So it is written in Genesis: "Whatsoever the man called every living creature, that was the name thereof."

Jesus taught and demonstrated that man is master of a kingdom far beyond the consciousness of the natural man, but accessible to those who open their mind to its laws and observe those laws in thought and act.

The official declarations of a representative of a country are recognized by all as worthy of credence. Jesus represented the kingdom of the heavens, and we, His agents, take possession of that kingdom in His name and declare that we are vested with authority to bring spiritual forces to bear that will restore man to his primal perfection.

In the 3d chapter of Acts is recorded the healing by Peter of a man lame from his birth; and Peter says, "In the name of Jesus Christ of Nazareth, walk. . . . And immediately his feet and ankle-bones received strength. And leaping up, he stood, and began to walk; and he entered with them into the temple, walking, and leaping, and praising God."

When the people were greatly astonished at this marvelous healing and gathered around Peter and John, Peter explained, "Ye men of Israel, why marvel ye at this man? or why fasten ye your eyes on us, as though by our own power or godliness we had made him to walk? . . . And by faith in his name hath his name made this man strong."

Shakespeare says, "Good name in man and woman . . . is the immediate jewel of their souls." But even Shakespeare, with his psychological insight, never realized how good a name would be or to what heights of power it could lift one who applies the laws of Spirit in its use.

Those who have searched diligently to know God and His Son Jesus and have prayed for the light of Spirit find that they possess a certain confidence and faith in the very name Jesus Christ and that to the one who speaks it the name draws creative forces far beyond mental comprehension. Hence we should have confidence in the promises of Jesus that those who in faith use His name shall do the marvelous wonders that He did and even greater works of a spiritual character.

Read in the 16th chapter of Mark what are the signs of a real follower of Christ and see if you are measuring up to them: "And these signs shall accompany them that believe: in my name shall they cast out demons; they shall speak with new tongues; they shall take up serpents, and if they drink any deadly thing, it shall in no wise hurt them; they shall lay hands on the sick, and they shall recover."

By the grace of God through Christ Jesus I am made whole.

Jesus knew what He had accomplished in breaking the

mortal mesmerism of the race, and He boldly proclaimed His ability to help all those who join Him in seeking to effect a direct union with creative Mind.

As Jesus healed in Galilee so He is healing in the same spiritual realm of radiant health today. "To him that over-cometh, to him will I give to eat of the tree of life, which is in the Paradise of God." "I am the way, and the truth, and the life."

Chapter 12

ALL THE WAY (1937)

WHEN WE SING, "I'll go with Him all the way," we do not always realize the mighty import of our words. Jesus went all the way from the human to the divine. He went all the way to immortality. He raised not only His own consciousness from despair and hopelessness to assurance and confidence in the presence and continued help of a loving Father-God, but He opened the way for the whole race to do likewise. When we determine to follow Him all the way we undertake the mighty work of the ages, a revolution of character before which the famous tasks of Hercules pale into insignificance.

As a matter of fact no one has ever followed Jesus all the way in the revolution in our race thought that He initiated. Many devout, sincere men have attempted to do so, but Jesus is yet to be understood and imitated in His work of salvation.

In the first place we have not understood the depth of our bondage to error and evil, nor the enormity of the consequences if it is allowed to continue. But Jesus knew how the human mind wraps itself up in its own error thought and brings darkness and desolation beyond redemption, unless

the light of divine understanding is released in the consciousness. Jesus knew how to quicken this inner light by
being Himself the great Light, and He showed us how to attain the same spiritual brightness. In the face of ignorance,
superstition, and persecution He boldly proclaimed: "I am
the light of the world." "Ye are the light of the world." "Even
so let your light shine before men; that they may see your
good works, and glorify your Father who is in heaven."

To understand Jesus' experiences in their spiritual significance and their effect on our human bondage we should become better acquainted with the real character of the man
and His relation to us, because the many claims of Jesus'
spiritual superiority made by His followers and Himself must
have a basis of Truth.

That Jesus had elements of greatness far beyond those of
any other man that has ever lived on this earth is universally
accepted by both the religious and the secular world. Some
Christians claim that He came direct from heaven; that He
was very God incarnate. Other Christians see in Him simply
the fulfillment of the ideal man designed by Divine Mind.
Neither of these views quite meets the logic of unbiased reason considered in connection with the events of Jesus' life.

If Jesus was very God and had all power, why did He suffer the agony in Gethsemane and cry out to His Father for
help? If He was a mere man, an evolved representative of our
race, why did He lay claim to an existence prior and superior
to the Jesus incarnation, "And now, Father, glorify thou me
with thine own self with the glory which I had with thee before the world was." "Before Abraham was born, I am."

He claimed the whole human race as his "flock" and compared them to sheep with Himself as the shepherd:

"I am the good shepherd; and I know mine own, and
mine own know me, even as the Father knoweth me,

and I know the Father; and I lay down my life for the sheep. And other sheep have I, which are not of this fold: them also I must bring, and they shall hear my voice; and they shall become one flock, one shepherd. Therefore doth the Father love me, because I lay down my life, that I may take it again. No one taketh it away from me, but I lay it down of myself. I have power to lay it down, and I have power to take it again. This commandment received I from my Father."

But they did not understand. "There arose a division again among the Jews because of these words. And many of them said, He hath a demon, and is mad; why hear ye him? Others said, These are not the sayings of one possessed with a demon. Can a demon open the eyes of the blind?"

Men in Jesus' time could not understand how what appeared to be an ordinary man could be the beginning of a whole new race of men as Jesus claimed to be. So they thought He was crazy when He made the assertion. We in our day do not fully understand how one man and one woman increase their species. It is a divine mystery, yet we bear witness to it.

In the 1st chapter of John's Gospel it is written:

"He was in the world, and the world was made through him, and the world knew him not. He came unto his own, and they that were his own received him not."

The fact is that the relationship which Jesus bears to the human family is quite beyond our present intellectual comprehension.

In order to understand the status of Jesus we have to visualize a universe like that in which we live as having existed during billions of years in the past, as having fulfilled its mission in the evolution of a superrace of men, and as then passing away leaving as its fruit God-men with creative power. Jesus was one of the God-men of that ancient creation, and it was His destiny to bring forth from the depths of Being a race of potential gods, place them in an environment where they could grow as He grew and become, like Him, a Son of God. As stated by Paul, "we are also his offspring."

The beginning of our race evolution is given in the allegory of Adam and Eve in the Garden of Eden. Jehovah is Christ, who formed man out of the dust of the ground and breathed into his nostrils the breath of life.

When the Adamic race reached a point in their evolution where they had personal-will volition, they began to think and act independently of the Jehovah or Christ Mind. Then the sense consciousness began to rule and the materialization of the body resulted. Degeneration of the whole man followed. Loss of ability to draw constantly on the one and only source of life threw the whole race into an anemic condition. Their bodies began to disintegrate, and death came into the world. Then Satan, the mind of sense, began to rule; sin was in the saddle. The people like sheep had gone astray; they were lost in the wilderness of sense; they were in the throes of race extinction. New life had to be imparted; a blood transfusion was imperative. Christ then began a series of physical incarnations, beginning prehistorically and ending with His Jesus incarnation.

Why does the all-powerful God have to resort to the limitations of law to attain creative ends? We can only reply that there is no evidence anywhere in nature that any end has ever been accomplished except through the work of law. As men make civil laws and enforce them with penalties, even to death, so the human race has formed laws of physical birth and death, laws of sickness and physical inability, laws making food the source of bodily existence, laws of mind recognizing no other source of existence except the physical, the material.

The total of these race laws has formed a race consciousness separate from and independent of creative Mind, and when that Mind sought to help men spiritually, the mind of the flesh opposed it and made every effort to solve its problems in its own way.

The way of the flesh always proved futile and disastrous because of human selfishness and greed.

Thus it became absolutely necessary for Christ, the Father of us all, to make closer contact with our physical or fleshly consciousness and pour into it a new life current. So Christ Himself, the Jehovah of the Old Testament, incarnated in Jesus and brought to our immediate attention both spiritually and physically the abundant life of primal being, Elohim God. Hence the proclamation of Christ in Jesus, "I came that they may have life, and may have *it* abundantly."

Modern scientists explain that the atoms that build molecules, cells, and tissues are composed of electrical units; that these units seem to contain the elements that convey life to all creation; that the cells of our body are energized by these life-giving atoms; and that the ether filling all space is heavily charged with this life-giving electricity. Science does not say that this omnipresent energy is divine life, nor does it admit that it is moved by mind, either divine or human. But spiritual discernment reveals that there is but one life and one intelligence penetrating and permeating man and the universe and that where there is evidence of life there is evidence of Being. Consequently the life-giving atom is the life-giving God, whom we conceive according to our degree of spiritual unfoldment.

If we have developed the mind of the Spirit, we see and feel the quickening life of the energy at the center of the atoms of our body. All spiritual concepts begin in the mind and are translated into atomic life in the body. Here we have the point of contact between the Christ life and the race life. It also explains why our life as a people was no longer receiving the energy flow from the parent stream. Like the prodigal son, we had gone into a country far from the Father, and there was a famine in that land. We were starving for the divine substance and got no satisfaction out of the husks, the food of the swine.

Because of the gulf between the Mind of Being and the sense mind of the race, no life flow was possible. Then Christ incarnate in the flesh through Jesus offered His body as a life or electrical transformer. The atomic units of His body were sundered and sown as points of life and light in our mind and body atmosphere, to the end that anyone who concentrates his thoughts on Christ in faith will attract as a spiritual magnet one or many of His body atoms. These Christ atoms, appropriated by the individual, become food and drink and form the nucleus of a regenerated body for the person appropriating them.

This casting forth of His life and body for the regeneration of His people is promised in the use of the bread and wine as symbols, in the Last Supper, as described in the 26th chapter of Matthew. "And as they were eating, Jesus took bread, and blessed, and brake it; and he gave to the disciples, and said, Take, eat; this is my body. And he took a cup, and gave thanks, and gave to them, saying, Drink ye all of it; for this is my blood of the covenant, which is poured out for many unto remission of sins."

Thus Jesus gave His life and body substance as a kind of blood transfusion to a dying race, and the agony in Gethsemane was the contemplation of the wrenching of the central ego of the trillions of living electrons, protons, atoms, molecules, and cells composing His organism. Thus the body and life elements of the Christ body were sown as seed in the soil of our race mind, and it is our privilege to appropriate and incorporate these precious elements into our mind and body.

The body of Christ Jesus is not to be subject to permanent disintegration and death; in the creative processes of God it must be made part of our redeemed body and restored to its parent source, the Christ. As He said, "Therefore doth the Father love me, because I lay down my life, that I may take it again."

Here also we have made clear the mystery of salvation through the blood of Christ. It is not a miracle nor a personal sacrifice, but a meeting of a crisis in the race evolution by the transfusion of life from a Father to His perishing children. Understanding this in the sense of its scientific reality should make us every one more energetic in taking advantage of our only means of escape from the ills of the flesh and insuring our ultimate salvation. "Pray that ye enter not into temptation" is translated by Fenton, "Pray, for fear trial should overtake you." The same idea is brought out in the Lord's Prayer, which in the King James Version reads, "Lead us not into temptation," but which, according to good authorities should be, "You would not lead us into temptation, nor forsake us in trial." The petition is for strength to overcome trial.

As Paul so tellingly wrote to the Philippians: "Finally, brethren, whatsoever things are true, whatsoever things are honorable, whatsoever things are just, whatsoever things are pure, whatsoever things are lovely, whatsoever things are of good report; if there be any virtue, and if there be any praise, think on these things."

Part Four

PNEUMATOLOGY: THE NATURE OF THE HOLY SPIRIT

Pneumatology: The Nature of the Holy Spirit

T HE HOLY SPIRIT has been relatively neglected in theological discussions, compared to the controversies surrounding the other two persons of the Holy Trinity, the Father and the Son.

The nature of Jesus Christ, the Son of God, has been hotly debated by nearly every generation of Christian theologians. The earliest generations debated about his equality with God the Father, whether or not he was "truly man" and/or "truly God." The most heated debate of the twentieth century has been about who Jesus was as a historical person.

God the Father has in some respects remained the most remote person of the Trinity and in other respects the most agreed upon. The Father has been associated with the unknown and unknowable aspect of God, yet there is almost universal agreement that He is omnipotent, omniscient, omnipresent, good, Creator, and Director of the universe, who sent His Son to save humanity. Discussions of salvation, the "problem of evil," and the "end of time" have tended to center around Father and Son, with the Holy Spirit remaining something of an afterthought.

The Holy Spirit has usually been associated with God's immanance. Believers receive the Holy Spirit. The Holy Spirit guides and empowers the faithful. The Holy Spirit links believers with God and each other. The main controversies surrounding the Holy Spirit center on the behavior of humans, rather than the nature of God. Is speaking in an unintelligible tongue a gift of the Holy Spirit or a false sign or a psychological aberration? Are "spiritual healings" signs of the Holy Spirit, or can they be signs of false prophets or even demonic influences? Is the Holy Spirit given to believers automatically or must they receive it from a charismatic Spirit-filled preacher? Questions about the Holy Spirit tend to center on phenomena in the experience of believers rather than larger issues of salvation and the nature of the cosmos.

Charles Fillmore's views on the Holy Spirit are consistent with that emphasis on phenomena in the experience of the faithful and perhaps shed some light on related questions. I say "perhaps shed some light" because Fillmore tended to take a very broad perspective on phenomena related to the Holy Spirit. For him, any phenomenon which involves an experience of the divine is activity of the Holy Spirit, and that activity is not related to whether or not a person holds "correct" Christian doctrine or even whether or not a person is a Christian. Activities of the Holy Spirit, for Fillmore, include, but are not limited to, the healing power of nature, spiritual dreams, and the law of God in action in general. For those who insist upon true Christian beliefs as a prerequisite for the help of the Holy Spirit, Fillmore's views would be false and possibly even blasphemous. For those who are open to the possibility that God's loving concern is not limited to those who are theologically acceptable, Fillmore's views open up a new world of understanding and experience of the Divine. Fillmore's views imply more than "tolerance" of varieties of religious experience; his views imply that we ought to rejoice in any spiritual experience that leads to stronger character, a more loving heart, or greater wholeness in life.

We should also note that Fillmore does not speak of the Trinity in the traditional terms of One God in three persons, but rather in terms of three aspects of the One God. The Father is the Infinite Mind of God, or God as unchanging Principle. The Son is God's perfect creative Idea for the universe and humanity, or the Principle revealed in a creative plan. The Holy Spirit is the expression of the Idea or Plan, the activity of Mind and Idea carrying out the Idea in manifestation or experience. At this level of description, the Trinity seems somewhat abstract and impersonal. But the two chapters included in this section reveal a more concrete and personal understanding of God, especially in regard to God as Holy Spirit.

The chapter called "The Holy Spirit" (from *Talks on Truth*) represents Fillmore's views in the 1920s. He speaks of the Holy Spirit in masculine terms as *He* and calls the Holy Spirit the "personality" of God. Fillmore describes the Holy Spirit as having a direct interest in and as guiding human affairs. The Holy Spirit guides us through visions and dreams. The Holy Spirit's mission is to help us become "God incarnate," equal in power with Jesus Christ. The Holy Spirit comes to us through our earnest seeking in prayer and not from others, no matter how illumined they may be.

The chapter called "Holy Spirit Fulfills the Law" (from *Jesus Christ Heals*) represents Fillmore's views in the late 1930s. Here we see Fillmore's views have expanded and shifted to some degree. The Holy Spirit is not only a "personality" who comes to guide us when we pray, but is also the healing power of nature and of Divine Mind. The Holy

Spirit is not so much the "law" of God as the love of God. The Holy Spirit is not masculine, but rather the loving, nurturing feminine aspect of God, God as Mother.

We might note here that the Holy Spirit as Mother is an idea found not only in New Thought writings, but also in second-century C.E. Christian Gnostic writings[1] and some of the Christian Mysticism of the Middle Ages.[2] From the fourth century onwards, Christian theology has tended to relegate notions of the divine feminine to the Virgin Mary, "the Mother of God," whose sole purpose is to be a passive, chaste vessel through which the Holy Spirit may give birth to the Son of God. The traditional doctrine of the Trinity seems somehow metaphorically deficient, with its Father and Son and masculine nonrelational "Spirit." A trinity of "Father-Son-Mother" has better symmetry as a metaphor and makes better sense as a relational description. After all, "father" and "son" are no more than relational descriptions. Perhaps Fillmore's notion of the Holy Spirit as the feminine aspect of God will help satisfy some of the current generation's longing for a more "nurturing" and less "gender-biased" theology.

Chapter 13

THE HOLY SPIRIT (1926)

GOSPEL is an Anglo-Saxon word derived from *God* (good) and *spell* (story, tidings). It is now universally identified with Jesus Christ's mission and the doctrine that has grown out of it. So when we speak of the gospel it is understood that we refer to that system of religious beliefs that has centered about the teachings of Jesus of Nazareth.

But as to what that gospel is in detail, there are many opinions. Many believe that it is the plan of salvation for men outlined in the dogmas and creeds of the churches. But those doctrines, creeds, and dogmas were formulated three hundred years after Jesus taught and demonstrated. There is no authority from Him or from His immediate disciples attesting the genuineness of many of these later enunciations interpreting the original teachings. They are the work of men who had to sustain an industry known as the church, who had to provide for a privileged class called the clergy. These had become an important part of the body politic, and it was thought best to organize them according to human ideas; hence, church creed and church government. Thus originated the Catholic Church; the Protestant churches are its offspring. All that the Protestants count dear as doctrine they borrowed from the Catholics, who had patched it together from early Christianity and from paganism. These teachings are not the pure Christianity of Jesus Christ, and He did not authorize the ecclesiastical structure called the Christian church.

It is safe to assert that no one can know the doctrine of Jesus Christ without going direct to Him for information. The writings of the New Testament known as the four Gospels are the most reliable external guide. When these are studied with unbiased mind, it is perceived that Jesus delegated no ecclesiastical power to anybody; that He did not formulate His doctrine or authorize any other human being to do so. Jesus appointed one teacher: "The Comforter, *even* the Holy Spirit, whom the Father will send in my name, he shall teach you all things, and bring to your remembrance all that I said unto you."

The Holy Spirit is the only authorized interpreter of the gospel of Jesus Christ, and no man can know what His doctrine is unless he gets it direct from this one and only custodian. It is not to come secondhand, but each for himself must receive it from the Holy Spirit, who is sent by the Father in the name of the Son.

The question is frequently asked: "Who is the Holy Spirit, and what relation does He bear to God and to Christ?"

The early disciples knew the Holy Spirit as the third person of the Trinity. The Father is always first, the Son second, and the Spirit third. The terms Father and Son express an eternal, reciprocal relation. The Spirit is the infinite "breath" of God, as the Son is His infinite "Word."

We may understand the relation and office of the Father, the Son, and the Holy Spirit by analyzing our own mind and its apparent subdivisions during thought action, because each one of us is a perfect copy in miniature, an image and likeness, of the great universal first cause—Being.

The source of all my manifestations is my mind. This source is exactly like the Father—is the Father in degree. An idea arises in my mind of something that I want to do; this idea is the Son. I express that idea in definite thought; that is Spirit going forth to accomplish that whereto I have sent it.

The Father is Principle. The Son is Principle revealed in a creative plan. The Holy Spirit is the executive power of both Father and Son, carrying out the creative plan.

Thus we might also say that Father is Being in the absolute, the unlimited, the unrelated. Son is the I AM identity of Being. Holy Spirit is the personality of Being. In its last analysis, Holy Spirit is the personality of God. The Holy Spirit is neither the all of Being nor the fullness of Christ, but is an emanation, or breath, sent forth to do a definite work. Thus circumscribed, He may be said to take on, in a sense, the characteristics of personality, a personality transcending in its capacity the concept of the intellectual man.

The Holy Spirit is designated in Scripture as personality and as not always existing for the consciousness of humanity in uniform degree. The mission of Jesus was to open the way for the Holy Spirit to enter into the minds of men. "But when the Comforter is come, whom I will send unto you from the Father, *even* the Spirit of truth, which proceedeth from the Father, he shall bear witness of me."

"Nevertheless I tell you the truth: It is expedient for you that I go away; for if I go not away, the Comforter will not come unto you; but if I go, I will send him unto you. And he, when he is come, will convict the world in respect of sin, and of righteousness, and of judgment."

The function of the Holy Ghost, or Spirit of Truth, implies distinct personal subsistence: He speaks, searches, selects, reveals, reproves, testifies, leads, comforts, distributes to every man, "searcheth all things, yea, the deep things of God."

What writers of the old Testament ascribe to Jehovah, the

writers of the New Testament ascribe to the Holy Spirit. (Compare Isa. 6:9 with Acts 28:25, and Jer. 31:31-34 with Heb. 10:15; see Acts 5:3, 4.)

The Holy Spirit is the law of God in action; in that action He appears as having individuality. From this fact the Hebrews got their concept of the personal, tribal God, Jehovah. Their prophets and mystics came into conscious mental touch with this executive lawgiver of God, and He used them as the mouthpieces through which He guided and directed His people. Adam talked to Him as Jehovah God. In this we understand that by means of the harmony and perfectness of the sinless man's mind, he was always conscious of the omnipresent Holy Spirit. Discord had not entered his innocent world—he was in the Eden of infancy. The desire for independent experience entered his mind; he began to get knowledge from experimenting blindly with the powers of Being, and in so doing severed the connection between his mind and the mind of the Holy Spirit.

Then the Holy Spirit found other means of communicating with men, the most common being the visions of the night, or dreams. "And he said, Hear now my words: if there be a prophet among you, I Jehovah will make myself known unto him in a vision, I will speak with him in a dream."

The Bible records a long line of prophets, mystics, and dreamers, who for thousands of years communicated the word of the Holy Spirit to the people. Jacob "dreamed," and "behold, a ladder set up on the earth, and the top of it reached to heaven . . . And, behold, Jehovah stood above it, and said, I am Jehovah, the God of Abraham thy father, and the God of Isaac . . . And, behold, I am with thee, and will keep thee whithersoever thou goest, and will bring thee again into this land."

Joseph dreamed, and he interpreted the dreams of others. Solomon was instructed by the Lord in dreams. Daniel prophesied through instruction received from the Lord in dreams. Joseph, the husband of Mary, was instructed in dreams, and he saved the life of the young child Jesus by following the warnings given him in this way. Peter had visions of the night. "And the Lord said unto Paul in the night by a vision, Be not afraid, but speak and hold not thy peace." "And the night following the Lord stood by him, and said, Be of good cheer: for as thou hast testified concerning me at Jerusalem, so must thou bear witness also at Rome."

The Children of Israel depended upon the Holy Spirit to guide and direct them, and from Genesis to Revelation the Bible is filled with incidents bearing testimony to the direct and personal interest of the Holy Spirit in the affairs of men.

Jesus Christ, the resurrected Adam, reconnected man with the Lord, opening the way by which man might at any time enjoy that communion with his Creator which he had had in the Edenic state, before his season of experimenting had begun.

Jesus prayed much by Himself and spent long hours in silent communion with God. Those who have even in a slight degree opened the Christ consciousness in themselves, so that it flows forth and recognizes the universal Mind, can readily understand that Jesus was in the silence with God, getting the power and wisdom necessary to do His work. The normal condition of man is one of opened inner communion, such as was enjoyed by Jesus, a condition in which he can say of every thought and word: "The word which ye hear is not mine, but the Father's who sent me."

It is the mission of the Holy Spirit to bring all men and all women into this open communion; but it is a difficult attainment. "And the light shineth in the darkness; and the darkness apprehended it not." He who is buried in sense limitations must find the way out of them into the place where the light shines in the light and man perceives it clearly. It is the mission of the Holy Spirit so to guide man in order that man will not mistake the way into that light or wander off into the darkness of the many delusive bypaths of mortal sense.

The Holy Spirit comes to men in this day, as in the past, and reveals to them in various ways how to overcome the erroneous states of consciousness that they have evolved, or in which they are cast through association. A higher and more farseeing guide than mere intellect is necessary, and that guide has been provided in the Holy Spirit.

The Holy Spirit is the one factor that His disciples and immediate followers counted absolutely necessary to their success in preaching the gospel of Jesus Christ. They looked to Him for power and guidance in all their work. They announced Him as the special gift promised by Jesus Christ, an endowment that could be given by them to those who believed on His name. By the laying on of hands they transferred Holy Spirit power to others, who upon receiving it went about preaching, teaching, prophesying, and healing. Even to this day many in the orthodox Christian church believe that only those are fitted to preach who are inspired of the Holy Spirit. But in some cases the inspirations of Spirit are so turned away by minds filled with scholastic dogma and creed learned in ecclesiastical colleges, that when given forth it is not recognized by the soul seeking the pure bread of life.

But the Holy Spirit is in the world today with great power and wisdom, ready to be poured out upon all those who look to Him for guidance. The Holy Spirit is authority on the gospel of Jesus Christ. He is the only authority ever recognized by Jesus Christ, and whoever attempts to set forth the Christ gospel from any other standpoint is in the letter and not in the Spirit.

Jesus gave His words into the keeping of this universal receptive agency, the Spirit of Truth, whose mission it is to carry those words directly into the understanding of everyone who accepts the Christ way into the kingdom of heaven. The Holy Spirit gave His words to the writers of the New Testament, and they wrote them out for the comprehension of the intellectual man. But this does not signify that the mission of the Holy Spirit ended there—that after giving this message He then withdrew from the world. On the contrary, it was just the beginning, the primary step of that larger, more comprehensive teaching that Spirit is ever ready to impart to every soul. The soul needs instruction, and the Father has provided a perfect way for us to get it. That way is the Jesus Christ way; whoever follows the steps outlined in Christ's gospel, now brought to each of us by the Holy Spirit, will finally reach the same place that Jesus reached.

The fact is that everybody has a soul to save, not from the hypothetical hell after death, but from the sins and the delusions of the sense consciousness that make hell here and now. There is a way to bring that salvation about, and it is the mission of the Holy Spirit to reveal that way to every one of us. The revelation begins the moment we turn from the letter of the gospel and seek for its spirit. To know that every word and sentence of Scripture veils a spiritual Truth is the first step in unraveling the gospel. Spiritual truths cannot be expressed in language that will carry correct concepts to the mind. No attempt to describe the Holy Spirit is made in Scripture, because language might be expanded indefinitely, description and illustration fill volumes, yet the Holy Spirit would not be compassed or apprehended on the intellectual plane where human language passes current. The Holy Spirit is the whole Spirit of God; He can be known by man only through his spiritual nature. When he tries to bring Spirit down to the plane of things, he always falls short.

So those who attempt to learn of the Holy Spirit by reading about Him, or from the teachings of others, will fail. The

Holy Spirit comes only to those who earnestly seek Him. If you are depending for spiritual enlightenment on some book or on church ritual and doctrine or on some teacher or leader, you need not expect to have the Holy Spirit fall upon you. It is the prayer and supplication of the soul alone in its upper room (state of high spiritual aspiration) that brings the Holy Ghost.

The doctrine of Jesus Christ is so intimately associated with the Holy Spirit that they are inseparable. The Holy Spirit is the interpreter of the Christ, and the Christ is the thing interpreted. They are omnipresent and cannot be separated in spirit or in works. Hence, to preach the gospel of Jesus Christ is to set forth that the Holy Spirit of God is ready and willing to bring all men and all women into the kingdom. It is the proclamation to everybody: "The kingdom of God is come nigh unto you."

All down the ages, ministers of the gospel have assumed that the requirements are met when men have been persuaded to believe in the Lord Jesus Christ as the Saviour of their souls, and to keep on believing this until they pass out of their bodies; then, the teaching runs, believers are received into the arms of the Lord. But the Holy Spirit does not indorse this assumption, neither does the letter of the Scriptures.

In the 17th chapter of John are these words of Jesus: "Neither for these only do I pray, but for them also that believe on me through their word; that they may all be one; even as thou, Father, *art* in me, and I in thee, that they also may be in us: that the world may believe that thou didst send me. And the glory which thou hast given me I have given unto them; that they may be one, even as we *are* one." Here Jesus opens the door of unity with the Father to all who believe on Him. It is thought by nearly everybody that Jesus was the only Son of God, but here He prays that we all may be in God as He is in Him and may realize our sonship.

Jesus wants companions in power, dominion, and glory, that it may be demonstrated to the world, this world, that what He claimed about man and his relation to God is true. Jesus was one with the Father—was the Father incarnate, and His prayer was "that they may be one, even as we *are*," that the world may believe.

The gospel of Jesus Christ is that all men shall become God incarnate. It is not alone a gospel of right living; it shows the way into dominion and power equal to, aye, surpassing that of Jesus of Nazareth.

Paul also saw it in this light. In the 2d Chapter of Philippians, he says: "Have this mind in you, which was also in Christ Jesus: who, existing in the form of God, counted not the being on an equality with God a thing to be grasped."

"But," we are asked, "do you mean to say that living upright, moral lives in the sight of God will not fulfill the requirement of the gospel of Jesus Christ; that believing on Him as our Saviour will not bring us into the kingdom of heaven?"

Jesus answered this question when He said that if our righteousness did not exceed that of the scribes and Pharisees we could in no wise enter into the kingdom of heaven.

How can one be in the Father, where Jesus Christ is, without being right with Him in consciousness? That is, to be one with the Father, as He is one, and thereby fulfill His prayer, we must be equal with Jesus Christ. If we have a sense of inferiority, if we believe that He has greater wisdom, or power, or love, then we are not fulfilling the requirements. So long as we feel any difference between ourselves in the Father and Jesus in the Father, we have fallen short of that "mind . . . which was . . . in Christ Jesus."

The cry goes up: "This is foolish, sacrilegious, to put man beside Jesus Christ and claim that they are equals." The claim is not that mortals, in their present consciousness, are

equal with Jesus, but that they must be equal with Him before they will emerge from the sense of delusion in which
they now wander.

We know that health is the normal condition of man and
that it is a condition true to his real being; we claim and declare this Truth, right in the face of appearances to the contrary. We have proved by experience many times repeated
that our words in this way reveal that health is potential in
Being.

If man is the son of God, he must be that son right now;
sonship must be just as real, just as omnipresent, as the
health that God has revealed through His Word. How shall
man reveal his sonship to himself and to others except by
claiming it; by declaring that he is not a son of mortality, but
a son of God; that the Spirit of God dwells in him and is now
shining through him; that this Spirit is Christ, who said
through Jesus: "Neither for these only do I pray, but for
them also that believe on me through their word"?

Your word is the power through which you make your belief manifest. Simple belief in or assent to the truth of a
proposition never gave understanding to anyone. There
must be mental action; organic changes in the mind are necessary before the new state of consciousness takes up its
abode in you.

If you can convince yourself that you are a son of God,
your next step is to declare it in word and to carry it out in
the acts of your daily life. After declaring this, if you fall short
in demonstrating yourself to be a son of God, you are to find
out why. "Ask, and it shall be given you . . . knock, and it
shall be opened unto you." You have neglected some of your
spiritual powers. You may be dissipating in the lusts of the
flesh some transcendent energy given you by the Father.

Here comes the mission of the Holy Spirit. When you ask
in the silence of Spirit to be shown why you do not manifest

the powers that Jesus of Nazareth manifested, the Holy Spirit will in some way reveal to you the lack. How that revealment will come about no one can tell you. But if you are patient and trustful you will be guided and directed so that all the links in the chain of your being will be brought together and harmoniously joined, and the Son of God will be revealed in you.

"Arise, shine; for thy light is come, and the glory of Jehovah is risen upon thee. For, behold, darkness shall cover the earth, and gross darkness the peoples; but Jehovah will arise upon thee, and his glory shall be seen upon thee. . . .

"Whereas thou hast been forsaken and hated, so that no man passed through thee, I will make thee an eternal excellency, a joy of many generations. . . For brass I will bring gold, and for iron I will bring silver, and for wood brass, and for stones iron. I will also make thy officers peace, and thine exactors righteousness. Violence shall no more be heard in thy land, desolation nor destruction within thy borders; but thou shalt call thy walls Salvation, and thy gates Praise. The sun shall be no more thy light by day; neither for brightness shall the moon give light unto thee: but Jehovah will be unto thee an everlasting light, and thy God thy glory. Thy sun shall no more go down, neither shall thy moon withdraw itself; for Jehovah will be thine everlasting light, and the days of thy mourning shall be ended."

HOLY SPIRIT FULFILLS THE LAW (1939)

HE SPIRIT OF WHOLENESS quickens and heals me. The Spirit of wholeness is called the Holy Spirit in the New Testament. In classical mythology it is called Hygeia. Modern medical men refer to it as the restorative power of nature. It has been recognized by savage and civilized in every land and age. It has many names, and they all identify it as a universal urge toward perfection in man and the universe and toward keeping things going regardless of any interfering force.

We may look on this restorative power as merely the tendency of the cells in an organism to retain their homogeneity, and when we look at it in this light our consciousness robs it of any of the divine qualities it may possess. This is the way the scientific world regards what we call the Holy Spirit. To such a view the Holy Spirit has no warm heart. To persons holding such a view the Holy Spirit is not the Comforter referred to by Jesus but merely an abstract principle that works just the same way whether it is praised or blamed.

But to the Christian metaphysician the Holy Spirit is just what the name implies, the whole Spirit of God in action. In

Hebrew *Jehovah* is written *Yahweh, Yah* being masculine and *weh* feminine. In the New Testament Christ stands for Jehovah. Jesus talked a great deal about the Holy Spirit: that it would bear witness of Him, come with Him, and help Him to the end of the age.

Do not be misled by the personality of the Holy Spirit and the reference to it as "He." This was the bias of the Oriental [Middle Eastern] mind, making God and all forms of the Deity masculine.

Holy Spirit is the love of Jehovah taking care of the human family, and love is always feminine. Love is the great harmonizer and healer, and whoever calls upon God as Holy Spirit for healing is calling upon the divine love.

Just here, in connection with the Holy Spirit is an important point for a good Christian healer to consider. Do not regard the Holy Spirit altogether as a restorative principle without feeling, sympathy, or love. This reduces your healing method to intellectual logic and the slow process of mental science. Under this method the patient must always be educated in Truth principles before he can be healed. No instantaneous healing ever takes place under this method.

The Holy Spirit is sympathetic, comforting, loving, forgiving, and instantly healing.

> "Who forgiveth all thine iniquities;
> Who healeth all thy diseases."

Do not fear to call mightily upon the Holy Spirit, "our Mother-God," who has all compassion and healing power of the Father at "Her" command.

Thy perfect plan of bodily perfection is now made manifest in me.

That Mind, which designed the universe, must have planned for man, its leading citizen, a body in harmony with the universe is good logic. This conclusion does not require inspiration but merely common sense.

The religions of every race have taught this perfection of the body but have usually assumed that it was to be given to God's elect in some heavenly place after death. They have not thought it possible that the body of flesh with its many apparent defects could be transformed into an ideal body. In consequence man has put the stamp of inferiority upon his body, and through the creative power of thought he has built into the race mind a consciousness of corruptible flesh instead of the inherent incorruptible substance of God-Mind.

This race thought of man's body as impure and perishable in time became so dense that no human thought could penetrate it. It was gradually consuming the little life left in human bodies and would have ended with their total destruction if it had not been for Jesus, who was incarnated as demonstrator of the perfection and immortality of man's body.

That the body of flesh had within it life elements that could be released and incorporated into a much finer body has always been beyond the comprehension of the sense mind, and it required a physical demonstration to convince men that it could be done. Jesus made that demonstration, and some of His followers were convinced that the body with which He appeared to them after the Crucifixion was the identical body that suffered on the cross. Thomas, for example, was allowed critically to examine that body for the marks and wounds of the cross, and he found them and was convinced.

But the majority still doubted and do so to this day. Not understanding that the body that Jesus occupied for the thirty-three years of His earthly incarnation could be transformed into an imperishable body, they have assumed that Jesus really died on the cross and went to heaven where God gave Him a glorious body. There is no foundation for this in the facts given in the New Testament.

"God is Spirit," said Jesus. "Know ye not that your body is

a temple of the Holy Spirit which is in you, which ye have from God?" wrote Paul. Here are two statements by accepted authorities on fundamental Christian principles. If God is Spirit and He dwells in man's body, that body must have within it certain spiritual principles. Here modern science comes to the rescue of primitive Christianity, telling us that the atoms that compose the cells of our body have within them electrical units that, released, can change the whole character of the organism. Jesus had attained an understanding of the law that releases these electrical units, and He knew before the Crucifixion that He could thus make His body unkillable; which He did.

When Elohim God created man in His likeness, He imprinted upon man's supermind two body pictures: first the picture of a natural body, and secondly the picture of a spiritual body. In the primal cell He then enclosed the elements necessary to the building of the natural and the spiritual body; that is, electricity on the inside and flesh on the outside. Then to man was given dominion and authority over these living atoms and cells out of which he must build mind and body into visibility. As God created man, His image and likeness, by the power of His word so man, God's image and likeness, projects his body by the same power.

Our physical bodies are carried in our minds as "ideas" and they obediently reflect every mental attitude. When in the course of our evolution we discern that an allwise Creator must have designed perfection for all His creation and we begin to affirm that perfection, then the transformation from the natural to the spiritual body begins, and it continues until our body is wholly regenerated and appears objectively in its divine perfection.

Thou art the strength of my life, and I am made whole.

The mighty truth that everything in this universe is the product of thought few persons let sink deeply into their minds. Mankind have wandered in thought so far from the parent Mind that they do not reflect or observe that everything they do originates in mind. A very little observation and reflection will convince anyone that mind acts on matter in every part of life. The story of creation begins in the first chapter of the Bible with God's command that the dry land appear. Then in the second chapter Jehovah God formed man out of the dust of the ground. Not only here in the beginning do we find mind molding matter; all through the Bible runs the same story. Jesus said of His body that He could raise it up.

When the Truth dawns on man that mind rules matter in both the great and the small, he has the explanation of myriad mysteries, strange episodes, reputed miracles. This great Truth that mind is the source and moving factor in all creation would, if studied and practiced, prove of tremendous worth to religion, science, and art. Jesus taught the supremacy of mind in many illustrations, but His followers have not understood the metaphysical significance because they have not analyzed the mind or directly applied its spiritual powers. When Jesus said that the Father was within Him and that the words He spoke were not His but the Father's, He must have referred to God as an interpenetrating mind.

Everything in this universe has both its mental and its physical side. Heaven and earth are parallel everywhere. Even the so-called elemental forces of nature are dual. Our men of science are puzzled because light sometimes appears as waves in space and again as particles. To a metaphysician the waves express the mind and the particles the matter. When Jesus walked on the water He blended His mind with the mind of the water and it obeyed His concentrated will.

Nature's mind is always the servant of man's mind when man lifts his thoughts to Spirit. Nature will even obey a determined will on an inferior plane of consciousness. Concentration of will as practiced by metaphysicians of the Orient, African witch doctors, and a horde of occult adepts bears testimony to the power of the mind of manipulate matter visible and invisible.

> "I sow no seeds of care and strife;
> But those of love, and joy, and life."

It is reported that a great philosopher, Herbert Spencer, once said substantially that he would gladly turn his life over to any creative force that would plan and carry it forward without his having to take any responsibility.

Because of the many blunders that the natural man makes in his life, such a shifting of responsibility would be popular on the part of many who have ideals that they are unable to fulfill because they are bound by material limitations. Also in the secret recesses of all of us there lurks the conviction that there is a power somewhere that may be invoked to show us a hidden way into the city of success. We think we should willingly follow any path in life if we were sure that we were being led by the hand of supreme wisdom.

In his famous soliloquy Hamlet heaps up the measure of the burdens of life with the subtle argument that they could be shifted by death:

> For who would bear the whips and scorns of time,
> The oppressor's wrong, the proud man's contumely,
> The pangs of despised love, the law's delay,
> The insolence of office and the spurns
> That patient merit of the unworthy takes,
> When he himself might his quietus make
> With a bare bodkin? who would fardels bear,
> To grunt and sweat under a weary life,
> But that the dread of something after death,

> The undiscovered country from whose bourn
> No traveler returns, puzzles the will
> And makes us rather bear those ills we have
> Than fly to others that we know not of?

Spiritual insight reveals that Hamlet is right. We cannot escape life's experiences, be they ever so rough, by fleeing to another environment. All the conditions in this world have been constructed by the people who inhabit the world, and each individual is a builder of it and personally responsible for his immediate environment.

It is the mind that makes the man, and the mind and the thoughts of the mind endure even though the body be dissolved. So let no man think that he can escape the creations of his mind by breaking the physical chains that bind him to the earth. Nor does death in any of its phases relieve him of the states of mind that dominated him at the time of passing. The law of God is not mocked at any time or under any circumstances. "Whatsoever a man soweth, that shall he also reap." What we have sown in the flesh we shall reap in the flesh unless we repent, change our minds. When we do repent, we shall break mortal thoughts and ascend into a spiritual thought realm, the kingdom of God. This ascension we do not attain by dying physically but by dying to ill thoughts and living in true, good thoughts while still in the flesh. "Yet in my flesh shall I see God."

"The Word became flesh, and dwelt among us," says John in the very first chapter of his gospel.

Of all the great spiritual teachers of the ages Jesus has given us the most vivid and vital evidence of God as Father and guide. We say as Philip did, "Show us the Father, and it sufficeth us." The disciples were looking for a flesh-and-blood God. Do not the majority of Christians today look forward to seeing sometime, somewhere, a flesh-and-blood

God sitting on a throne? Jesus replied, "He that hath seen me hath seen the Father."

He then explained that He was in the Father and the Father in Him. Yet His listeners did not understand, because they had not been trained to think metaphysically. God is Spirit, omnipresent Spirit-Mind; and in Him "we live, and move, and have our being."

> "God lives in me; no more I pine;
> For love, and health, and joy are mine."

That God is the animating principle of all creation is not a new or startling teaching. It has been the conclusion of thinking minds ever since the birth of logic, and it will never be discarded so long as the faculty of logic continues to be exercised. Where there is an effect there must be a cause, and no amount of sophistry will erase the straight line from premise to conclusion. Timid men will cry pantheism and scare both themselves and others with a bugaboo they do not understand. Nevertheless the fact remains that intelligence and design and all the other evidences of an omnipresent planning Mind are so palpable in us and the world about us that we cannot boast of our sanity and at the same time deny them.

When logic presents these mighty truths to us and we begin to turn our attention to the omnipresent principle eternally active and flashing its presence into us and the whole universe, we awaken within ourselves a consciousness of it, and it begins to think and plan through us. This is the first movement of Omnipresence, creating man as a self-conscious replica of itself, that is, of God. This replica is the Son of God or Christ, the exact reproduction in miniature of the mighty cosmic Mind. When this man of cosmic Mind arrives at full manifestation of Himself in habitation and place, we have Jesus Christ, the Son of God or God glorified in man. Jesus in ecstasy beholding this climax exclaimed "Glorify thou me with thine own self with the glory which I had with thee before the world was."

So if we have not begun our glorification by realizing this quickening life within, let us commence right now to recognize it in thought and word. James Russell Lowell wrote, "It may be that the longing to be so helps make the soul immortal." A great Truth, spoken by a great man. Desire from within shoots a ray of energy from the imprisoned I AM to the all-enfolding Spirit, and a thread of golden light unites parent and child. Darwin taught that desire for light in the protoplasmic cell shot a ray from its center to its surface and formed the primary eye. If this be true, and it seems logical, it is possible for us to animate the thirty-nine trillion cells estimated by Doctor Crile to be present in the body and eventually make them all luminous, as did Jesus. Thus science is revealing to us the movements of mind in forming the primary or physical body, which by the quickening of the Spirit is raised to the glorified immortal body.

We should not lose sight of the fact that the completion of this glorified body that God has planned for us devolves on us. We must become conscious of God-Mind and cooperate with it in making His plan manifest in us. As Jesus said, "My Father worketh even until now, and I work."

The childlike simplicity of this primary work seems so insignificant that great men who have delved into philosophy and worked with weighty intellectual problems deem it beneath them to become as a little child and concentrate their thoughts on nursery rhymes. They do not realize that instead of molding and animating the cells of their bodies they have projected their thoughts outwardly in speculating about the universe and its laws. So the cells left to themselves gradually starve for want of mind stimulation and finally die.

If you, dear reader, have attained eminence in some earthly field of action and yet have not demonstrated health, it may be that you need to take sound words in some simple form and go unto your Lord.

The Spirit of Him that raised up Jesus dwells in me, and I am made whole.

Paul wrote, "But if the Spirit of him that raised up Jesus from the dead dwelleth in you, he that raised up Christ Jesus from the dead shall give life also to your mortal bodies through his Spirit that dwelleth in you."

Few Christians realize the vital truth in this statement by Paul, although it is but one of many of like character to be found in his writings. Paul taught that what Spirit did for Jesus it would do for all who follow Him and adopt His methods of spiritual self-development.

Jesus claimed like results for His followers. In Matthew 19:28 it is written, "Verily I say unto you, that ye who have followed me, in the regeneration when the Son of man shall sit on the throne of his glory, ye also shall sit upon twelve thrones, judging the twelve tribes of Israel."

The promises of the power of Spirit to transform man from a mortal to an immortal state are producing a great company of spiritual-minded persons in the world today who work in the silence and speak but little about their heavenly experiences. In this way Spirit is forming a mighty Christian army that, when the need arises, will come out of its obscurity and save our civilization from extinction.

Although these spiritually quickened souls, often widely separated, may be working alone, they are bound together by the Holy Spirit, and the bond of brotherhood that unifies them is far more enduring than any human relationship. They are developing latent faculties of the soul that will make them superpowered men and women.

In order to establish and perpetuate the new order of life

that is being poured into earth's mental atmosphere from on high it is absolutely essential that a people be prepared who can make use of the finer forces of the mind. The great initial outpouring of Spirit took place at the Pentecostal baptism more than nineteen centuries ago. The few who received this primal baptism are the seed from which has sprung a multitude. The trillions of cells forming the body of Jesus swim in omnipresence awaiting our appropriation. They are the living, quickening seeds of new life.

I am strengthened and healed by the power of the Spirit in the inner man.

We all need a better acquaintance with that phase of creative Mind that reveals and forms a connecting link between the Most High and the mind of the natural man. Most of us have not made conscious contact with the Spirit within but are thinking and acting in the outer crust of our being. Consequently we cannot hold communion with God in His omnipotence but must have a mediator or equalizer of the light and power that proceeds from the originating source of existence.

This is illustrated in high-powered electric systems: a transformer is necessary to lower the voltage and adapt it to the capacity of a small industrial motor. If the full current from one of the big electric cables were turned directly into our small motors it would burn them up.

If the full current of God life were turned directly into the ordinary man's nervous system, it would destroy it. An equalizer has been provided—the Holy Spirit or Spirit of Truth—through Jesus Christ.

Our human family has lost contact with the Spirit of Truth, and our only salvation is through a soul strong enough to re-establish the connection. Jesus Christ released the electric atoms in His body and formed a conduit in the ether through which divine life is again flowing to the inhabitants of this planet. Without this purified life substance we should be unable to receive life or any message direct from God.

In John 14:16 Jesus said, "And I will pray the Father, and he shall give you another Comforter, that he may be with you for ever, *even* the Spirit of truth: whom the world cannot receive." Again in John 16:14 He makes His identity with the Spirit of Truth stronger: "He shall glorify me: for he shall take of mine, and shall declare *it* unto you."

All who have faith enough to believe these things are comforted and guided by the Spirit of Truth. Read John 17:20: "Neither for these only do I pray, but for them also that believe on me through their word."

It is the Spirit of Truth that talks to us in dreams, visions, and inner urges. The more we acknowledge the Spirit as our indwelling inspiration and life the stronger its consciousness will be to us.

Through the Spirit of Truth God moves the whole creation; hence any man may constantly increase his understanding of the source and relation of all things by claiming his unity with the Spirit of Truth.

Part Five
COSMOLOGY: LAWS OF MIND

COSMOLOGY:
LAWS OF MIND

Cosmology is the branch of metaphysics that is concerned with ideas related to the nature of creation, space, time, laws, and causality.

Christian theology dominated cosmological thinking for over 1000 years, from about the fifth century to the sixteenth century. Christian cosmology was based on the Bible, especially Genesis, with the addition of some philosophical ideas, first mainly from Plato then, after the Crusades, from Aristotle. The basic cosmology held that a few thousand years ago God created the world in seven days, as described in Genesis 1. According to Christian cosmology, the sun, moon, and stars all revolved around the earth and creation itself revolved around humanity. The appearance of comets and other "signs in the heavens" were all seen as ominous signs from God to humanity, signifying important events in human history. God made the universe to declare His Glory and Majesty, but God's ultimate purposes concerned the salvation of humanity.

In the sixteenth century a new cosmology began to develop that seemed to undermine both the cosmology and theology of the Christian church. "Natural Philosophy" became mathematical and eventually came to be known as "science." The science of Copernicus, Kepler, Galileo, and Newton demonstrated that the earth was just a tiny planet in the vast cosmos, revolving around a medium-sized star. Comets and other "heavenly signs" proved to be mathematically predictable and scientifically explicable, without reference to God's sending portents to humanity. Humanity itself seemed to lessen in significance along with the earth's relative shrinkage and displacement from the center of the cosmos. It began to seem more and more ridiculous to place humanity at the center of significance in God's purposes. Reasoning from the new science, it seemed that God created the cosmos, decreed its physical laws, and withdrew from participation in its events to other unknown projects or purposes.

Adding to the indignity of humanity's being withdrawn from the center of the physical cosmos was Darwin's theory of evolution put forth in the nineteenth century. Now scientists maintained that not only was humanity removed from the center of things, but also humanity was just another species of animal, derived from apelike creatures in a process of natural selection. Was the original "image and likeness of God" an ape?

Understandably, Christian theologians and preachers, both Catholic and Protestant, resisted these new theories.[1] It was not possible to square the story of Genesis and other Bible passages with the new theories of science. While the church eventually had to concede the picture of the cosmos depicted by astronomy and physics, to this day there is a concerted effort in some quarters of Christianity to overthrow the theories of evolution.

Charles Fillmore was too rational to retreat into denial of scientific evidence, but too much the man of faith and mysticism to wholly reject the Bible as ancient superstition. His solution to the dilemma was to accept science and search for an inner, spiritual meaning to the Genesis account of creation. There is historical precedent for taking that approach, notably the great third-century theologian Origen and the eighteenth-century scientist-theologian Emanuel Swedenborg. While the works of both Origen and Swedenborg have not been acceptable to traditional Christianity, there is another overlooked precedent that can hardly be dismissed by the church—St. Paul.

In the letter to the Galatians, Paul does a spiritual, nonliteral interpretation of the story of Abraham (Gal. 4:21-31). Indeed, Paul's doctrine that Gentiles can be children of the promise, equal to the Jews as God's chosen, depends upon the premise that through faith the uncircumcised can share in all the promises given to the children of Abraham. In other words, Gentiles, though not literally descendents of Abraham, are children of Abraham through faith, a position that can *only* be maintained by a *spiritual*, as opposed to a literal, interpretation of Scripture. So here is, within the Bible itself, precedent for spiritual (or metaphysical) interpretation of the Bible.

Fillmore's interpretation of Genesis was based on the metaphysical theory that reality is ultimately spiritual or mental. Interpreting the natural creation as symbolic of spiritual-mental actions, Fillmore concluded that Genesis 1 is a metaphorical account of the creative process. The first chapter in this section, "Spiritual Man" (from *Mysteries of Genesis*) gives Fillmore's interpretation of Genesis 1.

There is no way to prove that the meaning Fillmore derives from Genesis is the meaning intended by the human author of that work or by the Spirit that inspired the work. Just like when psychologists derive meaning from dreams and mythology, any attempt to derive symbolic meaning from scriptures is necessarily subjective to a great degree and dependent upon some theory of reality. Psychologists tend to base their interpretations of dreams and mythology on either Freudian or Jungian theories of the human psyche. Just as the validity of those psychological interpretations is dependent upon the validity of the theoretical foundations, even so the validity of Fillmore's type of interpretation is dependent upon the validity of his cosmological theory.

An additional problem for this type of metaphorical interpretation is the fact that stories and natural objects and occurances can have multiple symbolic meanings. For example, Jung once interpreted a hat in a dream as representing "the universal and everlasting man as distinct from the ephemeral and 'accidental' mortal man."[2] In his interpretation, Jung notes that "the hat, as a covering for the head, has the general sense of something that epitomizes the head."[3] So a hat *could* represent *anything* connected to the functioning of the mind. A hat could *also* be a symbol for protection, status, or any number of other ideas. A hat could also be *just* a hat.

The validity of this type of interpretation depends to a great extent on a much larger context. For Jungian analysis, the larger context is human mythology in general and the specific life and dreams of the individual whose dream is being interpreted. For Fillmore's Bible interpretation, the larger context is the general metaphysical theory and the total stories, language, and symbolism of the Bible. Furthermore, the validity of both Jungian and Fillmorean interpretation ultimately depends upon whether or not the interpretations have beneficial practical consequences for individuals. Psychological or spiritual therapy gains validity only if it bears the fruit of beneficial consequences, and Fillmore clearly has spiritual therapeutic intentions in his work. From the perspective of pragmatic epistemology, the question of the validity of Fillmore's interpretation resolves itself ultimately into the question: If I use these ideas, does it help me create what I want in my experience? Therefore I suggest that the reader can put Fillmore's theory to the test in his or her own life.

How would one go about testing the theory of "Mind Action"? According to Fillmore, the key to spiritual development and demonstration of the laws of mind action is prayer. Just as Fillmore used the phrase "the law of mind action" to include a wide range of principles (including the seven-step process described in Genesis 1), even so he used the word *prayer* to encompass a wide range of mind activities used to demonstrate the laws of mind action. For him, prayer included asking in faith, affirming the Truth, denying error, contemplating God, concentrating on centers in the body, visualizing, and waiting in the Silence. The chapter called "The Omnipotence of Prayer" (from *Jesus Christ Heals*) gives a good overview of Fillmore's teachings on this subject.

In addition to the teachings on prayer, "The Omnipotence of Prayer" also includes further discussion of Fillmore's cosmology. Included in his cosmology and mentioned in this chapter are ideas of realms of Spirit, soul and matter, the ethers, angels, and auras. The chapter also emphasizes the importance of relaxation, peace of mind, and persistence in effective prayer.

"Realization Precedes Manifestation" (also from *Jesus Christ Heals*) discusses many of the themes already mentioned in "The Omnipotence of Prayer." The "Realization" chapter is included here for its discussion of the stage of prayer in which the metaphysician realizes that his or her work is done. Students of Unity metaphysics often wonder how much they should pray about something or when one should let go of the desire and let God finish the work. This chapter gives a description of the mental state at which "one can let go and let God." It also includes some interesting points about the subconscious and other "psychic realms."

The final chapter in this section is called "Right Giving, the

Key to Abundant Receiving" (from *Prosperity*). This chapter is included to illustrate the point that Fillmore's notion of practical application of Christian metaphysics is not all about sitting and praying. Fillmore believed in practical physical action as part of the whole picture of the creative process. Any action, to be effective, must have right thinking behind it, in Fillmore's view. Furthermore, any activity, including business and personal economics, can have behind it right thinking, which will align that activity with spiritual principles.

This chapter indicates Fillmore's vision for "spiritual economics" and community, based on the elimination of greed and fear from consciousness and the establishment of love and justice in consciousness. He argues that The Gospels' vision of a community holding all things in common can only successfully be established through those changes in consciousness aided by "freewill offering" economics. While this notion may seem completely impractical, the Fillmores operated Unity on that basis. Even today the Unity School of Christianity receives most of its operating income in the form of "love offerings." The School today does charge specific fees for publication, retreat, and educational services, but offerings still exceed the fees from those activities.

This chapter also indicates that Fillmore rejected the popular notion of charity as a relationship between benefactors and dependents. Instead of that concept of charity, he advocated developing a consciousness of stewardship in which one sees all things belonging to God—God's work for us being the loving, cheerful, and equitable distribution of resources to God's children.

Chapter 15

SPIRITUAL MAN (1936)

THE WORD *genesis* means "source" or "origin." It points to new birth and to the perfection of man in the regeneration. The law of generation is undoubtedly one of the mysteries in human consciousness. Men have probed with more or less success nearly every secret of nature, but of the origin of life they know comparatively nothing. In the matter of life we discover that the clues given us by our own experience point to intelligence as well as force. In other words, life falls short of its mission if it is not balanced by intelligence.

Man is constantly seeking to know the origin of both the universe and himself. But nearly all his research of a scientific nature has been on the material plane. As a rule, he has ascribed the beginning to matter, to atoms and cells, but much has eluded his grasp because their action is invisible to the eye of sense. Now we are beginning in the realm of mind a scientific search for the origin of all things. We say "scientific" because the discoveries that come from a right understanding of mind and its potentialities can be arranged in an orderly way and because they prove themselves by the application of their laws.

What is stated in the Book of Genesis in the form of allegory can be reduced to ideas, and these ideas can be worked out by the guidance of mental laws. Thus a right understanding of mind, and especially of Divine Mind, is the one and only logical key to an understanding of the beginnings of man and the universe. In this book we have many symbols explained and their meaning interpreted, so that anyone who sets himself the task can understand and also apply to his own development the rules and laws by which ideas are related to one another and discover how they are incorporated into man's consciousness, thus giving him the key to the unfoldment of the primal ideas implanted in him from the beginning.

It is found that what is true in the creation of the universe (as allegorically stated in Genesis) is equally true in the unfoldment of man's mind and body, because man is the microcosmic copy of the "Grand Man" of the universe.

The Bible is the history of man. In its sixty-six books it describes in allegory, prophecy, epistle, parable, and poem, man's generation, degeneration, and regeneration. It has been preserved and prized beyond all other books because it teaches man how to develop the highest principle of his being, the Spirit. As man is a threefold being, Spirit, soul, and body, so the Bible is a trinity in unity. It is body as a book of history; soul as a teacher of morals; and Spirit as a teacher of the mysteries of Being.

The student of history finds the Bible interesting, if not wholly accurate; the faithful good man finds in it that which strengthens his righteousness, and the overcomer with Christ finds it to be the greatest of all books as a guide to his spiritual unfoldment. But it must be read in the Spirit in order to get its lesson. The key to its spiritual meaning is that back of every mentioned thing is an idea.

The Bible will be more readily understood if the fact is

kept in mind that the words used have both an inner and an outer significance. Studied historically and intellectually, the external only is discerned, and the living inner reality is overlooked. In these lessons we shall seek to understand and to reveal the within, and trace the lawful and orderly connection between the within and the without.

Genesis, historically considered, falls into three parts: first, the period from the creation to the Flood; secondly, the period from the Flood to the call of Abraham; and thirdly, the period from the call of Abraham to the death of Joseph.

The 1st chapter describes creation as accomplished in six days, and refers to a seventh day of rest. There is no reason to believe that these days were twenty-four hours in length. "One day is with the Lord as a thousand years, and a thousand years as one day." They simply represent periods of development or degrees of mind unfoldment.

Numbers are used throughout the Bible in connection with faculties or ideas in Divine Mind. There are twelve divine faculties. They are symbolized in the Old Testament by the twelve sons of Jacob and in the New Testament by the twelve disciples of Jesus Christ. All of these have a threefold character: first, as absolute ideas in Divine Mind; secondly, as thoughts, which are ideas in expression but not manifest; and thirdly, as manifestations of thoughts, which we call things. In man this threefold character is known as Spirit, soul, and body. Therefore in studying man as the offspring of God it is necessary to distinguish between the faculties as they exist in the Spirit and as they are expressed in the soul and manifested in the body. We find heaven to be the orderly arrangement of divine ideas within man's true being. Earth is the outer manifestation of those ideas, this manifestation being man's body.

In the 1st Chapter of Genesis it is the great creative Mind

at work. The record portrays just how divine ideas were brought into expression. As man must have an idea before he can bring an idea into manifestation, so it is with the creations of God. When a man builds a house he builds it first in his mind. He has the idea of a house, he completes the plan in his mind, and then he works it out in manifestation. Thus God created the universe. The 1st chapter of Genesis describes this ideal creation.

The 1st chapter shows two parts of the Trinity: mind, and idea in mind. In the 2d chapter we have the third part, manifestation. In this illustration all theological mystery about the Trinity is cleared away for we see that it is simply mind, idea in mind, and manifestation of idea. Since man is the offspring of God, made in the image and likeness of Divine Mind, he must express himself under the laws of this creative mind. The law of manifestation for man is the law of thought. God ideates: man thinks. One is the completion of the other in mind.

The man that God created in His own image and likeness and pronounced good and very good is spiritual man. This man is the direct offspring of Divine Mind, God's idea of a perfect man. This is the only-begotten Son, the Christ, the Lord God, the Jehovah, the I AM. In the 2d chapter this Jehovah or divine idea of perfect man forms the manifest man and calls his name Adam.

The whole of the 1st chapter is a supermental statement of the ideas upon which evolution is based. Mind projects its ideas into universal substance, and evolution is the manifestation of the ideas thus projected. The whole Genesiac record is an allegory explaining just what takes place in the mind of each individual in his unfoldment from the idea to the manifest. God, the great universal Mind, brought forth an idea, a man, perfect like Himself, and that perfect man is potentially in every individual, working himself into manifestation in compliance with law.

> *Gen. 1:1-5.* "In the beginning God created the heavens and the earth. And the earth was waste and void; and darkness was upon the face of the deep: and the Spirit of God moved upon the face of the waters. And God said, Let there be light: and there was light. And God saw the light, that it was good: and God divided the light from the darkness. And God called the light Day, and the darkness he called Night. And there was evening and there was morning, one day."

To understand the creation of the universe by God we must know something of the character of God. Jesus said, "God is Spirit." The works of God, He said, were done in Him (Jesus) and through Him. "The Father abiding in me doeth his works." That God is an intelligent force always present and always active is the virtual conclusion of all philosophers, thus corroborating the statements of Jesus. God is eternally in His creation and never separate from it. Wherever there is evidence of creative action, there God is.

God is Mind, and He created through His word or idea, and this is the universal creative vehicle. It is plainly stated in this 1st chapter of Genesis that "God said." Jesus corroborated this creative power of the word or idea again and again. He said that His words were so powerful that if we let them abide in us we might ask whatsoever we would and it should be done to us.

God is mind force carrying forward creation under mental law. That law may be known to anyone who will follow the example of Jesus. Jesus said, "Be perfect, as your heavenly Father is perfect." This means that we should strive for the perfection that God is. We are the image and likeness of this great creative Mind, and being in a certain aspect of our mind just like it, we can through mental adjustment attain the same conscious unity that Jesus did.

God creates through action of His Mind, and all things rest on ideas. The idea back of the flower is beauty. The idea back of music is harmony. The idea back of day is light or the dispensation of intelligence.

This whole chapter is a statement of the creative ideas involved in the universe. It deals with involution. Evolution is the working out in manifestation of what mind has involved. Whatever mind commands to be brought forth will be brought forth by and through the law of evolution inherent in being. This applies to the great and the small. In mind there is but one.

The first step in creation is the awakening of man to spiritual consciousness, the dawning of light in his mind, his perception of Truth through the quickening of his Spirit. Light is wisdom; and the first day's work is the calling of light or wisdom into expression. Light represents intelligence, and darkness represents undeveloped capacity. Symbolically these are "day" and "night."

The word *God* in this instance stands for Elohim, which is God in His capacity as creative power, including within Himself all the potentialities of being. The "beginning" indicates the first concept of Divine Mind. "Created" means ideated. The "heavens" is the realm of ideas, and the "earth" represents ideas in expression. Heaven is the ideal and earth the mental picture. A comparison is found in the activity of our own mind: we have an idea and then think out a plan before we bring it forth.

Ferrar Fenton, the well-known student of Hebrew and Greek, says that the first verse should read: "By periods God created that which produced the Suns; then that which produced the Earth. But the Earth was unorganized and empty; and darkness covered its convulsed surface; but the breath of God vibrated over its fluid face." From this we are to understand that God created, not the earth as it appears, but that which produced the earth. Elohim, Spirit, creates the spiritual idea, which is afterward made manifest through Jehovah God.

The earthly thought was not yet clear. Harmony of form had not yet come into expression. "The deep" represents the capacity of the earth idea to bring forth. "The face of the deep" represents its intelligence. Understanding has not yet come into expression, and there is no apparent action. "The Spirit of God" or divine intelligence moved upon the "face of the waters." "Waters" here represents unexpressed capacities, the mental element out of which all is produced. Man is conscious of unexpressed capacities within himself, but only as he moves upon mind substance with intelligence, are his inherent spiritual qualities molded into forms. "Light" is intelligence, a spiritual quality. It corresponds to understanding and should precede all activity. At the beginning of any of our creating we should declare for light. Our declarations of Truth are instantly fulfilled in Spirit.

James says in his Epistle, "Every good gift and every perfect gift is from above, coming down from the Father of lights." The Evangelist John speaks of the "true light . . . which lighteth every man, coming into the world."

All that emanates from God is good. In the process of bringing forth our ideas we need a certain degree of understanding in order properly to regulate our thoughts. The light must be divided from the darkness, as in Divine Mind the light was separated from the darkness.

"Day" represents that state of mind in which intelligence dominates. "Night" represents the realm of thoughts that are not yet illuminated by the Spirit of God. "One day" represents a certain degree of mind unfoldment.

Gen. 1:6-8. "And God said, Let there be a firmament in the midst of the waters, and let it divide the waters from the waters. And God made the firmament, and divided the waters which were under the firmament from the waters which were above the firmament: and it was so. And God called the firmament Heaven. And there was evening and there was morning, a second day."

The second step in creation is the development of faith or the "firmament." The "waters" represent the unestablished elements of the mind.

The second day's creation is the second movement of Divine Mind. The central idea in this day's creation is the establishment of a firmament in the "midst of the waters" dividing the "waters from the waters." "Waters" represent unexpressed possibilities in mind. There must be a "firm" starting point or foundation established. This foundation or "firmament" is faith moving upon the unformed capacities of Spirit consciousness. The divine Logos—God as creative power—gives forth the edict "Let there be a firmament." The first step or "day" in creation involves "light" or understanding, and the second step, faith in the knowing quality of mind.

The word is instantly fulfilled in Spirit. "And God made the firmament." This does not refer to the visible realm of forms but to the mental image in Divine Mind, which deals only with ideas. In every mental state we have an "above" and a "below." Above the firmament are the unexpressed capacities ("waters") of the conscious mind resting in faith in Divine Mind. Below the firmament are the unexpressed capacities ("waters") of the subconscious mind.

The word "Heaven" is capitalized in this passage because it relates directly to Divine Mind. Faith ("firmament") established in consciousness is a state of perfect harmony, therefore Heaven. Another degree of mind unfoldment has been attained. "And there was evening and there was morning, a second day." "Evening" represents completion, and the "morning" following represents activity of ideas.

> *Gen 1:9-13.* "And God said, Let the waters under the heavens be gathered together unto one place, and let the dry land appear: and it was so. And God called the dry land Earth; and the gathering together of the waters called he Seas; and God saw that it was good. And God said, Let the earth put forth grass, herbs yielding seed, *and* fruit-trees bearing fruit after their kind, wherein is the seed thereof, upon the earth: and it was so. And the earth brought forth grass, herbs yielding seed after their kind, and trees bearing fruit, wherein is the seed thereof, after their kind: and God saw that it was good. And there was evening and there was morning, a third day."

The third step in creation is the beginning of the formative activity of the mind called imagination. This gathers "the waters . . . together unto one place" so that the "dry land" appears. Then the imagination begins a great multiplication of forms and shapes in the mind.

The first day's creation reveals the light or inspiration of Spirit. The second day establishes faith in our possibilities to bring forth the invisible. The third day's creation or third movement of Divine Mind pictures the activity of ideas in mind. This is called expression. The formative power of mind is the imagination, whose work is here represented by the dry land. There is much unformed thought in mind ("the heavens") that must be separated from the formed.

In this proclamation "earth" is the mental image of formed thought and does not refer to the manifest world. God is Di-

vine Mind and deals directly with ideas. "Seas" represents
the unformed state of mind. We say that a man is "at sea"
when he is in doubt in his mental processes. In other words
he has not established his thoughts in line with the principle
involved. The sea is capable of production, but must come
under the dominion of the imagination.

Divine Mind images its ideals definitely and in every detail. The ideal precedes the fulfillment. "Let there be" represents the perfect confidence necessary to demonstrate.

Ideas are productive and bring forth after their kind. They
express themselves under the law of divine imagery. The
seed is within the thought and is reproduced through
thought activity until thought habits are formed. Thoughts
become fixed in the earth or formed consciousness. In Divine Mind all is good.

Again a definite degree of mind unfoldment has been attained. Man, in forming his world, goes through the same
mental process, working under divine law. Jesus said, "The
seed is the word of God."

> *Gen. 1: 14-19.* "And God said, Let there be lights in the
> firmament of heaven to divide the day from the night;
> and let them be for signs, and for seasons, and for days,
> and years: and let them be for lights in the firmament
> of heaven to give light upon the earth: and it was so.
> And God made the two great lights; the greater light to
> rule the day, and the lesser light to rule the night: *he
> made* the stars also. And God set them in the firmament
> of heaven to give light upon the earth, and to rule over
> the day and over the night, and to divide the light from
> the darkness: and God saw that it was good. And there
> was evening and there was morning, a fourth day."

The fourth step in creation is the development of the "two
great lights," the will and the understanding, or the sun (the

spiritual I AM) and the moon (the intellect). These are but reflectors of the true light; for God had said, "Let there be light: and there was light"—before the sun and the moon were created.

The "firmament of heaven" is the consciousness of Truth that has been formulated and established. In the second day's creation a firmament was established in heaven (realm of divine ideas). This firmament divides the day (illumined consciousness) from the night (unillumined consciousness). Through faith the "lights" are established; that is, understanding begins to unfold. The "signs," "seasons," and "days and years" represent different stages of unfoldment. We gain understanding by degrees.

The "earth" represents the more external processes through which an idea passes, and corresponds to the activity of an idea in mind. In man the "earth" is the body consciousness, which in its real nature is a harmonious expression of ideas established in faith-substance. "And it was so"; that is, an idea from divine consciousness is instantly fulfilled.

The "greater light," in mind, is understanding and the "lesser light" is the will. The greater light rules "the day," that realm of consciousness which has been illumined by Spirit. The lesser light rules "the night," that is, the will; which has no illumination ("light" or "day") but whose office is to execute the demands of understanding. The will does not reason, but in its harmonious relation acts easily and naturally upon the inspiration of Spirit. Divine will expresses itself as the I AM in man.

The "stars" represent man's perceptive faculties, including his ability to perceive weight, size, color, sound, and the like. Through concentrating any one of the faculties ("stars") at its focalizing point one may come into an understanding of its action.

Divine Mind first images the idea, then perceives its fulfillment. Man, co-operating with Divine Mind, places himself under the same creative law and brings into manifestation his ideas.

The idea is the directing and controlling power. Every idea has a specific function to perform. When our ideas are constructive and harmonious we see that they are good and realize that their power to rule is dominant in consciousness.

"Evening" stands for the fulfillment of an idea and marks another "day" or degree of unfoldment in consciousness.

Again referring to Fenton's translation of the 1st verse of Genesis, "By periods God created that which produced the solar systems; then that which produced the earth," we see that God did not create the worlds directly; He created that which produced or evolved them. Then God said, "Let there be light." The Hebrew word of light is *owr,* meaning "luminosity" either literally or metaphysically. On the fourth day God said, "Let reflectors appear in the expanse of the heavens." Then God made two large "luminaries." The Hebrew word here used to express light is *maowr,* "a luminous body." The author of Genesis made a distinction between the source of light and how it was to be bodily manifested. But both were concepts in Divine Mind.

Our modern dynamos produce luminosity out of the ether equal to sunlight. The earth whirling on its axis generates electricity. Modern scientists are accepting analogy then, holding that bodies in motion generate energy that under certain conditions becomes luminous, and the conclusion is that the primal force that produces light existed before its manifestation through matter. This conclusion is in harmony with the symbolic story of creation as found in Genesis.

Modern critics have questioned the accuracy of Scripture on these points. Robert Ingersoll in his book *Some Mistakes of Moses* calls attention to the creation of light before sources of light, the sun and the stars, were created, as evidence of the ignorance and inaccuracy of Moses. But scientific research and study of the original Hebrew reveals their harmony.

Gen. 1:20-23. "And God said, Let the waters swarm with swarms of living creatures, and let birds fly above the earth in the open firmament of heaven. And God created the great sea-monsters, and every living creature that moveth, wherewith the waters swarmed, after their kind, and every winged bird after its kind: and God saw that it was good. And God blessed them, saying, Be fruitful, and multiply, and fill the waters in the seas, and let birds multiply on the earth. And there was evening and there was morning, a fifth day."

The fifth step in creation is the bringing forth of sensation and discrimination. The "creatures" are thoughts. The "birds . . . in the open firmament of heaven" are ideas approaching spiritual understanding.

"Water" represents the unformed substance of life, always present as a fecundating element in which ideas ("living creatures") increase and multiply, just as the earth produces a crop when sown with seed. The "birds" represent the liberated thoughts or ideas of mind (heaven).

In connection with the body, "water" represents the fluids of the organism. The "sea-monsters" are life ideas that swarm in these fluids. Here is pictured Divine Mind creating the original body idea, as imaged in the 20th verse. In the 2d chapter of Genesis we shall read of the perfect manifestation of this idea. Idea, expression, and manifestation are the steps involved in bringing anything forth under divine law. The stamp of good is placed upon divine ideas and their activity in substance.

In the fifth day's creation ideas of discrimination and judgment are developed. The fishes and fowls represent ideas of life working in mind but they must be properly related to the

unformed (seas) and the formed (earth) worlds of mind.
When an individual is well balanced in mind and body, there
is an equalizing force flowing in the consciousness, and harmony is in evidence.

Another orderly degree of mind unfoldment is fulfilled.
Another step in spiritual growth is worked out in individual
consciousness, when the individual enters into the quickening of this judgment and seeks to conform his ideas to those
of Divine Mind.

> *Gen. 1:24-31.* "And God said, Let the earth bring forth liv-
> ing creatures after their kind, cattle, and creeping things,
> and beasts of the earth after their kind: and it was so.
> And God made the beasts of the earth after their kind,
> and the cattle after their kind, and everything that creep-
> eth upon the ground after its kind: and God saw that it
> was good. And God said, Let us make man in our image,
> after our likeness: and let them have dominion over the
> fish of the sea, and over the birds of the heavens, and
> over the cattle, and over all the earth, and over every
> creeping thing that creepeth upon the earth. And God
> created man in his own image, in the image of God cre-
> ated he him; male and female created he them. And
> God blessed them: and God said unto them, Be fruitful,
> and multiply, and replenish the earth, and subdue it;
> and have dominion over the fish of the sea, and over the
> birds of the heavens, and over every living thing that
> moveth upon the earth. And God said, Behold, I have
> given you every herb yielding seed, which is upon the
> face of all the earth, and every tree, in which is the fruit
> of a tree yielding seed; to you it shall be for food: and to
> every beast of the earth, and to every bird of the heav-
> ens, and to everything that creepeth upon the earth,
> wherein there is life, *I have given* every green herb for

food: and it was so. And God saw everything that he had made, and behold, it was very good. And there was evening and there was morning, the sixth day."

The sixth step in creation is the bringing forth of ideas after their kind. When man approaches the creative level in his thought, he is getting close to God in his consciousness, and then the realization that he is the very image and likeness of his Creator dawns upon him. This is the consciousness in man of Christ.

On the sixth day of creation ideas of life are set into activity. "Cattle" represent ideas of strength established in substance. "Creeping things" represent ideas of life that are more subtle in their expression, approaching closer to the realm of sense. They are the micro-organisms. The "beasts" stand for the free energies of life that relate themselves to sensation. Divine ideas are always instantly set into activity: "and it was so."

Underlying all these ideas related to sensation, which in their original purity are simply ideas of life functioning in substance, is the divine idea of life. When life is expressed in divine order it is pronounced good. What is termed "sense consciousness" in man is not to be condemned but lifted up to its rightful place. "As Moses lifted up the serpent in the wilderness, even so must the Son of man be lifted up; that whosoever believeth may in him have eternal life," When the ideas of life are properly related to love and wisdom, man will find in them eternal satisfaction instead of sense pleasure.

Wisdom and love are the two qualities of Being that, communing together, declare, "Let us make man in our image, after our likeness." This is the mental image of man which in Truth we call the Christ. The Christ man has dominion over every idea emanating from Divine Mind.

The creation described in these six days or six "steps" or

stages of God-Mind is wholly spiritual and should not be confounded with the manifestation that is described in the succeeding chapters. God is Mind and all His works are created in mind as perfect ideas.

This statement of man's creation, "And God said, Let us make man in our image, after our likeness," has always been a puzzle to people who read the Scriptures literally. The apparent man is so at variance with the description that they cannot reconcile them. Theologians began first to admit that the Garden of Eden story was an allegory, and now they are including the whole of Genesis.

But this is more than an allegory; it is a description of the ideal creation. In their calculations engineers often use mathematical symbols, like the letters $x, y,$ and $z,$ to represent quantities not yet given precise determination but carried along for development at the proper time. Involved in these symbols are ideas that are to be brought out in their proper order and made visible when the engineer's plans are objectified. So man plans in his mind that which he proposes to build. First the idea, then the visible. This is the process through which all creation passes. God makes all things in His mind first, which is involution; then they are made into form and shape, and this is evolution.

In some such way then we can think of man as represented by an x in God's plan or calculations. God is carrying man along in His mind as an ideal quantity, the image-and-likeness man of His creation, and His divine plan is dependent for its success on the manifestation by man of this idea. The divine plan is furthered by the constant idealism that keeps man moving forward to higher and higher achievements. The image-and-likeness man pours into "mankind" a perpetual stream of ideas that the individual man arranges as thoughts and forms as substance and life. While this evolutionary process is going on there seem to be two men, one ideal and spiritual and the other intellectual and material, which are united at the consummation, the ideal man, Christ.

When the mind attains an understanding of certain creative facts, of man's creative powers, it has established a directive, intelligent center that harmonizes these two men (ideal and spiritual vs. intellectual and material). This directive center may be named the I AM. It is something more than the human *I*. Yet when this human *I* has made union with the image-and-likeness *I*, the true I AM comes into action, and this is the Christ Jesus, the Son of God, evolved and made visible in creation according to divine law.

God ideated two universal planes of consciousness, "the heavens and the earth." One is the realm of pure ideas, the other of thought forms. God does not create the visible universe directly, as a man makes a concrete pavement, but He creates the ideas that are used by His intelligent "image and likeness" to make the universe. Thus God's creations are always spiritual. Man's creations are both material and spiritual, according to his understanding.

Mental activity in Divine Mind presents two phases: first, conception of the idea and secondly, expression of the idea. In every idea conceived in mind there is first the quickening spirit of life, followed by the increase of the idea in substance. Wisdom is the "male" or expressive side of Being, while love is the "female" or receptive side of Being. Wisdom is the father quality of God and love is the mother quality. In every idea there exists these two qualities of mind, which unite in order to increase and bring forth under divine law.

Divine Mind blessed the union of wisdom and love and pronounced upon them the increase of Spirit. When wisdom and love are unified in the individual consciousness, man is a master of ideas and brings forth under the original creative law.

"Seed" represents fundamental ideas having within themselves reproductive capacities. Every idea is a seed which, sown in the substance of mind, becomes the real food upon which man is nourished. Man has access to the seed ideas of Divine Mind, and through prayer and meditation he quickens and appropriates the substance of those ideas, which were originally planted in his I AM by the parent mind.

Provision is made for the sustenance of all the ideas emanating from Divine Mind. The primitive forms of life are fed upon the "herbs," they have a sustaining force that is food to them, even as the appropriation of divine ideas is food for man.

Divine Mind, being All-Good itself, sees only its own creation as good. As man co-operates more fully with Divine Mind, imaging only that which is good, he too beholds his productions with the "single" eye or sees them only as good. The sixth step in creation, is the concentration, in man, of all the ideas of Divine Mind. Man is given authority and dominion over all ideas. Thus is completed another degree of mind unfoldment.

In the six mind movements, called days, Elohim God creates the spiritual universe and spiritual man. He then rests. He has created the ideals, patterns, for the formed universe that is to follow. . . .

Chapter 16

THE OMNIPOTENCE OF PRAYER (1939)

TO A PERSON in the understanding of Truth prayer should be an affirmation of that which is in Being.

What is the necessity of the prayer of affirmation if Being already is? In order that the creative law of the Word may be fulfilled. All things are in God as potentialities. It is man's office under the divine law to bring into manifestation that which has been created or planned by the unmanifest. Everybody should pray. Through prayer we develop the highest phase of character. Prayer softens and refines the whole man. A prominent skeptic once said that the most unattractive thing in existence was a prayerless woman.

Prayer is not supplication or begging but a simple asking for that which we know is waiting for us at the hands of our Father and an affirmation of its existence. The prayer that Jesus gave as a model is simplicity itself. There is none of that awe-inspiring "O Thou" that ministers often affect in public prayer but only the ordinary informal request of a son to his Father for things needed.

"Father . . . Hallowed be thy name." Here in the Lord's

Prayer is a recognition of the all-inclusiveness and completeness of Divine Mind. Everything has its sustenance from this one source; therefore "the earth is the Lord's, and the fullness thereof."

We need supplies for the day only. Hoarding for future necessity breeds selfishness. The Children of Israel tried to save the manna, but it spoiled on their hands.

The law "Whatsoever a man soweth, that shall he also reap" is here shorn of its terrors. If we forgive others we shall be forgiven, and the penalty of suffering for sins will be eliminated.

It does not seem possible that God would lead us into temptation. The statement about temptation follows closely that regarding the forgiveness of sin, and it is evidently a part of it. "Let not temptation lead us" is a permissible interpretation.

Jesus advised asking for what we want and being persistent in our demands. People ignorant of the relation in which man stands to God wonder why we should ask and even importune a Father who has provided all things for us. This is explained when we perceive that God is a great mind reservoir that has to be tapped by man's mind and poured into visibility through man's thought or word. If the mind of man is clogged with doubt, lethargy, or fear, he must open the way by persistent knocking and asking. "Pray without ceasing," "continuing instant [constant] in prayer." Acquire in prayer a facility in asking equal to the mathematician's expertness in handling numbers and you will get responses in proportion.

We give our children what we consider good gifts from our limited and transitory store, but when the gifts of God are put into our minds we have possessions that are eternal and will go on being productive for all time.

Undoubtedly the one thing that stands out prominently in the teaching of Jesus is the necessity of prayer. He prayed on the slightest pretext, or in some such manner invoked the presence of God. He prayed over situations that most men would deal with without the intervention of God. If He was verily God incarnate, the skeptic often asks, why did He so often appeal to an apparently higher God. To answer this doubt intelligently and truly one must understand the constitution of man.

There are always two men in each individual. The man without is the picture that the man within paints with his mind. This mind is the open door to the unlimited principle of Being. When Jesus prayed He was setting into action the various powers of His individuality in order to bring about certain results. Within His identity was of God; without He was human personality.

The various mental attitudes denoted by the word prayer are not comprehended by those unfamiliar with the spiritual constitution of man. When the trained metaphysician speaks of his demonstrations through prayer, he does not explain all the movements of his spirit and mind, because the outer consciousness has not the capacity to receive it.

When we read of Jesus spending whole nights in prayer, the first thought is that He was asking and begging God for something. But we find prayer to be many-sided; it is not only asking but receiving also. We must pray believing that we shall receive. Prayer is both invocation and affirmation. Meditation, concentration, denial, and affirmation in the silence are all forms of what is loosely termed prayer.

Thus Jesus was demonstrating at night over the error thoughts of mind. He was lifting the mortal mind up to the plane of Spirit through some prayerful thought. The Son of man must be lifted up, and there is no way to do this except through prayer.

One who exercises his thought powers discovers that there is a steady growth with proper use. The powers of the mind are developed in much the same way that the muscles of the body are. Persistent affirmation of a certain desire in the silence concentrates the mental energies and beats down all barriers.

Jesus illustrates the power of such affirmative prayer, of repeated silent demands for justice, for instance, by the case of the widow bereft of worldly protection and power. To the widow's persistence even the ungodly judge succumbs. The unceasing prayer of faith is commanded in the Scriptures in various places.

If a man's prayers are based on the thought of his own righteousness and the sinfulness of others, he does not fulfill the law of true prayer. Self-righteousness is an exclusory thought and closes the door to the great Father love that we all want. We are not to justify ourselves in the sight of God but let the Spirit of justice and righteousness do its perfect work through us.

That God and angels and heaven exist is accepted by all who believe the Scriptures, but there is wide diversity of thought about their character and abode. Those who read the Bible after the letter have invented all kinds of imaginary notions as to the conditions under which God and His angels live and as to the location of heaven. Their minds being fixed on things, they have not conceived of the realm of ideas, and they are therefore totally ignorant of the true teaching of the Scriptures. To understand the Bible one must know about the constitution of man. This is the key to all mysteries, the knowledge of man's true Self. "Know thyself."

Man is Spirit, soul, body. These are coexistent. God is the principle of being as an axiom is a principle of mathematics. God is not confined to locality. Is a mathematical principle confined to a particular place and not found elsewhere? "The kingdom of God is within you." God is the real of man's being. It follows that all the powers that are attributed to God may become operative in man. Then we live right in the presence of God and angels and heaven. What seems a desert place is filled with angelic messengers, and like Jacob we know it not.

Man sets into action any of the three realms of his Being, Spirit, soul, and body, by concentrating his thought on them. If he thinks only of the body, the physical senses encompass all his existence. If mind and emotion are cultivated he adds soul to his consciousness. If he rises to the Absolute and comprehends Spirit, he rounds out the God-man.

Spirit is the source of soul and body, hence the ruling power. Its works are so swift and so transcend the limitations of matter that the natural man cannot comprehend them and hence calls them "miracles." But all things are done under law. "Prayer was made earnestly of the church unto God for him," and Peter was delivered from prison by an angel. The earnest prayers of the devout believers in the power of supreme Spirit brought about the result. The history of Christianity is full of instances of so-called miracles wrought through prayer. The hour-long prayer of Luther by what was supposed to be the deathbed of his friend Melanchthon is a famous instance of importunate pleadings. It was Luther's firm belief that Melanchthon's years of continued life were the direct answer to his prayers.

Mighty things have been wrought in the past by those who had mere blind faith to guide them. To faith we now add understanding of the law, and our achievements will be a fulfillment of the promise of Jesus: "He that believeth on me, the works that I do shall he also do; and greater *works* then these shall he do." The prayer of Luther and its results are now being duplicated every day. As we go on in the exercise of the spiritual faculties we shall strengthen them and understand them better, and we shall cease to talk about anything miraculous. All things are possible to man when he exercises his spiritual power under the divine law.

When man directs the power of exalted ideas into his body, he exalts the cells, releases their innate spiritual energy, and causes them finally to disappear from physical sight into the omnipresent luminous ether. This is what Jesus accomplished at His ascension. The promise was that all who follow Him in the regeneration of the body would do likewise. It is true that even the followers of Jesus have not always understood the scientific import of His doctrine. They have mentally absorbed His exalted ideas and looked to their fulfillment in a faraway heaven in the skies. By thus projecting their ideas toward a fulfillment outside of the body they have separated their soul or mind consciousness from its companion, the body, and the deserted cells have been resolved into their mother principle, the earth.

The mind of man is constantly projecting thought energies or waves through brain cells into the ether or space element in which we live. Every person lives in an environment of radiant energy that circulates through the cells of his organism like bees in a hive. Ordinarily we cannot see the radiations of the mind, but we almost universally feel them. When a discordant mind impinges upon our mind radiations we instinctively shrink away. But we are radiantly happy in the presence of an exalted mind.

"No man hath beheld God at any time." Seers, prophets, preachers, and holy men and women in all ages are a unit in saying that they have become acquainted with God through prayer, expressed in the Spirit of their minds.

This testimony to God's spiritual presence is so unanimous that no one seeks His help in any way other than through the Spirit of the mind; and the fact that we know

God with our minds and not with our senses proves that God is Spirit.

In its higher functioning the mind of man deals with spiritual ideas, and we can truthfully say that man is a spiritual being. This fact explains the almost universal worship of God by men and makes possible the conjunction of the heaven and the earth by those who understand the underlying laws of prayer. Jesus stated this emphatically in John 4:24: "God is Spirit; and they that worship him must worship in spirit and truth."

Then the real foundation of all effective prayer is the understanding that God is Spirit and that man, His offspring, is His image and likeness, hence spiritual.

Such a concept of God gives man a point of contact that is never absent; in all places and under all conditions he has the assurance of the attention and help of God when he realizes the Father's spiritual presence and comradeship.

When it has a spiritually poised mind to work through, Spirit is not limited in its power by any material environment. "With God all things are possible." To make this strong statement of Jesus come true we must study the laws of God and strive to carry them out through a quickened consciousness.

The Bible is replete with situations where men and women seemed beyond any material help, but through faith and prayer they triumphed right in the face of seemingly insurmountable obstacles. The author of the 11th chapter of Hebrews builds pyramids of faith demonstrations. Hear the climax:

"And what shall I more say? for the time will fail me if I tell of Gideon, Barak, Samson, Jephthah; of David and Samuel and the prophets who through faith subdued kingdoms, wrought righteousness, obtained promises, stopped the mouths of lions, quenched the power of fire, escaped the edge of the sword, from weakness were made strong, waxed mighty in war, turned to flight armies of aliens."

Paul might have added to his pyramid of faith the long list of miraculous healings of diseases and many superhuman works recorded in the Bible, among which are restoration of the leper Naaman and the resurrection of the Shunammite's son by Elisha; the control of the elements by Elijah; the overcoming of gravity in the floating of the workman's ax-head from the bottom of the Jordan by Elisha, and Moses' causing the water to gush from the rock.

The majority of people think that great spiritual faith is necessary to get marvelous results. But Jesus taught differently. "The apostles said unto the Lord, Increase our faith. And the Lord said, If ye had faith as a grain of mustard seed, ye would say unto this sycamine tree, Be thou rooted up, and be thou planted in the sea; and it would obey you."

The mustard is among the smallest of seeds, and the comparison would indicate what a tiny bit of real faith is necessary to cause motion in material things. Paul and Silas in the Roman jail prayed and sang until their bonds fell off, the doors flew open, and they walked out both free men. On the day of Pentecost the followers of Jesus prayed and sang until the ethers were so accelerated that tongues of fire flashed from the bodies of the worshipers, and they were miraculously quickened in mental ability.

Prayer liberates the energies pent up in mind and body. Those who pray much create a spiritual aura that eventually envelops the whole body. The bands of light painted by artists around the heads of saints are not imaginary; they actually exist and are visible to the sharp eye of the painter. The Scriptures testify in Luke 9:29 that when Jesus was praying "his countenance was altered, and his raiment *became* white *and* dazzling." After Moses had been praying on the mountain his face shone so brightly that the people could not look on it, and he had to wear a veil.

Thus prayer is obviously dynamic and actuates the spiritual ethers that interpenetrate all substance. Prayer is related directly to the creative laws of God, and when man adjusts his mind and body in harmony with those laws, his prayers will always be effective and far-reaching. The activity of the mind that is named the understanding is essential in righteous prayer. Spirit is omnipresent, but the individual consciousness gives it a local habitation and a name.

If in thinking about God we locate Him in a faraway heaven and direct our thoughts outward in the hope of reaching Him, all our force will be driven from us to that imaginary place and we shall become devitalized.

"The kingdom of God is within you." The pivotal point around which Spirit creates is within the structure of consciousness. This is true of the primal cell as well as of the most complex organ. The throne on which the divine will sits is within man's consciousness, and it is to this inner center that he should direct his attention when praying or meditating. David called this spiritual center of the soul "the secret place of the Most High," and all the defense and power of the 91st Psalm is promised to the one who dwells in the consciousness of the Almighty within. Paul says, "Know ye not that ye are a temple of God, and *that* the Spirit of God dwelleth in you?"

In the 6th chapter of Matthew, in giving His disciples directions for prayer, Jesus called attention to the God center in man in these words: "But thou, when thou prayest, enter into thine inner chamber, and having shut the door, pray to thy Father who is in secret, and thy Father who seeth in secret shall recompense thee." He also told them not to use vain repetitions: "For your Father knoweth what things ye have need of, before ye ask him."

If Divine Mind knows our needs, why should we have to ask to have them supplied? We do not ask expecting God to hand us the things we want, but we realize that He has made provision in the very nature of things for our every need to be fulfilled. When we realize this and go about our work in perfect confidence, the fulfillment of the divine law of support and supply is often demonstrated in ways we had not dreamed of.

Do not supplicate or beg God to give you what you need, but get still and think about the inexhaustible resources of infinite Mind, its presence in all its fullness, and its constant readiness to manifest itself when its laws are complied with. This is what Jesus meant when He said, "Seek ye first his kingdom, and his righteousness; and all these things shall be added unto you."

We all need a better understanding of the nature of God if we are to comply with the laws under which He creates. We must begin by knowing that "God is Spirit." Spirit is not located in a big man called God but is everywhere the breath of life and the knowing quality of mind active in and through all bodies, "over all, and through all, and in all." The highest form of prayer is to open our minds and quietly realize that the one omnipresent intelligence knows our thoughts and instantly answers, even before we have audibly expressed our desires.

This being true, we should ask and at the same time give thanks that we have already received. Jesus expressed this idea in Mark 11:24: "Therefore I say unto you, All things whatsoever ye pray and ask for, believe that ye receive them, and ye shall have them." Before He broke the miraculously multiplied loaves and fishes and fed the five thousand He looked up to heaven and gave thanks. When He raised Lazarus He first said: "Father, I thank thee that thou heardest me. And I knew that thou hearest me always." Then He commanded Lazarus to come forth.

We observe that all things come out of the formless, but our knowledge of the formless is so limited that we do not conceive of its infinite possibilities. When we think or silently speak in the all-potential ethers of Spirit, there is always an unfailing effect. "Whatsoever ye have said in the darkness shall be heard in the light; and what ye have spoken in the ear in the inner chambers shall be proclaimed upon the housetops."

Silent prayer is more effective than audible, because by silent prayer the mind comes into closer touch with the creative Spirit. James says, "The prayer of faith shall save him that is sick, and the Lord shall raise him up." Countless thousands are applying this faith prayer today and are being healed as men were in the time of Jesus.

The strange thing is that this very important proof of the Spirit's work in Christian healing should have been neglected for so many hundred years when Jesus gave it as one of the signs of a believer: "These signs shall accompany them that believe; in my name shall they cast out demons; they shall speak with new tongues; they shall take up serpents, and if they drink any deadly thing, it shall in no wise hurt them; they shall lay hands on the sick, and they shall recover."

The history of the Christian church records that during its first three hundred years the followers of Jesus healed the sick by prayer and that healing was gradually dropped as the church became prosperous and worldly. A layman from a rural district was being shown, by a bishop, the riches of a cathedral. The bishop said, "The church can no longer say, 'Silver and gold have I none.'" "No," said the layman. "Neither can it say, 'Take up thy bed, and walk.'"

It is found by those who have faith in the power of God

that the prayer for health is the most quickly answered. The reason for this is that the natural laws that create and sustain the body are really divine laws, and when man silently asks for the intervention of God in restoring health, he is calling into action the natural forces of his being. Doctors agree that the object of using their remedies is to quicken the natural functions of the body. But medicine does not appeal to the intelligent principle that directs all the activities of the organism, hence it fails to give permanent healing.

However a conscious union with the natural life forces lying within and back of all the complex activities of man gets right to the fountainhead, and the results are unfailing if the proper connection has been made.

The first step in prayer for health is to get still. "Be still, and know that I am God." To get still the body must be relaxed and the mind quieted. Center the attention within. There is a quiet place within us all and by silently saying over and over, "Peace, be still," we shall enter that quiet place and a great stillness will pervade our whole being. Jesus Christ said, "Peace be unto you. . . . Receive ye the Holy Spirit." That is, He spoke to the within. He said also, "whatsoever ye shall ask in my name, that will I do, that the Father may be glorified in the Son."

"For my thoughts are not your thoughts, neither are your ways my ways, saith Jehovah. For as the heavens are higher than the earth, so are my ways higher than your ways, and my thoughts than your thoughts." This verse from Isaiah gives us an insight into the difference between the mortal thinker and the divine. Divine Mind is serene, orderly, placid, while sense mind is turbulent, discordant, and violent. We can readily understand from this comparison why we do not get divine guidance even though we strive ever so hard for it. The best of us are subject to crosscurrents of worry that interfere with the even flow of God's thoughts into our consciousness. Jesus warned His followers not to be anxious about what they should eat, drink, or wear. In all literature there is no finer comparison than that given by Jesus when He pointed to the flowers and said: "Consider the lilies of the field, how they grow; they toil not, neither do they spin; yet I say unto you, that even Solomon in all his glory was not arrayed like one of these."

If God so clothes the lilies, shall He not much more clothe His children? This argument holds good with reference to all human needs. There is a natural law whose chief purpose is to take care of the human family. But the divine order of creative Mind must be observed by man before he can receive the benefits of his natural inheritance.

Metaphysicians, who study the mind and its many modes of action, find that when they refuse to let thoughts of worry, anxiety, or other distraction act in their minds, they gradually establish an inner quietness that finally merges into a great peace. This is the "peace of God, which passeth all understanding." When this peace is attained, the individual gets inspirations and revelations direct from infinite Mind.

Any method that will hush the external thought clamor will achieve unity with the inner peace. When we are in peaceful sleep, the outer clamor of thought is stilled and the great Spirit of the universe communicates its higher vision to the inner consciousness of man.

The ancient peoples seem to have been more open than moderns to revelations in sleep. Long ago Job wrote in the 33d chapter of his book:

"In a dream, in a vision of the night,
　When deep sleep falleth upon men,
　In slumberings upon the bed;
　Then he openeth the ears of men,
　And sealeth their instruction."

It is written in 1 Kings, Chapter 3, that the Lord appeared to Solomon in a dream and said, "Ask what I shall give thee." Solomon did not ask for riches, for honor, or for the glory that kings usually seek, but in meekness he asked the Lord to give him an "understanding heart" so that he might discriminate between good and evil and be a wise judge of his people. Riches and honor followed of course, as they always do when a man is earnestly striving to be honest and just in all ways.

We get our most vivid revelations when in a meditative state of mind. This proves that when we make the mind trustful and confident, we put it in harmony with creative Mind; then its force flows to us in accordance with the law of like attracting like.

The agonizing, supplicating, begging prayer is not answered, because the thoughts are so turbulent that Divine Mind cannot reach the pleader. Jesus prayed with a confident assurance that what He wanted would be granted, and He established a mode of prayer for His followers that never fails when the same conditions and relations are attained and maintained with reference to the Father-Mind.

Through His spiritual attainments Jesus formed a spiritual zone in the earth's mental atmosphere; His followers make connection with that zone when they pray in His "name." He stated this fact in John 14:2: "I go to prepare a place for you." Simon Peter said, "Lord, whither goest thou?" Jesus answered him, "Whither I go, thou canst not follow me now; but thou shalt follow afterwards."

When Jesus had purified His body sufficiently, He ascended into this "place" in the spiritual ethers of our planet. In our high spiritual realizations we make temporary contact with Him and His spiritual character, represented by His "name." But we, like the apostles, are not yet able to go there and abide, because we have not overcome earthly attachments. We shall however attain the same freedom and spiritual power that He attained if we follow Him in the regeneration. But we should clearly understand that we cannot go to Jesus' "place" through death. We must overcome death as He did before we can be glorified with Him in the "heavens," the higher realms of the mind.

We should not cease to pray to the Father in the name of Christ Jesus; He said that man should "pray always." Prayer lifts our thoughts on high and sets us free from the narrow limits of matter, just as the electromagnetic impulse is lifted and carried by the ether and caught by any receptive station. Spiritual-minded people are being united today, as in the past, by zones of spiritual force that will eventually become the permanent thought atmosphere of the planet. In Revelation this is typified as the New Jerusalem descending out of the heavens into the earth.

Jesus said we could ask whatsoever we wished in His name and it should be done unto us: "Verily, verily, I say unto you, If ye shall ask anything of the Father, he will give it you in my name. Hitherto have ye asked nothing in my name: ask, and ye shall receive, that your joy may be made full."

Jesus taught in parables because the people did not understand that spiritual forces, acting through mind, make race conditions. But He told them: "The hour cometh, when I shall no more speak unto you in dark sayings, but shall tell you plainly of the Father."

The time prophesied by Jesus—when we should plainly understand the character of the Father—is now at hand, and it behooves all Christians to come out of parables and to realize that scientific laws govern the material, mental, and spiritual realms of Being.

"Pray without ceasing; in everything give thanks," wrote Paul to the Thessalonians. The idea is that we should be persistent in prayer. We know it is always the will of the air to give us all that we can breathe into our lungs. Jesus compared the Spirit to the air in describing the new birth to Nicodemus. It requires lung capacity to breathe deeply of the oceans of air; so it requires spiritual capacity to realize how accessible and ready omnipresent Spirit is to fill us full of itself. The lack is in us. God is more willing to give than we are to receive.

To acquire the mind that is always open to Spirit we must be persistent in prayer. It is written in the 18th chapter of Luke: "And he spake a parable unto them to the end that they ought always to pray, and not to faint." He then told of the judge who feared not God nor man yet who was worn out by the persistency of a woman who demanded justice.

By experimentation modern metaphysical healers have discovered a large number of laws that rule in the realm of mind, and they all agree that no two cases are exactly alike. Therefore one who prays for the health of another should understand that it is not the fault of the healing principle that his patient is not instantly restored. The fault may be in his own lack of persistency or understanding; or it may be due to the patient's dogged clinging to discordant thoughts. In any case the one who prays must persist in this prayer until the walls of resistance are broken down and the healing currents are tuned in. Metaphysicians often pray over a critical case all night, as history says Luther prayed for the dying Melanchthon and brought about his recovery.

Persistency in prayer awakens the spiritual consciousness and sets into perpetual glow the core of the soul. When this has been accomplished, one is in a constant state of thanksgiving and praising, and the joy of a conscious union with creative Mind is realized.

Chapter 17

REALIZATION PRECEDES MANIFESTATION (1939)

OD'S MAN IS HALE, whole, hearty. This is Truth. A spiritual realization is a realization of Truth. A spiritual realization of health is the result of holding in consciousness a statement of health until the logic of the mind is satisfied and man receives the assurance that the fulfillment in the physical must follow. In other words, by realizing a healing prayer man lays hold of the principle of health itself and the whole consciousness is illumined; he perceives principle working out his health problems for him.

However when man lays hold of the principle of wholeness, he finds that he is automatically working with God and that much new power is added. He realizes: "My Father worketh even until now, and I work." After man has applied his mind diligently for a season, he exhausts his resources or powers of realization for the time being and rests from all his work; but his accumulated thought energy is completed or fulfilled in a higher realm, and he has a double assurance that health must become manifest.

Jesus understood and demonstrated this law perfectly. He

was so much at one with the principle of health that He needed only to say, "Thy faith hath made thee whole" or "Lazarus, come forth," in order to bring into evidence the perfect demonstration.

Realization means at-one-ment, completion, perfection, wholeness, repose, resting in God. A realization of health brings to the consciousness an inner knowing that the divine law has been fulfilled in thought and act. Then as man lays hold of the indwelling Christ he is raised out of the Adam or dark consciousness into the Christ consciousness. This at-one-ment with God brings a lasting joy that cannot be taken away.

God-Mind rests in a perpetual realization of health, and that which seems to be sickness does not exist in Truth. When man becomes so much at one with God-Mind that he abides in the consciousness of health he enters the eternal peace in which he knows that "it is finished."

In order to understand God-Mind we need to study our own mind. The more we analyze the processes of the mind the more plainly the mind with its mental "compounds" appears as the source of health and of all other things. In the realms of dense matter intelligence may be so faint as to have lost all contact with Mind. Yet the poet sings about there being "sermons in stones." Again science announces that life is present in and is disintegrating the solid rocks and the whole earth groans and creaks in her struggle with inertia. So if we want to know the secrets of health and how right thinking forms the perfect body, we must go to the mind and trace step by step the movements that transform ideas of health into light, electrons, atoms, molecules, cells, tissues, and finally into the perfect physical organism.

Although there is almost universal skepticism with reference to the mind's ability to know consciously how relative substance is formed, there are those who have made contact with the thought processes and can apply them in transforming the cells and tissues of their own body. The almost insurmountable obstacle to explaining to others how this is accomplished is the paucity of language. The mind functions in ways that are so strange and unbelievable that the pioneers on this frontier of metaphysics choose as a rule to remain silent.

Jesus is the outstanding pioneer in this realm where the health-producing processes of cells are released and imbued with supermind vitality.

He spent years in becoming acquainted with His body and freeing its cells from the material bondage to which the race thought had bound them.

Yet He gave no scientific explanation of the purifying through which He put His body to transform it before Peter, James, and John, as stated in Luke 9:29: "And as he was praying, the fashion of his countenance was altered, and his raiment *became* white *and* dazzling." Modern metaphysicians do not excuse their ignorance by claiming that this and many other instances in which Jesus showed mastery over His body were miracles. Scientific Christians regard as mortal superstition the prevalent view that miracles are the abrogation by God of His laws and are performed as a sort of *legerdemain* to attract and astonish the people. The marvelous things that Jesus did we can do when we understand the law. "The works that I do shall he do also; and greater" still holds good.

Much that is attributed to the subconscious, strictly speaking, springs from the all-knowing or spiritual Mind. When we cannot intellectually account for our knowledge we assume the subconscious to be its source. Yet we should know that the subconscious is the storehouse of past knowledge and past experiences. So it knows only what has filtered through the conscious mind. It cannot therefore be the source of knowledge except through reflection or memory. This memory of what man has passed through in the aeons of his experience is often called intuition; it is the instinct of the animal soul.

The world today looks up to science; that is, it does not accept or believe anything unless it can be demonstrated by well-known universal laws. There are no known laws governing religion that can be scientifically explained; hence it is not acceptable to the scientific mind. But there is a technique for molding thought stuff by means of the mind, and metaphysicians follow it in their scientific thinking and in healing. The metaphysician handles omnipresent Spirit life and substance very much as the electrician handles electricity. Energy is locked up in all this life and substance and its release enables the metaphysician to utilize it in demonstrating health and in achieving success.

All the chemical elements adhere to their particular form and endeavor to retain it. Electricity is supposed to be a universal invisible energy whose unity can be broken up by the whirl of a dynamo. The electronic units exert all the force of their nature in a pull to regain their original status. Thus the power generated by a dynamo is gained from the force exerted by the electrical units in their rush to establish their primal equipoise.

Only a certain percentage of this energy is utilized because of the pull of the electrical units to get back home to their mother principle. The dissipation of energy is one of the great problems of the engineer. The loss of electricity in transmission is so great that only a small part of the original current reaches its destination.

We exist right in the midst of forces that would yield us power to do all our work if we knew how to conserve and properly utilize their energies. This is not only true of our use of the many elements in the natural world all about us but especially of our utilization of the energy generated by our minds. If we could utilize this dissipated energy constructively it would restore the body, illumine the mind, and establish us in a lasting consciousness of dominion and mastery.

With every thought there is a radiation of energy. If a person is untrained in thinking and lets his mind express all kinds of thoughts without control, he not only uses up his thought stuff but fails also to accomplish any helpful result.

Conservation of thought stuff is essential to right thinking. Right thinking is using the mind to bring about right ends idealized by the thinker. All the elements necessary to the restoration of health exists in the higher dimensions of the mind. Through concentration and conservation of thought force man regains the consciousness of health in his mind, and health then becomes manifest in his body.

Laws fixed by infinite Mind automatically accomplish whatever man desires when he becomes obedient to the inner guide. Concentration, one-pointed attention, forms a mental magnet in the mind to which thought substance rushes like iron filings to a lodestone. Then follows confidence or faith in one's ability to accomplish the desired end. According to the Scriptures this is the law by which the universe was brought into manifestation. In the 11th chapter of Hebrews it is written: "By faith we understand that the worlds have been framed by the word of God."

Modern science by its most daring proponents is launching out into the deeps of the invisible and describing in detail the electrical processes that ultimate in the atom and its aggregations in visible things. In substance they tell us that when points of light gather about a certain nucleus an atom is created, and from this a cell, and cell aggregations make tissues and these merge into the realm of things.

Here we have the scientific explanation and the Christian metaphysician's formula for making the invisible visible. The greatest of all physicists cannot tell what electricity is. Even Edison said he was ignorant of its real nature. Some find it sometimes acting very much like mind and have so stated. The head of the General Electric research department was asked by a reporter to give him a definition of electricity. The professor replied that to his mind electricity was like what the Christians describe as faith.

The scientific metaphysician fixes his attention powerfully on the consummation of a certain idea until he has a realization, which means that the idea has nucleated a certain amount of thought substance. When this realization is had the metaphysician rests "from all his work." Through faith and work he has fulfilled the law of mind and he rests in the conviction that his ideal of health will appear in manifestation in due season.

To a metaphysician realization is the conviction that a person gets when he has persistently concentrated his attention on an ideal until he feels assured of the fulfillment of that ideal. Elohim God pronounced His spiritual creation "very good"; then rested from all His work. There was as yet no manifestation, "no herb of the field had yet sprung up," and "there was not a man to till the ground"; yet the planning Mind had the realization that the spiritual law had been fulfilled and that it should rest from all its works.

That all things visible are held in place by a force invisible is the conviction of the majority of logical thinkers. In other words, everything is ensouled. When we understand that the soul has consciousness, that it thinks, we have the explanation of many mysterious phenomena. Some 150 years ago Franz Mesmer announced in Germany that under certain conditions he could induce a magnetic sleep in persons and control their minds. His demonstrations attracted the attention of doctors and mental scientists the world over. In this day the system is practiced under the name of hypnotism. It is full of pitfalls for both operator and patient because its tendency is to weaken the positive control that the mind should always exercise over its own brain structure. However it is one of the many proofs that the mind can produce conditions in the mental world that ultimate in the material world. A great physical scientist stated recently that it may be that the gods that determine our fates are our own minds working on our brain cells and through them on the world about us. This is very close to the Truth.

Every Christian metaphysician knows that back of the personal mind there is a great creative Mind that also recreates. This creative Mind has been named and described by men all down the ages. God-Mind not only can restore and heal but can establish us in the consciousness of permanent health. Do not allow your conception of God to be handicapped by what men have said about Him.

"There is a spirit in man,

And the breath of the Almighty giveth them understanding."

Let the Spirit of God in you reveal to you His true character. God was never sick a day; He is the source of life and health and joy. God wills that we express His "image" and "likeness," in which we were created.

The prayer for realization attains its consummation when with concentrated spiritual attention one has affirmed that God Spirit is present, that with all His power He is bringing to pass the perfect health desired, and that all is well. When your thoughts radiate with the speed of spiritual light, they blend with creative Mind (called by Jesus "heaven"), and the thing you have asked for will be done. Jesus told Peter that whatever he bound (affirmed) in earth would be bound in heaven and whatever he loosed (denied) in earth would be loosed in heaven. Peter had unbounded faith in Jesus (who represents spiritual man). When any man has unbounded faith in spiritual power his words, uttered in the limitations of matter, are flashed to heaven (creative Mind) and they accomplish whatever he puts into them. The fulfillment of this spoken word in the world of activities may take moments, hours, days, years, centuries; Jesus said that the Father only knew when these things would come to pass. Do not think because you do not get an instant response to your prayers that they are not answered. Every sincere desire and every effectual prayer for health that has ascended to heaven (creative Mind) is fulfilled, and will be made manifest whenever material limitations permit. Shakespeare had an inkling of this law of the relation of thoughts and words when he wrote,

"My words fly up, my thoughts remain below:
Words without thoughts never to heaven go."

The kingdom of heaven (the heavens) so often referred to by Jesus and described by Him as very near to us is far more accessible and is more often contacted by us than we imagine. Not only those who pray but those who persistently concentrate their thoughts on mathematics, music, or philosophies based in principle, are often rewarded with the marvelous intuitions of genius. These persons apparently break into a realm where no effort is required to gain the answer to their questions. The mathematical genius is called a prodigy. He solves instantly the most complex mathematical problem, yet cannot explain how he does it. He simply knows the answer, often before the statement of the problem has been completed.

Henri Poincaré in his book *Science and Method* says that his discoveries in mathematics came to him in flashes after he had spent long periods of study and concentration on the subject. Concentrated attention of the mind on an idea of any kind is equal to prayer and will make available the spiritual principle that is its source in proportion to the intensity and continuity of the mental effort. Anyone can attain spiritual understanding and become conscious of the light who will persistently pray for it. "He that cometh to God must believe that he is, and *that* he is a rewarder of them that diligently seek him." The emphasis here is on the word *diligently.*

The mind is the seat of perfection, not only of health but also of talents like music, art, writing, and the like. The idea of health and the idea of music are interblended, for instance. Music is a great aid to the healing force. Musical and health ideas interblend, and their establishment in order produces this kingdom of the heavens.

Our spiritual realizations produce that silent shuttle of thought which, working in and through cell and nerve, weaves into one harmonious whole mind and body and is expressed as health and wealth and genius.

The musical genius says he hears the music in a flash and is often at his wit's end to transcribe it fast enough. Many an immortal poem and prose work as well has been flashed from the mind of the author without any apparent effort on his part. But if all the prayers and mind efforts of literary geniuses were inquired into, it would be found that there had been heroic mental effort somewhere at some time. So it is with healing. The realization of perfection takes root in the soul and may come forth in a flash as perfect health. We should not confine ourselves to the present life of the individual but go into previous incarnations in which the work was done that made the genius in this incarnation.

Professor Einstein was considered the greatest mathematical genius of our time. The scientific world does not connect his insight into scientific principles with his religious life, but he freely stated that he worshipped God. He said: "The voice of God is from within. Something within me tells me what I must do every day." For him God is as valid as a scientific argument. On the subject of spiritual realization he once said:

"Every man knows that in his work he does best and accomplishes most when he has attained a proficiency that enables him to work intuitively. That is, there are things that we come to know so well that we do not know how we know them. Perhaps we live best and do things best when we are not too conscious of how and why we do them."

The supreme realization of man is his unity with God. Jesus had this realization and proclaimed it before there was any manifestation. When He told His followers, "I and the Father are one" and "He that hath seen me hath seen the Father," they demanded that He show them the Father. They could not understand that He had spiritually united with creative Mind. Men in our day are having this realization in a more universal way than ever before in the history of the race, and they are affirming it in the face of ridicule and condemnation. When this inner consciousness is attained by any man the foundation has been laid of the Peter church or temple that is man's immortal body, which will never pass away.

Metaphysically realization is expectancy objectified. The mind conceives a proposition and then marshals all its forces to make that conception a reality in the objective world. All things material are first thought pictures, carved by the imagination from omnipresent thought substance. Shakespeare in *Much Ado About Nothing* brings out the idea as follows:

"The idea of her life shall sweetly creep
  Into his study of imagination,
  And every lovely organ of her life,
  Shall come appareled in more precious habit,
  More moving-delicate and full of life
  Into the eye and prospect of his soul."

This realm of realization is so real to the mind that it requires a trained metaphysician to detect the difference between its creations and the manifest realm of things. We all have a body in the ether that is the counterpart of the physical. It is through this psychic body that we have sensation in the physical. It is possible to think of the psychic body and cultivate its sensations until it appears as real as the physical. Many persons have done this until they have formed a psychic world consciousness and they are often unable to separate it from the physical. They search materially for the treasures they see psychically. To them the realm of thought forms is the finality of creation instead of the mental pictures of that which is about to appear.

The trained metaphysician is no stranger to this picture gallery of the mind and he is not deceived into believing that it is any more than a mental reflection. One who enters the realm of spiritual ideas does not allow his consciousness to become confused with the mind pictures that flash into psychic sight. They are part of the process of making ideas manifest. When a Christian healer realizes that his treatment has firmly formed the picture of health, he relaxes his decrees and statements of Truth and trusts the divine law to make health manifest.

Paul urges in many of his writings that we have the Mind of Christ: that we let Christ be formed in us. This has usually been taken to mean that we are to imitate Christ. This is good as far as it goes, but it does not go far enough. To follow Jesus Christ in the regeneration or new birth we must fulfill the law of body building, which is a reconstruction of the corrupt cells: "This corruptible must put on incorruption." To accomplish this and make the body conform to His perfect body we must see Him as He is in His perfect body. This perfect body exists as an ideal body in us all. By mentally concentrating on this perfect body and focusing all our powers on it as the vital life of the physical a transformation will begin that will finally raise the physical to divine stature. Paul points the way in 2 Corinthians:

"But we all, with unveiled face beholding as in a mirror the glory of the Lord, are transformed into the same image from glory to glory, even as from the Lord the Spirit."

Chapter 18

RIGHT GIVING, THE KEY TO ABUNDANT RECEIVING (1936)

HERE IS A LAW of giving and receiving and it requires careful study if we would use it in our prosperity demonstrations. It is a law of mind action, and it can be learned and applied the same as any other law. The teaching of Jesus stands out prominently, because it can be practically applied to the affairs of everyday life. It is not alone a religion in the sense that word is usually taken but is a rule of thinking, doing, living, and being. It is not only ethical but practical, and men have never yet sounded the depths of the simple but all-inclusive words of Jesus. To some people it is unthinkable to connect the teaching of Jesus with the countinghouse and the market place, but a deeper insight into their meaning and purpose, which the Spirit of Truth is now revealing to the world, shows that these lofty teachings are the most practical rules for daily living in all departments of life. They are vital to modern civilization and the very foundation of business stability. The law of giving and receiving that Jesus

269

taught, "Give, and it shall be given unto you," is found to be applicable to all our commercial as well as our social relationships.

We have not been more successful in making this doctrine of Jesus a practical standard for everyday guidance because we have not understood the law on which it is based. Jesus would not have put forth a doctrine that was not true and not based on unchanging law, and we can be sure that this doctrine of giving and receiving is powerful enough to support all the affairs of civilization. We have not gone deeply enough into the teaching but have thought we understood it from a mere surface study. "Ye look at the things that are before your face," says Paul, and Jesus also warned us to "judge not according to appearance." We should form no conclusions until we have gone thoroughly into the causes and the underlying laws. The things we see outwardly are the effects that have arisen from causes that are invisible to us. There is an inner and an outer to everything: both the mental and the material conditions pervade the universe. Man slides at will up and down the whole gamut of cause and effect. The whole race slides into an effect almost unconsciously and so identifies the senses with the effect that the causes are lost sight of for thousands of years.

An awakening comes in time and the cause side of existence is again brought to the attention of men, as set forth, for example, in the doctrine of Jesus Christ. But men cannot grasp the great Truth in a moment and cling to what is plainly visible to them, the effect side. The Truth that things have a spiritual as well as a material identity and that the spiritual is the cause side and of greatest value, is a revelation that may be slow in coming to most people. In this instance it is the material side that they cling to, thinking it to be all and refusing to let go. Men have taken the letter or appearance side of the Jesus Christ doctrine and materialized it to fit their beliefs and customs. That is the reason why the Christ message has not purified commerce, society, and government. But it should be made spiritually operative in those fields. It will easily do the work desired when its mental side is studied and when it is understood and applied from the spiritual viewpoint.

There is need for reform in economics more than in any other department of everyday life. Money has been manipulated by greed until greed itself is sick and secretly asks for a panacea. But it does not look to the religion of Jesus Christ for healing. In fact that is the very last place it would apply for aid, because many of the advocates of the Jesus Christ doctrine are themselves economic dependents and have no solution for the economic problem—not understanding the power of their own religion. Yet no permanent remedy will ever be found for the economic ills of the world outside a practical application of the laws on which the doctrine of Jesus Christ is based.

The correctness of the solution of any problem is assured by the right relation of its elements. All true reform begins with the individual. Jesus began there. He did not clamor for legislation to control men or their actions. He called His twelve apostles and through them individually instituted that reform which has as its basis an appeal to the innate intelligence, honesty, and goodness in every man. He told them, "Go ye into all the world, and preach the gospel to the whole creation."

As people learn more definitely about the dynamic effect of thought and how ideas pass from mind to mind, they see more and more the wisdom of the Christ teaching. They are beginning to understand that there is one undeviating law of mind action and that all thinking and all speaking is amenable to it. Thus when Jesus said, "By thy words thou shalt be justified, and by thy words thou shalt be condemned," He taught the power of thoughts and words to bring results in accordance with the ideas back of them.

Following the metaphysical side of the teaching of Jesus, we have found that certain thoughts held in the minds of the people are causing widespread misery, disease, and death. We have also found that these thoughts can be dissolved or transformed and the whole man made over through his conscious volition. Paul well understood this process. He said, "Be ye transformed by the renewing of your mind."

Among the destructive thoughts that men indulge in and exercise are those forms of selfishness which we know as avarice, covetousness, money getting, the desire for financial gain and for possessing the things of the world. These thoughts threaten seriously to disturb the civilization of the world and the stability of the whole race. The sole thought of money getting is being allowed by men and women to generate its cold vapor in their souls until it shuts out all the sunlight of love and even of life. The remedy for the misery caused by destructive thoughts is not far to seek. It lies in constructive thinking along the lines that Jesus laid down. Indeed the remedy for all the ills to which flesh is heir lies in conformity to the divine law that Jesus revealed to His true followers. It is said of these true followers (Acts 4:32) that they were "of one heart and soul: and not one of them said that aught of the things which he possessed was his own; but they had all things common."

Many true Christians have observed this righteous law and sought to conform to it in community life. Such efforts have not always been successful, because there was not the necessary recognition of the mental factor and the discipline of ideas. So long as the idea of covetousness is lodged in the human mind as its dominant generating factor, there can be no successful community life. That idea must be eliminated from the mental plane first; the next step, the outer practice, will then be safe and successful.

Everywhere true metaphysicians are preparing themselves to be members in the great colony that Jesus is to set up, by working to eliminate from their mind all selfish ideas, along with all other discordant vibrations that produce inharmony among members of the same group. A step in this direction is the gradual introduction of the "freewill offering" plan to replace the world's commercial standard of reward for services. We are striving to educate the people on this question of giving and receiving and to let their own experience prove to them that there is a divine law of equilibrium in financial matters that corresponds to the law of balance and poise that holds the suns and the planets in place. In order to make a success of this great effort we must have the loving cooperation of everyone to whom we minister. The law is based on love and justice, and it equitably and harmoniously adjusts all the affairs of men. It goes even further, for it restores a harmony and balance in both mind and body that results in happiness and health as well as prosperity. Love and justice are mighty powers, and all things must eventually come under their influence, because even a few men and women of right motive can, by right thinking and consequent just action, introduce these ideas into the race consciousness and pave the way for their universal adoption. The movement has already begun and is rapidly gaining headway. Every student and reader is asked to give it impetus by resolving to be unselfish and just without compulsion.

The race consciousness is formed of thought currents and the dominant beliefs of all the people. A few men and women rise above these currents of thought and become independent thinkers. The dominating race idea of money getting as the goal of success is now being replaced by the idea of usefulness and good works. This idea must be carried out by individuals who have resolved to think and to act in the Jesus Christ way. To be one of these individuals and to contribute to the change in the race consciousness, first dedicate yourself in Spirit to the ministry of Jesus and resolve to carry forward the great work He has commissioned you to do. This does not mean that you must preach like Paul or necessarily carry on any extensive work in the outer. In the silence of your "inner chamber" you can do a mighty work of power by daily denying the beliefs in avarice and covetousness and affirming the universal sway of divine love and justice. You can make the idea of exact equity and justice between man and man the central theme of all your saying and doing. When you see examples of greed and avarice or when thoughts of these seek a place in your mind, remember the words of the Master: "What is that to thee? follow thou me."

Never for a moment allow yourself to entertain any scheme for getting the better of your fellows in any trade or bargain. Hold steadily to the law of equity and justice that is working in and through you, knowing for a certainty that you are supplied with everything necessary to fulfill all your requirements. Give full value for everything you get. Demand the same for everything you give, but do not try to enforce that demand by human methods. There is a better way: think of yourself as Spirit working with powerful spiritual forces, and know that the demands of Spirit must and will be met.

Do not plan to lay up for the future; let the future take care of itself. To entertain any fears or doubts on that point saps your strength and depletes your spiritual power. Hold steadily to the thought of the omnipresence of universal supply, its perfect equilibrium and its swift action in filling every apparent vacuum or place of lack. If you have been in the habit of hoarding or of practicing stringent economy, change your thought currents to generosity. Practice giving, even though it may be in a small way. Give in a spirit of love and give when you cannot see any possibility of return. Put real substance into your gift by giving the substance of the heart with the token of money or whatever it is. Through the power of your word you can bless and spiritually multiply everything that you give. See yourself as the steward of God handing out His inexhaustible supplies. In this manner you are setting into action mental and spiritual forces that eventually bring large results into visibility. Be happy in your giving. God loves a cheerful giver because his mind and heart are open to the flow of the pure substance of Being that balances all things.

Do not give with any idea that you are bestowing charity. The idea of charity has infested the race consciousness for thousands of years and is responsible for the great army of human dependents. Do all you can to annul this mental error. There is no such thing as charity as popularly understood. Everything belongs to God and all His children are equally entitled to it. The fact that one has a surplus and gives some of it to another does not make the one a benefactor and the other a dependent. The one with the surplus is simply a steward of God and is merely discharging the work of his stewardship. When one asks for divine wisdom and understanding about giving, it becomes a joy both to the giver and the recipient.

Followers of Jesus who are doing His work of teaching and healing should, like Him, receive freewill offerings for their ministry to the people. The majority of those who apply to teachers and healers recognize this law of giving and receiving, but there are quite a number who do not understand it. First there are those who are in bondage to the idea of avarice, and secondly, there are those who still are in bondage to the idea of charity. Both these classes need education and treatment to release them from mental limitation and mental disease. The avaricious suffer most in body and are the most difficult to heal, because of the mental bias that prompts them to get everything as cheaply as possible, including the kingdom of heaven. They must be patiently educated to be just because it is right, and to learn to "let go" of the acquisitive spirit and replace it with the spirit of generosity. They will do this readily enough as a mental drill but are not so willing to let go of the money symbol. However, continued treatments in the silence, supplemented with oral and written instruction, will eventually prevail and heal them.

There are many examples that could be given to prove the outworking of the law. The covetous idea has a great power over the body. It would avail little to treat the outer manifestation before first removing the inner cause from the mind. The salvation of such people is to learn to give generously and freely, not from compulsion or for the sake of reward but from a love of the giving. Some metaphysicians think to cure their patients of the hold of avaricious thoughts by charging them a good round price for their treatments. By the same token the medical doctor who charges the most is surest to heal his patients, and any service for which an exorbitant price is charged is the best! Surely this would be a foolish idea. Metaphysical healing has become so popular that hundreds have gone into it as a business and are making of it an industry founded on the old commercial idea, just as cold and calculating, as hard and unyielding as the idea is in the ranks of the money-changers of mammon.

Surely there is a "more excellent way," one more in harmony with divine law, a way that permits the heart as well as the head and hand to be used in the grace of giving and receiving. Those who are using the freewill offering method meet with some criticism and opposition from those who hold to the commercial method and say that charging a definite sum is the legitimate way. They accuse Unity of fostering charity and poverty and keeping alive the spirit of getting something for nothing that is manifested by so many people. Our reply is that we are pursuing the only course that could ever effectually eradicate these erroneous states of consciousness and bring people into an understanding of the spiritual law of prosperity through giving in love.

Everyone should give as he receives; in fact, it is only through giving that he can receive. Until the heart is quickened at the center and the mind is opened up to Truth there is no permanent healing. Everyone can make a fair return for everything he gets. We aim to show moneyless paupers that they can give something in return for the good that has been done them. It may be to pass the true word to some other needy one, or merely to lift up their voice in thanksgiving and praise where before they were dumb. We recognize the necessity of some action of the mammon-bound mind. It must be made to let go somewhere before it can receive the light and the power of Spirit.

Our work is to bring men and women to the place of true and lasting dominion where they are superior to both riches and poverty. We can do this by showing them that they are spiritual beings, that they live in a spiritual world here and now, and that through the apprehension of the Truth of their being and their relation to God this dominion is to be realized.

The central and most vital fact that they must come to realize is that an idea has the power of building thought structures, which in turn materialize in the outer environment and affairs and determine every detail of their existence. Every man is a king ruling his own subjects. These subjects are the ideas existing in his mind, the "subjects" of his thought. Each man's ideas are as varied and show as many traits of character as the inhabitants of any empire. But they can all be brought into subjection and made to obey through the I AM power that is the ruler of the kingdom. In your domain of mind there may be colonies of alien ideas—the Philistines, Canaanites, and other foreign tribes, that the Children of Israel found in their Promised Land when they attempted to take possession of it. The story of the Children of Israel and how they gained the possession of that land is a symbolical representation of the experience of everyone who seeks to reclaim his own consciousness in the name of the Lord. The meaning in Hebrew of the name *Canaanite* is "merchant" or "trader"; in other words, a set of ideas that has to do with the commercial phase of life. Study the Children of Israel (spiritual ideas) in their experiences with these Canaanites and you will get many valuable hints on subduing and handling your own money-getting ideas.

You may allow avariciousness and stinginess to develop in your mind domain until the very blood in your body starts to dry up and your nerves are shaken and palsied with the fear of future poverty. If so, it is time these ideas were driven out and a new set of ideas settled in your domain to become active in building up a new state of consciousness (nation). Begin at once to let go of your all-consuming thoughts of gain. Think about generosity and begin to be generous for your own sake. "It is more blessed to give than to receive" will prove itself to you as the law, for you will be blessed by a new influx of ideas of life, health, and prosperity when you start giving.

Instead of being grasping and avaricious, perhaps you have gone to the other extreme and have cultivated ideas of small things financially. You may have been fostering poverty by holding ideas of pennies instead of dollars or of hundreds instead of thousands. You may be thinking that you cannot give because your income is small or your supply is limited. Your remedy is to cultivate ideas of abundance. Claim God as your inexhaustible resource; that all things are yours. But in order to set in motion the accumulated energy of your thought you must also begin to give. You may be able to give only pennies at first, but give them in the name and the spirit of your opulent God. Send them forth with all the love of your heart and say to them as they go, "Divine love through me blesses and multiplies you."

Your consciousness is like a stream of water. If the stream is in any way dammed up, the water settles in all the low places and becomes stagnant. The quickest way to purify and reclaim the low, "swampy" places in your consciousness is to let in the flood from above by opening the dam. Many people try to demonstrate God as their supply by repeating affirmations of abundance now present, but fail to deny and thus to let go of the old condition and old belief in lack by beginning to give as generously as possible. It is not the amount you give measured by standards of the world, it is the good will you send forth with the gift; which can be measured only by spiritual standards.

"God loveth a cheerful giver." The Greek word here translated cheerful is *hilarion*, which means really "hilarious, joyful." The gift may be measured in dollars and cents but God looks not on such standards, He looks on and loves the "joyful" giver. We read in Deuteronomy 28:47, 48, "Because thou servedst not Jehovah thy God with joyfulness, and with gladness of heart, by reason of the abundance of all things; therefore shalt thou serve thine enemies . . . in hunger, and in thirst, and in nakedness, and in want of all things." This shows that there is a definite relation between the cheerfulness or joyfulness of our giving and our prosperity. Whether we make a large or a small gift, let us make it with largeness of cheer and joy, even of hilarity, remembering that God loveth a "hilarious" giver. "Keep therefore the words of this covenant, and do them, that ye may prosper in all that ye do."

BLESSINGS THAT MAY BE PLACED ON OUR GIFTS

Divine love, through me, blesses and multiplies this offering.

The Father gives abundantly; I receive thankfully, and give again generously.

This is the bounty of God, and I send it forth with wisdom and joy.

Divine love bountifully supplies and increases this offering.

I give freely and fearlessly, fulfilling the law of giving and receiving.

Part Six
SPIRITUAL DEVELOPMENT: PUTTING ON THE CHRIST

SPIRITUAL DEVELOPMENT: PUTTING ON THE CHRIST

Moving now from the more general theoretical concepts, we begin consideration of the practical ideas for living the spiritual life. What does it mean to live a spiritual life? What practices and objectives are involved?

Charles and Myrtle Fillmore lived relatively austere lives. They were vegetarians who did not indulge in the use of tobacco, alcohol, or coffee. They were not given to displays of wealth or fine clothing. Charles frequently preached against sense indulgence and advocated, if not absolute celibacy, then conservation of sexual energy, or what he called "vital fluids." They were not extreme ascetics, but they lived in a simple and unpretentious way.

At the same time, the Fillmores did not insist that other Unity leaders and students follow their example. Today some Unity ministers prefer a lifestyle similar to the Fillmores, while others prefer a more carnivorous, more opulent or less austere way of living.

Charles Fillmore's attitude about ways of living is illuminated in the first chapter of this section, "Ye Must Be Born

Again" (from *Talks on Truth*). In this article, we see that he advocated detachment from the realm of the senses and concentration on the joys of Spirit. That explains his relatively austere lifestyle. He also insists that those who choose a more "sense indulgent" way of life are not to be condemned. He is confident that eventually, if not in this life then in some other, the sensual appetites will be satiated, and everyone will come to choose a more spiritual focus.

It is doubtful that the mere external practice of an austere lifestyle can provide a true measure of relative spirituality. Is it really possible to judge the relative spiritual merits of the carnivorous, beer-drinking Martin Luther vs. the vegetarian, alcohol-abstaining Charles Fillmore based solely on what they consumed? Does the vegetarianism of the Hindu automatically signal spiritual superiority over the meat-eating Christian? Did Hitler's vegetarianism indicate a high spiritual consciousness? Clearly, Fillmore's notions of spirituality have deeper and broader meaning than can be summed up in the degree of sensuality exhibited in a given individual's lifestyle.

At perhaps a deeper level, Fillmore holds that what we call our perception of substance determines our conditions:

> There is a primal substance, and all states of consciousness are in it. We do not have to go anywhere to find it; it is here. We are basing our present experience upon it and calling it flesh. If we desire to see it as Spirit, we must so call it, and must seek to know the mental attitude on our part that is necessary to make it show forth the conditions of Spirit.

Note that Fillmore is not here moralizing in the conventional way, not condemning those more sensually oriented than he as sinners, nor is he admonishing his listeners to practice more willpower. He is instead advocating that we change our ways of thinking about the universe and of perceiving ourselves if we desire to experience more spiritual conditions. Being "born again" in this context is not a one-time conversion experience, but rather a conscious decision to start thinking *systematically* in new ways about God, ourselves, our relationships, and our world.

The *system* for new thinking advocated by Fillmore is reflected in the next article, "The Twelve Powers of Man" (from the book of the same title). Fillmore's basic metaphor for our spiritual potential is Jesus and the twelve disciples. Fillmore, like Jung, associates Jesus with the idea of the Self,[1] which is to be fully actualized or expressed. The disciples are associated with various qualities, attributes, faculties, or powers of the divine Self or Christ.

Fillmore's association of disciples with powers and physiological centers is derived from a partially intuitive analysis of the Greek or Hebrew meanings of their names, their character as illumined in the New Testament, and physiological symbolism in our language. For example, "John" is a name derived from Hebrew words for *God* and *grace*. John was known as "the beloved disciple," and his epistles emphasize the quality of love. Consequently, John represents love, which is associated with the heart in our language. Not all the symbolism of the disciples is as obvious as that of John, but the method of association is basically the same.

Fillmore believed that the Scriptures were inspired by the Holy Spirit to symbolically convey spiritual truths along with historical truths. So for him, the symbolism he discerned in Jesus and the disciples was not a mere exercise in allegorical interpretation, but rather an important part of the search for the divine plan for humanity. The method of focusing on physiological power centers while contemplating affirmations of the Christ qualities was not for Fillmore just an interesting meditation technique; the method was rather what he believed the Holy Spirit was directing him to do to develop Christ consciousness.

Whether or not we find Fillmore's account of the divine plan compelling, the twelve powers method of meditation does focus the mind on developing desirable and beneficial qualities as well as developing a positive and healthy consciousness of the body. Arguably, one could use different symbolism, but as a general method and discipline, the twelve powers method is a significant contribution to humanity's spiritual resources. The twelve powers method of meditation is a Christian discipline roughly analogous to the Hindu system of kundalini yoga and merits our consideration as a mystical path.

The rest of this section consists of amplifications of key Christ qualities: faith, love, wisdom, and zeal. Fillmore wrote extensively on those subjects, and I have simply chosen my personal favorite chapters. I realize that other Unity students may well question my selection of these particular chapters. Nevertheless, I am convinced that these chapters, if not the best choices, are at least well worth studying.

"Indispensable Assurance" (from *Jesus Christ Heals*) discusses the nature of faith. This chapter is rich in metaphors, insights, inspirational words, and practical ideas. Fillmore discusses how faith connects us to invisible realities and draws forth possibilities into substantial experiences and things. He compares the development of faith to the story of the apostle Peter, who wavered in his faith until he reached a point of powerful faith. Fillmore makes reference to the well-known "placebo effect" in medicine as an example of the power of faith. He uses the metaphor of growing plants to explain how thoughts "planted" in the subconscious mind "bring forth their fruit in due season." He discusses the relationship between faith and genius, faith and understanding, faith and thinking, faith and desire, faith and vitality, and faith and imagination. He also reveals his sense of humor in stories about a woman on board a ship during a storm and a lawyer who eats an eraser.

"The Development of Divine Love" (from *Talks on Truth*) begins with a discussion of the relationship among the faculties of love, faith, strength, and judgment; then moves into an analysis of love as a power. Fillmore notes that not all degrees and expressions of love are necessarily beneficial, to indicate the importance of developing love to its maximum effectiveness as universal and unconditional. He discusses how love can be developed by focusing on possibilities of good in even bad situations. He also suggests meditations for developing love in consciousness. Fillmore's optimistic vision of the cosmos is concisely expressed in a sentence in this chapter: "The earth shall yet be made paradise by the power of love."

In discussing the power of love in this chapter, Fillmore relies heavily on the metaphor of love as a magnet, emphasizing how we are drawn to what we focus our love on and, at the same time, what we love is drawn to us. That way of describing love is more like Socrates' discussion of love in "Symposium"[2] than Paul's discussion in 1 Corinthians. However, Fillmore also weaves some of Paul's ideas into the analysis. For good measure, Fillmore weaves in references to bhakti yoga, centrifugal and centripetal forces and, of course, teachings of Jesus. Thus this chapter is an excellent example of how Fillmore synthesized concepts from science, philosophy, and world religions to formulate his vision of practical Christianity.

"Judgment and Justice" (from *Christian Healing*) begins with a quote from the Sermon on the Mount, followed by a reference to the obscure biblical Urim and Thummim. The rather esoteric-sounding introduction is soon followed by a fairly lucid explanation of the spiritual and practical aspects of judgment. Fillmore, again like Emerson, advocates trust in a principle of justice (Emerson called it "compensation")[3] at work in the universe.

Noncondemnation is emphasized as an attitude in alignment with judging righteously. Even judgments against crime and sin are not to be seen as being about punishment, but rather as being about "purification through discipline." Fillmore argues that the biblical "hell" is figurative speech for such purification and so should not be taken as a place of eternal torment for those with whom God is displeased. The interpretation of hell as figurative for purification is arguably more consistent with the teachings of Jesus on love, forgiveness, and nonjudgment than is the literal view of hell advocated for so many centuries by the Christian church.

One might well take issue with Fillmore's notion that misuse of the judgment faculty causes liver problems. The idea reflects not only Fillmore's view that physical conditions are caused by habitual mental states, but also a belief prevalent among New Thought and Christian Science metaphysicians. See, for example Herbert Eustace's book *Christian Science: Its "Clear, Correct Teaching" & Complete Writings* and the recent popular work of Religious Science minister Louise Hay. While there is no scientific evidence for the specific claims of Fillmore, Eustace, Hay, and others; in principle the idea may not be so farfetched. Note for example scientific studies associating specific ailments with certain "personality types."

Finally, the "Healing Power of Joy" *(Jesus Christ Heals)* is included for its prescient insight regarding the therapeutic effects of humor, laughter, and music. The most famous case of the healing power of laughter is the story of the highly regarded author and magazine editor Norman Cousins, which is described in his book *Anatomy of an Illness as Perceived by the Patient.*[4] While Fillmore's writings tend to remain at a serious level, those who knew him or heard him speak usually noted his sense of humor and enjoyment of jokes as a significant aspect of his character. The "Healing Power of Joy" reveals his view of the close association among humor, happiness, health, and spirituality.

This chapter makes only brief reference to the idea that laughter is therapeutic. The practice of singing to bring joy is more emphasized, and those who knew Fillmore also noted how much he enjoyed music and singing. The chapter touches on a fairly wide range of subjects, including zeal, Pythagoras' concept of the "music of the spheres," vibrations, energy, the mathematical nature of the universe, the importance of peace of mind, the story of Eden, Christ, and the Spirit of Truth. While this wandering from topic to topic may not reflect the best writing skills, it does provide an appropriate recapitulation of significant ideas already covered in this book; for after this section we will move into "the final things."

Chapter 19

YE MUST BE
BORN AGAIN (1926)

"**A**ND NO ONE hath ascended into heaven,
Save he that out of heaven descended—
The Son of Man."
—John 3:13 (Rotherham translation)

Jesus said: "That which is born of the flesh is flesh; and that which is born of the Spirit is Spirit." "Except one be born of water and the Spirit . . ." Who and what is this that is subject to so many births?

This important invisibility that takes on these protean forms is man, according to Jesus. But what is man? Plato told his students that a good description of man was a "biped without feathers." Diogenes learned of this definition, procured a chicken, and after plucking its feathers, turned it loose before Plato's class with the words, "Behold Plato's man!" This is a peculiarly fitting illustration of the ignoble end of all definitions that circumscribe man to form.

Jesus evidently referred to an invisible something that was first born of flesh, then born of Spirit. The inference is that this something is capable of an infinite number of experiences in birth and rebirth.

What is this invisible something that says, "Before Abraham was born, I am"? Who are you, born into this round of experiences through which you are now passing, and whence came you? What is it that says "I am"?

When your voice says "I am," does it do so on its own responsibility, or is it moved by an invisible One? Who is this invisible One, and what is His relation to the voice through which He speaks? These are the most important questions that were ever put to any school on earth. When we begin to consider them, in even the most primary way, we are entering the realm of the gods.

Over the entrance to the Greek temple was written, "Know thyself," and it is always written over every door that opens from ignorance to wisdom. "Know thyself"; know who and what you are, where you came from, what you are doing here, and where you are going. If you want to know all this, meditate upon the I AM.

Your mind reverts to Moses and to Jehovah; you think of a mighty I AM away back in history. You do not connect that far-away I AM that inspired Moses with your own little everyday "I am" that struggles in the "brawl for bread." Yet there is but one I AM. It cannot be cut into parts; it is Principle. That which says "I Am" in all men, women, and children is identical. It is like the mathematical 1. All the combinations of figures that were ever conceived are but the repetitions of this digit. It is the son of the principle, mathematics. It is inspired by its principle and all the possibilities of that principle are open to it.

Your I AM is the Son of the God Idea, and all the possibilities of the Principle, through that Idea, are open to you. To "know thyself" is to know that you are I AM, and not flesh and blood.

It is this I AM that is born of flesh and born of spirit. It is not flesh, neither is it Spirit, if by Spirit is meant a state of consciousness. It is just I AM, the center from which all states of consciousness are generated. Speaking definitely, it is never born into any state of consciousness, because it always transcends all conditions. It is the supreme Dictator that determines the state of consciousness in and through which it will function. "I will be what I will to be" is its dictum.

I AM may choose to be born into the flesh, and it may choose to be born into the Spirit. By its decision it sets in motion the machinery of the universe to carry out its will. "Legions of angels" hasten to obey its call when it knows who and what it is.

It is evident that we have, at some time chosen to be born into the flesh or we should not be in it. If we have had enough of the flesh, it is our privilege to drop it out of our mind and to be born of Spirit. "That which is born of the flesh is flesh; and that which is born of the Spirit is spirit." The "flesh" is a state of consciousness; the "Spirit" is a state of consciousness.

The ego or I AM functions in these states of consciousness, according to its desire. The moving factor of the I AM is desire. It desires a certain experience; on the wings of that desire it carries itself to a place where it can be fulfilled. In the process of fulfillment the ego may forget that it has ever so desired, but the law never forgets.

If you are functioning in the flesh, you may be sure that you somewhere, sometime, desired an experience to which this answers.

There are no accidents in the laws of Being. "Whatsoever a man soweth, that shall he also reap" is another way of saying that for every cause there is an adequate effect. This law of sequence is the balance wheel of the universe. Like all other laws that inhere in Being, it is good.

The ego can have any experience that it wills to have. If it wills to revel in sensation, a state where sensation holds

high carnival is provided. If its appetite for sensation is satiated, other states are open to it; it may be "born of the
Spirit."

But before one can journey hence, the tangled ends of this
experience must be straightened out. "Let all things be done
decently and in order" is written over the door of all of God's
playhouses. If you choose to function in the realm of sensation, if through any cause you have brought about disorder,
you cannot leave until harmony is restored.

If you lack wisdom, there is a way provided to get it—"The
Spirit of truth . . . he shall guide you into all the truth."

Your real Self is that which says "I AM." It cannot be described, because description is limitation, and your real Self
is unlimited in its capacity to be. It is the all-possibility, yet
it is ignorant of the states of consciousness into which it is
ushered until it has experienced them. In the flesh consciousness it is will. In the spiritual consciousness it is love.
Both are blind unless will is married to intelligence and wisdom is married to love.

There are people who have had enough fleshly experience
and now desire to be born into the Spirit. That desire will
open the door into the Spirit. You have only to desire to be,
and you will surely find the way to be that which you desire.
There is no exception to this inherent principle of Being. You
have sometime polarized your desire in the direction of the
flesh, or you would not be having the experience of the
flesh.

Do not condemn the flesh or bewail your lot. The flesh is
an obedient servant, and it now expresses your idea of what
form should be. In its virgin purity it is the immaculate substance of Being. If it appears corrupt or subject to corruption,
humanity has made it so through ignorance, and humanity
must again purify it by restoring it to the heaven of its consciousness, when it will cease to be flesh. That which the

world conceives to be flesh has no existence whatever in Being. It is a malformation of the substance idea of Being, and must be transformed by right conception of divine perfection, before the mortal can put on the immortal.

Thus all things are right here, ready for our using, to function through, in the fulfillment of our desire to experience sensation. If we have failed to get satisfaction, the fault lies not in the substance but in our use of the substance. Now that we wish to transfer our experiences to the realm of Spirit, to light instead of to sensation, we have but to comply with the conditions of that realm in order to make the desired change.

There is a primal substance, and all states of consciousness are in it. We do not have to go anywhere to find it; it is here. We are basing our present experiences upon it and calling it flesh. If we desire to see it as Spirit, we must so call it, and must seek to know the mental attitude on our part that is necessary to make it show forth the conditions of Spirit.

"The kingdom of God is within you." It is not afar, nor is it hard to find, if your desire has headed you in its direction.

Do you really want to be born into the Spirit? The majority of people would answer this query in the affirmative without a moment's thought. But this is mere impulse, and does not involve a careful consideration of the most important matter ever presented to the I AM.

To be born into the Spirit is to come into an entirely new and different state of consciousness. This has a mighty meaning in back of it. What makes up your present consciousness? Is it not largely the things of sense?

Analyze your surroundings and see whether they are not based upon the perception of the five senses. You swing in your little orbit of family ties. You believe that you were born into the world through a chain of fleshly ancestors to whom you are bound by a filial love that to your present understanding is inviolable. Yet He who passed from the flesh consciousness into the Spirit looked back and said: "Call no man your father on the earth: for one is your Father, even he who is in heaven."

So the I AM that desires to function on the spiritual plane must drop all belief in fleshly parentage. It must count as rubbish all pride of ancestry and "blue blood." It must forever cease to talk about the social prestige of "our family"; it must not bolster up the mortal man by considering ancestral reputation to be of any weight. This form of human pride must all be denied as a dream of the night, because it is one of the strong cords that bind the I AM to the flesh.

Every tie of earthly relationship must be recognized as the passing condition of a brief fleshly experience. Your children are not yours as you have looked upon them. They are egos like yourself; through some similarity of desire they have been attracted to your mental stratum. They may be older than you in experience and in wisdom. Do not let your affections throw both them and you into a little vortex of family selfishness. You will love them with a love that will help to lift them into the eternal heaven when you know that they are not yours alone, but that all men and women compose one great common family with God as the Father-Mother. "For whosoever shall do the will of my Father who is in heaven, he is my brother, and sister, and mother."

The I AM was born into the flesh through desire, and desire keeps it in the consciousness of the flesh. The five senses are simply avenues of one great central desire—sensation. The I AM desired experience in sensation, and the five senses are the five formulated avenues through which it enjoys that experience.

Sensation is not an evil, except when you choose to let it crawl on its belly through the fleshly avenues. It is the serpent that beguiles man when he turns it outward into mere seeming—hearing, seeing, feeling, tasting, and smelling. In the wilderness of sense, Moses lifted it up. Moses was the law that the I AM sent forth.

You must make a law for this serpent that is holding you in the sensations of the flesh. You desire to be born into the Spirit, but you cannot rise out of the flesh. Something binds you down. Like a captive balloon, you are tugging at the guy ropes that fasten you to earth.

Mind is the only causative power. By the power of the Word, it makes and unmakes all laws governing in personal life. The I AM floats in mind and formulates the words that set mind in motion.

If you are bound to the flesh, the cords that hold you are words. If you want to be unbound, it must be accomplished by words. The cords are states of consciousness that you must dissolve. This dissolving process is accomplished by words that express denial—negations.

The denial looses the bond. In your cutting yourself free from the chains of Egypt (ignorance), your I AM must go forth and make laws of denial, the dominant idea of which is negation—"Thou shalt not."

"Thou shalt not commit adultery" is a denial that regulates the animal consciousness and helps it along the path to higher things; but Jesus said, "Ye have heard that it was said, Thou shalt not commit adultery: but I say unto you, that every one that looketh on a woman to lust after her hath committed adultery with her already in his heart."

He was laying down the law of the spiritual conscious-ness—instructing those who wanted to be born out of the flesh into the Spirit. In that realm the flesh man with his carnal sensations has no part. "And Jesus said unto them, The sons of this world marry, and are given in marriage: but they that are accounted worthy to attain to that world, and the resurrection from the dead, neither marry, nor are given in marriage."

Do not be deluded by those who cry, "All is good, therefore all the desires of the flesh are good and should be indulged." Jesus plainly said, "That which is born of the flesh is flesh; and that which is born of the Spirit is spirit," definitely indicating two states of consciousness.

The I AM is always the same. Your identity is preserved wherever you are, in the flesh or in the Spirit; but the two states are as distinct as America and Europe. When you are in Europe, you come into relation with people and surroundings quite different from those in America. So the one who has let go of the bonds of the flesh and come into the things of Spirit finds himself in a new and different country.

In the flesh, his sensation was turned outward through feeling, and man was bound to the eternally rolling wheels of birth and death by physical generation. When he is born into the Spirit, he cuts off the indulgence of the external, and is delighted to learn that sensation finds an interior faculty through which it expresses itself in perpetual ecstasy. Had he continued to indulge the desires of the flesh in the external, he would never have discovered the enduring faculty of the internal.

Jesus said, "In my Father's house are many mansions"; that is, there are many states of consciousness. Each state is good for him who enjoys it. Therefore we should not condemn the flesh consciousness, nor those who prefer to remain in it. Neither should we who are satiated with the flesh, continue to bow down and worship it, nor believe the subtle argument that it is Spirit because it came forth from mind.

In claiming your unity with Spirit, you must be willing to conform to the conditions of Spirit. If you are not sincere in your conformity, you will be torn in the conflict. You cannot worship two masters.

When you have renounced the fleshly consciousness and have resolved to live in the Spirit, you have made a covenant with the Most High to leave the domain of the flesh forever. You have entered into an agreement with your invisible Self that is far more binding than any man-made contract could possibly be.

If you agreed to go to California and to remain there for a consideration to be paid by your employer, you would be in honor bound to carry out your contract. You would arrange to leave the things of this region behind you; you would faithfully seek to prepare yourself for the new requirements in that country. This is exactly the attitude that you should take when you have agreed with the Father to do His will and to be born into the Spirit.

You are going into a country entirely new to you, and your experiences will be strange and wonderful. The customs that prevail in the flesh consciousness will not fit the spiritual consciousness.

Paul says, "The fruit of the Spirit is love, joy, peace, long-suffering, kindness, goodness, faithfulness, meekness, self-control; against such there is no law. . . . If we live by the Spirit, let us also walk."

Are you bringing forth this kind of fruit? If not, you may know that you are not being born of the Spirit, for "by their fruits ye shall know them."

A large number of students of Truth are at this time complaining because they are having trials. They say, "We have denied and affirmed for years. We have studied science and understand it. We are faithful to the hours of meditation and are stanch defenders of the Truth, yet we do not demonstrate. Why is it?

"If we live by the Spirit, by the Spirit let us also walk." Here is the key that will open the door of causes for you. Do you also walk by the Spirit? How about the habits of the flesh consciousness? Do you still give them rein?

Remember that you cannot perform a single act without putting your consciousness into it. All things are sustained by your conscious thought projection. Every time you indulge in any of the sensations of the flesh, you are binding the I AM to the fleshly consciousness.

Spiritual thinking is the pioneer that opens the way into the new birth, but it must be followed by spiritual acting on the part of every faculty.

"Present your bodies a living sacrifice, holy, acceptable to God, *which is* your spiritual service."

In the Sermon on the Mount, Jesus laid down the law for those who desire to follow Him into the regeneration—to be born again. If you seek this spiritual birth, examine your daily life and see whether you are conforming to its requirements.

If you are angry with your brother, you will be in danger of the judgment. "Agree with thine adversary quickly." Does this allow the intervention of the courts to settle your disputes? Did you ever know a man who went to law, to agree with his adversary quickly?

Judicial courts are not known in the Spirit, and you can never be born again or expect the help of the Spirit in your affairs so long as you believe in securing your rights through such contentious channels. If you are sincere in your desire to be born into the Spirit, shun all the entanglements of the world's legal machinery. It is a snare and a delusion. Your triumphs through its methods will in the end turn to dust and ashes. "If any man would go to law with thee, and take away thy coat, let him have thy cloak also." Trust the defense of your rights to the law of Spirit, and you will be victor in every instance. You may appear to lose both your coat and your cloak, but do not worry. Your judge is the almighty equilibrium of the universe, and all men and all things are obedient to it in its "day of judgment."

Do you love your enemies? Do you bless them that curse you, do good to them that hate you, and pray for them that despitefully use you? This is required of one who seeks the new birth

Are you laying up treasures for yourself upon earth, "where moth and rust consume, and where thieves break through and steal"? If so, remember the primal law of thought generation—the gluing of the ego to the things that it consciously seeks; "for where thy treasure is, there will thy heart be also." You cannot float out into the ethereal substance of the Spirit, with bags of gold in each hand.

Do you allow your mind to drift with the current criticism of the world, magnifying the error and minimizing the good? This mental habit of the ignorant flesh is carnal judgment— darkness and ignorance seeing themselves reflected in all the universe. Beware of this subtle adversary who goes forth ostensibly to reform the world.

According to Rotherham, Jesus said:

> "Why, moreover, beholdest thou the mote, in the eye of thy
>> brother, While the beam in thine own eye thou dost
>> not consider? Or how wilt thou say unto thy brother,
> Let me cast the mote out of thine eye,
> When lo! a beam is in thine own eye?
> Hypocrite! cast first out of thine own eye the beam,
> And then shalt thou see clearly to cast the mote out of
>> the eye of thy brother."

O Son of God and Son of man! realize what and who you are. Know consciously what Jesus so succinctly stated: "No one hath ascended into heaven, but he that descended out of heaven, even the Son of man," the one having his being in heaven.

Your being is in heaven—the spiritual consciousness. You descended from that high estate; you belong there now. You are there now if you will but realize it and will but comply with the laws of heaven. God is here now in our very midst. The Spirit is here, taking account of our every thought. The Father loves us with His infinite love. We are His in Truth, and must be His in consciousness.

Chapter 20

THE TWELVE POWERS
OF MAN (1930)

T HE SUBCONSCIOUS REALM in man has twelve great centers of action, with twelve presiding egos or identities. When Jesus had attained a certain soul development, He called His twelve apostles to Him. This means that when man is developing out of mere personal consciousness into spiritual consciousness, he begins to train deeper and larger powers; he sends his thought down into the inner centers of his organism, and through his word quickens them to life. Where before his powers have worked in the personal, now they begin to expand and work in the universal. This is the first and the second coming of Christ, spoken of in the Scriptures. The first coming is the receiving of Truth into the conscious mind, and the Second Coming is the awakening and the regeneration of the subconscious mind through the superconscious or Christ Mind.

Man expands and grows under divine evolution as an industrial plant grows. As the business expands, it is found that system is necessary. Instead of one man's being able to do the work with the assistance of a few helpers, he requires many helpers. Instead of a few helpers, he needs hundreds;

and in order to promote efficiency he must have heads for the various departments of the work. Scripture symbology calls the heads of departments in man's consciousness the twelve apostles.

Each of these twelve department heads has control of a certain function in soul or body. Each of these heads works through an aggregation of cells that physiology calls a "ganglionic center." Jesus, the I AM or central entity, has His throne in the top head, where phrenology locates spirituality. This is the mountain where He so often went to pray. The following outline gives a list of the Twelve, the faculties that they represent, and the nerve centers at which they preside:

Faith—Peter—center of brain.
Strength—Andrew—loins.
Discrimination or Judgment—James, Son of Zebedee—
    pit of stomach.
Love—John—back of heart.
Power—Philip—root of tongue.
Imagination—Bartholomew—between the eyes.
Understanding—Thomas—front brain.
Will—Matthew—center front brain.
Order—James, son of Alphaeus—navel.
Zeal—Simon the Cananaean—back head, medulla.
Renunciation or Elimination—Thaddaeus—abdominal
    region.
Life Conserver—Judas—generative function.

The physiological designations of these faculties are not arbitrary—the names can be expanded or changed to suit a broader understanding of their full nature. For example, Philip, at the root of the tongue, governs taste; he also controls the action of the larynx, as well as all vibrations of power throughout the organism. So the term "power" expresses but a small part of his official capacity.

The first apostle that Jesus called was Peter. Peter represents faith in things spiritual, faith in God. We begin our religious experience, our unity with Divine Mind, by having faith in that mind as omnipresent, all-wise, all-loving, all-powerful Spirit.

Faith in the spiritual man quickens spiritual understanding. Peter believed that Jesus was the Messiah; his faith opened his spiritual discernment, and he saw the living Christ back of the personal mask worn by Jesus. When asked, "Who do men say that the Son of man is?" the apostles, looking upon personality as the real, said: "Some *say* John the Baptist; some, Elijah; and others, Jeremiah, or one of the prophets." Then Jesus appealed to their own inner spiritual understanding and He said: "But who say ye that I am?" Only Simon Peter answered: "Thou art the Christ, the Son of the living God." And Jesus answered, "Thou art Peter, and upon this rock I will build my church, and the gates of Hades [the grave] shall not prevail against it. I will give unto thee the keys of the kingdom of heaven."

Spiritual discernment of the reality of man's origin and being is the only enduring foundation of character. It was to this faith in the understanding of the real being of man that Jesus gave power in earth and heaven. It was not to the personal Peter that Jesus gave the keys to His kingdom, but to all who through faith apply the binding (affirming) and loosing (denying) power of Spirit in the earth (substance consciousness). Right here and now the great work of character-building is to be done, and whoever neglects present opportunities, looking forward to a future heaven for better conditions, is pulling right away from the kingdom of heaven within himself.

People who live wholly in the intellect deny that man can know anything about God, because they do not have quickened faith. The way to bring forth the God presence, to make oneself conscious of God, is to say: *I have faith in God; I have faith in Spirit; I have faith in things invisible.* Such affirmations of faith, such praise to the invisible God, the unknown God, will make God visible to the mind and will strengthen the faith faculty. Thus faith (Peter) is called and instructed spiritually.

When a center loses its power it should be baptized by the word of Spirit. We are told in the Scriptures that Philip went down to Gaza ("the same is desert"), and there baptized a eunuch. Gaza means a "citadel of strength." It refers to the nerve center in the loins, where Andrew (strength) reigns. "Lo now , his strength is in his loins." Gaza is the physical throne of strength, as Jerusalem is the throne of love.

The back grows weak under the burden of material thought. If you are given to pains in your back, if you become exhausted easily, you may know at once that you need treatment for freedom from material burdens. Eliminate from your mind all thought of the burdens of the world, the burdens of your life, and all seeming labors. Take your burdens to Christ. "Come unto me, all ye that labor and are heavy laden, and I will give you rest."

We are pressed upon by ideas of materiality. Thoughts make things, and the material ideas that are pressing upon us are just as substantial in the realm of mind as material things are substantial in the realm of matter. Everything has origin in thought, and material thoughts will bring forth material things. So you should baptize and cleanse with your spiritual word every center, as Philip baptized the eunuch of Gaza. Baptism is cleansing. It always represents the erasing power of the mind.

When the baptizing power of the word is poured upon a

center, it cleanses all material thought; impotence is vitalized with new life, and the whole subconsciousness is awakened and quickened. The word of the Lord is there sown in the body, and once the word of the Lord is sown in any of these centers—the cells of which are like blank phonograph records—they take the thought that is given them, and send it through the whole organism. The baptism of strength goes to the uttermost parts of the body, and every one of the twelve powers, under the divine law, feels the new strength.

James, the son of Zebedee, represents discrimination and good judgment in dealing with substantial things. James is the faculty in man that wisely chooses and determines. It may be in the matter of food; it may be in the matter of judgment about the relation of external forces; it may be in the choosing of a wife or a husband—in a thousand different ways this faculty is developed in man. The spiritual side of the James faculty is intuition, quick knowing.

James and John are brothers, and Jesus called them "sons of thunder." These brothers preside over the great body brain called the solar plexus, or sun center. James has his throne at the pit of the stomach; and John just back of the heart. They are unified by bundles of nerves and are metaphysically closely related. Whatever affects the stomach will sympathetically affect the heart. People with weak stomachs nearly always think they have heart trouble.

Jesus called those two apostles "sons of thunder." Tremendous vibrations or emotions that go forth from the solar plexus. When your sympathies are aroused, you will find that you begin to breathe deeply and strongly, and if you are very sympathetic you can feel the vibrations as they go out to the person or thing to which you are directing your thoughts. All fervor, all the high energy that comes from soul, passes through these centers.

Bartholomew represents the imagination. The imagination

has its center of action directly between the eyes. This is the point of expression for a set of tissues that extend back into the brain and connect with an imaging or picture-making function near the root of the optic nerve. Through this faculty you can project an image of things that are without, or ideas that are within. For instance, you can project the image of jealousy to any part of your body and, by the chemistry of thought combined with function, make your complexion yellow, or you can image and project beauty by thinking goodness and perfection for everybody. Bartholomew is connected directly with the soul, and has great power in the pictures of the mind. Jesus saw him under a fig tree, a long way off, before he was visible to the natural eye. Do not imagine anything but good, because under the law of thought combined with substance it will sooner or later come into expression, unless you head it off, eliminate it by denial.

Man has faculties of elimination, as well as of appropriation. If you know how to handle them you can expel error from your thought body. The denial apostle is Thaddaeus, presiding in the abdominal region, the great renunciator of the mind and the body. All the faculties are necessary to the perfect expression of the man. None is despised or unclean. Some have been misunderstood; through ignorance man has called them mean, until they act in that way and cause him pain and sorrow. The elimination, by Thaddaeus, of the waste of the system through the bowels is a very necessary function.

Thomas represents the understanding power of man. He is called the doubter because he wants to know about everything. Thomas is in the front brain, and his collaborator, Matthew, the will, occupies the same brain area. These two faculties are jointly in occupation of this part of the "promised land." Like the land of Ephraim and Manasseh, their inheritance in undivided.

James, the son of Alphaeus, represents divine order. His center is at the navel.

Simon, the Cananaean, represents zeal; his center is at the medulla, at the base of the brain. When you burn with zeal and are anxious to accomplish great things, you generate heat at the base of your brain. If this condition is not balanced by the cooperation of the supplying faculties, you will burn up the cells and impede the growth of the soul. "For the zeal of thy house hath eaten me up."

Judas, who betrayed Jesus, has his throne in the generative center. Judas governs the life consciousness in the body, and without his wise co-operation the organism loses its essential substance, and dies. Judas is selfish; greed is his "devil." Judas governs the most subtle of the "beasts of the field"—sensation; but Judas can be redeemed. The Judas function generates the life of the body. We need life but life must be guided in divine ways. There must be a righteous expression of life. Judas, the betrayer of Jesus, must in the end be cleansed of the devil, selfishness; having been cleansed, he will allow the life force to flow to every part of the organism. Instead of being a thief (drawing to the sex center the vital forces necessary to the substance of the whole man) Judas will become a supplier; he will give his life to every faculty. In the prevailing race consciousness Judas drains the whole man, and the body dies as a result of his selfish thievery.

It is through Judas (the desire to appropriate and to experience the pleasure of sensation) that the soul (Eve) is led into sin. Through the sins of the sex life (casting away of the precious substance), the body is robbed of its essential fluids and eventually disintegrates. The result is called death, which is the great and last enemy to be overcome by man. Immortality in the body is possible to man only when he has overcome the weaknesses of sensation, and conserves his life substance. When we awaken to the realization that all indulgence for pleasure alone is followed by pain, then we shall know the meaning of eating of the tree of the knowledge of good and evil, or pleasure and pain.

If you would build up your faculties under the divine law, redeem Judas. First have faith in the power of Spirit, and then speak to Judas the word of purity. Speak to him the word of unselfishness; baptize him with the whole Spirit— Holy Spirit. If there is in you a selfish desire to exercise sensation, to experience the pleasures of sense in any of its avenues, give that desire to the Lord; in no other way can you come into eternal life.

These twelve powers are all expressed and developed under the guidance of Divine Mind. "Not by might, nor by power, but by my Spirit, saith Jehovah of hosts." You must keep the equipoise; you must, in all the bringing forth of the twelve powers of man, realize that they come from God; that they are directed by the Word of God, and that man (Jesus) is their head.

Chapter 21

INDISPENSABLE ASSURANCE (1939)

MAN CAN *BE* what he determines to be. He can be master or he can be serf. It rests with him whether he shall fill the high places in life or the low, whether he shall serve or be served, lead or be led, or be sickly or healthy. Of course we understand that these distinctions are relative only; in the sight of the Most High the servant may be prized more than his master, but there is within every one an inherent desire to be at the top, which desire has its root deep down in our very nature and is consequently legitimate. That it is frequently misdirected and used toward base ends is no reason why it should be depreciated. We all desire to excel. This desire is the inspiration of Spirit, which ever forces us up through earth toward heaven, and it should be encouraged and cultivated in the right direction.

A man without ambition is like a ship afloat on the waves without sails or power. Such a man simply drifts: if he reaches port safely it is by chance.

But a ship under full sail or power needs one other important thing and that is a rudder. Then it needs a man to handle that rudder, and that man needs faith.

In considering the character of faith we must start, as we do with everything else, in the one Mind. God must have had faith in order to ideate the universe before it was created; and man, being like God, must base his creations on faith. Faith is innate in man. A favorite definition of faith is that of Paul: "Faith is assurance of things hoped for, the conviction of things not seen." It is by works of faith that we develop our consciousness and heal ourselves. The important question with everyone of us is, How does faith work?

It is possible to have a reality and yet neither touch it nor smell it nor see it nor in any way come into consciousness of it in the outer realm. That is what faith is. It is the consciousness in us of the realities of the attributes of mind. Before we can have the substance of faith we must realize that the mind creates realities. How do we create realities without seeing them, or feeling them, or smelling them, or tasting them, or in any way coming into outer consciousness of them? Faith is the wonderful power that builds these eternally real things.

Faith is a power of the spiritual mind, but in all the realms of existence we find faith. The foundation of faith is in the spiritual, but wherever you find the mind at work you find faith. Faith in its highest form is an exalted idea. And what is the most exalted idea that man can have? That he is spiritual; that he is related directly to the one great Spirit, and that through that Spirit he can do mighty works by faith.

Jesus laid great stress on faith. He always tried to direct the attention of the people to the invisible, the spiritual, by statements like these: "Believe ye that I am able to do this?" "According to your faith be it done unto you." "Thy faith hath made thee whole." All through His works there runs a golden thread of faith. Jesus did not advocate faith in material forces of any character. Through faith He healed thousands. His command was "Have faith in God."

We would not destroy anyone's faith in the lesser things, but would give him a sure foundation for all faith by directing his attention to the one and only source of faith, Divine Mind. The question for us is how to increase our faith in Spirit. You will find that you have plenty of faith. All men have faith, but it is scattered here and there and everywhere by being placed in lesser things, and those lesser things finally fail us.

If you get a good strong perception of something that your inner mind tells you is true, act upon it, and you will find that it will come true.

In developing His apostles Jesus took Peter as the representative of faith, and proclaimed that upon this foundation (of faith), He would build the new man, His "church" or aggregation of spiritual ideas. The faith demonstrated by Peter in the beginning of his career was not of a very high type. When Truth (represented by Christ) was being tried, Peter denied Jesus: said that he did not know Him and swore at Him, showing that Peter's faith must have been at a very low ebb when put to the test. At the very last Jesus tried Peter again and again, asking three times. "Lovest thou me?" Faith and love are very closely related. You must love the Lord, and then you must have faith in His spiritual power and continuity. Peter finally unfolded a mighty healing power. Even his shadow healed.

Now this faith that we are all cultivating and striving for is built up through continuous affirmations of its loyalty to the divine idea, the higher Self. You must have faith in your spiritual capacity.

Many have learned how to hold the truth about health steadily in faith even in the midst of the most adverse appearances, and they clearly understand that they are not telling falsehoods when they deny sickness right in the face of the appearance of it. In the same way we achieve our victory over sin. When ill temper, vanity, greed, selfishness, and other sins of greater and lesser degree come up, they should be denied; and the unselfishness, the purity, the uprightness, and the integrity of the higher Self should be affirmed. Persons who are quickened spiritually can do very much greater works through the law of faith than those who are still in the material consciousness; and once having discerned the power of Spirit, we should be on our guard and send forth on every occasion exalted ideas of the spiritual.

"I am the living bread which came down out of heaven: if any man eat of this bread, he shall live for ever." Jesus Christ raised people who had let go of the life idea and brought them into such a consciousness of omnipresent life that they came out of the tomb.

This life consciousness that Jesus Christ quickens is as greatly needed in our day as it was in the time when He first worked in the souls of men. If you go to a medical doctor and ask him the cause of your ills, he will tell you that most of them come from lack of vitality, which means lack of life. We all need vitalizing. The question is, How shall we get life? What is the source of life? Those who teach the use of material remedies point us to various things as the source—food, air, water, and so forth; but those who depend on these remedies are fast losing faith in drugs and are reaching out to electricity and similar means of gaining more abundant life. They are thus getting a little closer to the healing system of Jesus, but they still lack the all-important Truth that God is life and that they who worship Him must worship Him in the life consciousness, that is, in Spirit. When we worship God in His way, we are vitalized all at once; there is no other way to get real, permanent life. We cannot get life from the outer man or from anything external; we must touch the inner current.

The life source is spiritual energy. It is deeper and finer

than electricity or human magnetism. It is composed of ideas, and man can turn on its current by making mental contact with it.

When Jesus came teaching the gospel of Spirit, people did not understand Him. They did not know that universal Spirit is Principle and that we demonstrate it or fail to demonstrate it according to the character of our thinking. It has taken the race two thousand years to find that we turn on the life current by means of thoughts and words. We can have fullness of life by realizing that we live in a sea of abundant, omnipresent, eternal life, and by refusing to allow any thought to come in that stops the consciousness of the universal life flow. We live and move and have our being in life, Mind life. You can think of your life as mental; every faculty will begin to buzz with new life. Your life will never wane if you keep in the consciousness of it as Mind or Spirit; it will increase and attain full expression in your body. If you have faith in the life idea in your consciousness, your body will never be run down but will become more and more alive with spiritual life until it shows forth the glory of Christ.

We must think life, talk life, and see ourselves filled with the fullness of life. When we are not manifesting life as we desire, it is because our thoughts and our conversation are not in accord with the life idea. Every time we think life, speak life, rejoice in life, we are setting free, and bringing into expression in ourselves more and more of the life idea. Here is the place of abundant life, and we can fill both mind and body, both our surroundings and our affairs, with glad, free, buoyant life by exercising faith in it. "According to your faith be it done unto you."

In this way we enter into the same consciousness of abundant, enduring, unfailing, eternal life that Jesus had, and we can readily understand His proclamation that those who believe in the indwelling Christ life will never die. If we are wise, we shall cultivate faith in and understanding of omnipresent life.

I know a man who is a natural pessimist, and if anyone mentions something that is not to be emulated he will say, "Now, let us be careful about that." If you speak of someone who has been doing a good work for the community, he will always throw in a little depreciation. His whole life has been like sodden bread. Everything falls flat in his affairs, and he does not understand why it is. He says, "I have been studying this Truth for years, and I do not understand why I do not succeed." Intellectually he is a Truth seeker, but it has not taken hold of his faith substance. He doubts, and down he goes. When Peter tried to walk on the water to meet Jesus, he went down in the sea of doubt. He saw too much wetness in the water. He saw the negative side of the proposition, and it weakened his demonstration. If you want to demonstrate, never consider the negative side. If mountains seem to oppose the carrying out of your plans, say with Napoleon that there shall be no Alps. The man who is grounded in faith does not measure his thoughts or his acts by the world's standard of facts. "Faith is blind," say people who are not acquainted with the real thing; but those who are in spiritual understanding know that faith has open eyes, that certain things do exist in Spirit and become substantial and real to the one who dwells and thinks and lives in faith. Such a one knows.

Many Christians are like the woman who was on a ship during a great storm. She went to the captain and said, "Now I want to know just how bad it is." He told her plainly that they were in a very desperate and helpless condition and finished by saying, "We shall have to trust in God." She exclaimed, "Oh, dear! has it come to that?"

A close analysis shows that faith is the foundation of all that man does. The doctor knows that the patient's faith in him and his method is essential to his success. I remember a story told me by a lawyer: A certain attorney was subject to periodical headaches. He had some capsules prescribed by his physician that would cure these headaches almost instantly. For emergencies he carried one of the capsules in his vest pocket, and immediately upon swallowing it the pain would disappear. Once when pleading a case he was seized with a headache. He reached into his pocket, secured the little antidote and swallowed it, and immediately the headache left him. He went on with his argument, and after he sat down he wished to make some corrections in his notes, and felt in his pocket for a little rubber pencil tip that he carried for that purpose. Instead of the rubber tip he brought out a capsule, thus discovering that he had swallowed his pencil tip instead of the capsule.

This was an exhibition of faith asserting itself unawares. Suppose we should concentrate such faith on the invisible, the real things, the things of Spirit, how wonderful would be our demonstrations! How effective we should become in using the mighty working power of Spirit!

Jesus told His followers (and we are all His followers) to go forth and do His works—raise the dead and the like—and that we should do even greater works than He did. How? By exercising spiritual faith, by increasing our power through exalted ideas. We must raise our faith to the very highest in us and rest in the "assurance" or substance of its reality.

Jesus had faith in God, and this gave Him faith in all men. Spiritual understanding reveals the universality of all things. When they brought to Him the lame man on the couch, letting him down through the ceiling, "Jesus seeing their faith," healed him, not because of the faith of the man himself but because of the faith of those who brought him. The faith of his neighbors in the power of Spirit did the work for the sick man.

We believe that doctors are doing the very best they know; but if they would only approach a little closer to the spiritual, what a wonderful work they might do! They are giving less and less medicine every year. They recognize more and more that there is something back of medicine that they call the healing power of nature.

Nearly every doctor of large experience will tell you that he can get the same result with a little sweetened water that he can with drugs if he has the confidence of the patient. If the patient can be made to believe that the drug is going to work in a certain way, he will carry out this belief to the letter. Thus the word, the imagination, and faith work together.

Jesus had this high spiritual realization, and He healed through the word. He is the Great Physician. He is the one whom we are to follow, whom we are seeking to emulate; and we do it through laying hold of Spirit. I would say to you that if you want to do the works of God, you must follow Christ. If you want to elevate yourself out of the physical, you must have faith in God and must cultivate that faith through affirmation of your spiritual power and faith. The Lord's Prayer is continual affirmation from beginning to end.

It has been our experience in developing the faculties of mind that the more we affirm a certain thing the stronger it becomes. But we must have the understanding that our relation to God is that of a son to his father; that we exist in the one Mind as an idea, and that this idea does work in us as in a superman, even Christ.

It is a metaphysical law that there are three steps in every demonstration; the recognition of Truth as it is in principle; holding the idea; and acknowledging fulfillment. Pray believing that you have received, and you shall receive.

From the teaching of Jesus it is clear that He accepted fully the proposition that God is our resource and that all things are provided for us by our Father. It is necessary to cultivate these ideas by considering them daily in all that we do.

It is recorded that a pupil of Socrates' once said to him: "Master, when we read what you have inscribed we are inspired; when we come into your presence we are moved to love; when we hear your words we are charmed, and when we touch your hand we are thrilled."

Socrates was a great soul, a master mind, and his soul radiation was very powerful. But Jesus was still greater in His soul radiation; He had through ages of discipline and thought projection in word and deed made Himself a master scientist in the mental and spiritual worlds. His soul radiation or aura was so powerful that it perpetually stimulates to greater achievement and thrills with new life all who enter its sphere of influence. Thought transference is an accepted fact to many persons, and it is sustained by the recent tests in measuring the force projected in the process of human thinking. Machines have been invented so sensitive that they respond to the thoughts of men and women under various emotions. The results are reported to be so pronounced in their order and regularity as to constitute a universal law in mind activity.

This power of the mind to project the results of thinking gives us the key to the work of Jesus in resurrecting His body and making it perpetually radiant in our mental and spiritual atmosphere.

As there are dimensions above that in which we live so there are levels of mind activity above and beyond the intellectual. Jesus said, "In my Father's house are many mansions"; that is, dwelling places in mind or consciousness: states of consciousness.

"I go to prepare a place for you . . . that where I am, *there* ye may be also."

The assertions by physical scientists that we have no assurance of any power that will increase our moral stature or save us from suffering and degeneracy is beyond comprehension to one who has gone deeply into the study of psychology and spiritual dynamics.

We may receive spiritual inspiration from within. By prayer and meditation on words of Truth in the silence we may so open our consciousness to the inner divine presence that the necessary understanding, love, and power may be given us to enable us to bring forth in our own lives the good results that we wish to see manifest. This is much better than waiting to see the demonstrations of others before believing and before attempting to bring forth demonstrations of our own.

After Thomas was shown the evidence he believed. After the outer reason sees the works accomplished by the I AM by means of faith and the word it accepts Truth. But there is a quicker way to grow in faith and in spiritual understanding, a way that has nothing to do with intellectual reasoning and belief. Jesus said, "Blessed *are* they that have not seen, and *yet* have believed." That way is the quickening of our innate spiritual faith.

True faith in God separates itself from all negative belief in the body as material, impure, transient.

With the growth of faith in the mind of the individual there comes a quickening of all his thoughts by the influx of Truth. "The word of God" increases.

God is never absent from you. He is constantly taking form in your life according to the exact pattern of your words, thoughts, and actions. Just as soon as you really bring your words and your expectations up to the measure of God's love for you, just that soon you will demonstrate.

Thoughts are seeds that, when dropped or planted in the subconscious mind, germinate, grow, and bring forth their fruit in due season. The more clearly we understand this Truth the greater will be our ability to plant the seeds that bring forth desirable fruits. After sowing the plants must be tended. After using the law we must hold to its fulfillment. This is our part, but God gives the increase. You must work in divine order and not expect the harvest before the soil has been prepared or the seed sown. You have now the fruits of previous sowings. Change your thought seeds and reap what you desire. Some bring forth very quickly, others more slowly, but all in divine order.

The law of spiritual healing involves full receptivity on the part of the one under treatment. God does not do things in us against our will, as will acts in both the conscious and subconscious realms of mind. However much it may appear that the word is thwarted in its original intent, this is never true; it goes on, and it enters where reception is given it. In this way men are quickened, and whether we see the result with our physical vision or not, the process is as sure as God Himself.

In treating others we are told to see our patients as perfect. So in actualizing our ideals we must see them as if they were part of our phenomenal life. We often hear it said that the genius lives in a world of his own, separate and apart from common minds. From the metaphysical standpoint we see that the genius is merely one who has caught onto the law of believing his dreams of health, perfection, and success to be true, and whose dreams have therefore become true.

A genius is one who lets the full Spirit within him speak out, regardless of how different its utterances may be from those of people who have posed as authority. He has absolute faith in his spiritual revelations and fearlessly proclaims them. He is a pioneer and a leader. He listens to his own inherent genius and has faith in his God-given ability. Not only must he listen but he must act. The world is filled with original dreamers. They have ideas brilliant beyond expression, but they do not clothe them in the habiliments of action.

You must not only perceive an idea; you must also give it form by infusing into it the substance of your living faith. Daydreamers may be found by the score in physics and metaphysics. They all fall short in failing to realize that there are two sides to every proposition, the image and the expression: and that the Lord God formed man out of the ground and breathed into his nostrils the breath of life.

So each one of us must not only see the image of his desires as a theory, but he must also form it into a living, breathing thing through every motive and act of his life. That is, if we have an idea, we must act just as if it were part of our life. We must be formed from the substance of our world, whether it be the dust of the ground or the ethers of the invisible. There must be an actual imaging of them in our consciousness before we shall ever see our ideas realized.

Here is where the dreamer and the divine scientist part company. One says, "I admire your theories greatly, but they can never be realized on this earth. Things are as they are, and they cannot be changed. We are here, and we shall just have to make the best of it."

He who has learned the meaning of man—who and what man is—never allows himself to make any such admissions. He knows that there is a way provided by which he not only can lift himself out of the swamp of belief in sin, sickness, and death but also through his efforts open the way for many others to find the way to perfection. No man ever demonstrated his God-given powers in even a small way who did not help many others to do likewise. Preaching is good, but practice is better. "I, if I be lifted up from the earth, will draw all men unto myself."

There is a work for everyone who will listen and obey the

Spirit. That work is important, because it is eternal and brings results eternal in their nature.

If you have heard the voice of the Lord and are obedient to it at any cost, you are chosen. Your life is hid with Christ in God, and the way into the kingdom is assured you.

This is no fanciful sketch, nor does it refer to a theoretical place or condition to be reached in some future state or under circumstances more propitious. This kingdom of God is now existing right here in our midst. It is being externalized little by little.

Whoever has a high, pure thought and affirms his allegiance to it as a part of his daily life is adding to the externality of that kingdom among men. Whoever says, *"I will be upright and honest in all that I think and do,"* is laying the foundation stones for one of the buildings of the New Jerusalem.

Whoever affirms his allegiance to the good, regardless of all appearance of evil, and in dealing with his brother declares by word and act that only the good exists, is building white spires to the one and only true God.

Whoever lays up in his mental storehouse the resolve *"I will do unto others as I would have them do unto me"* is paving the highways with pure gold in a heavenly city of equity and justice.

There will be no need of the sun or the moon in the city of the kingdom of God, because God, the good, will be the light thereof.

We are the temples of God, of good, and through us is this light to shine, which is so bright as to dim the rays of those shining orbs of the night and the day. Herein is God glorified that we love one another. Herein does the true light shine that we let love and peace and kindness shine forth forever and always. We are to be the very light itself and we can only be the light by becoming so pure that it cannot help but shine through us. This is possible to the highest and lowest in the world's roster of respectability. We are all the chosen of the Lord and we make the covenant that carries us into His visible presence by laying down the personal man and taking up the universal man. He it is that thunders in the depths of our soul. "Who say ye that I am?"

Chapter 22

THE DEVELOPMENT OF DIVINE LOVE (1926)

"**O** JERUSALEM, JERUSALEM, that killeth the prophets, and stoneth them that are sent unto her! how often would I have gathered thy children together, even as a hen gathereth her chickens under her wings, and ye would not!"

—Jesus

Jesus weeping over Jerusalem is the picture of a great love welling up in the heart and flowing out to all the earth—the love of the good Father for His erring and willful children. Such is the love of Christ for His own; such is the love of God through Christ for all creation.

We may talk about the wisdom of God, but the love of God must be felt in the heart. It cannot be described, and one who has not felt it can have no concept of it from the descriptions of others. But the more we talk about love, the stronger it grows in the consciousness, and if we persist in thinking loving thoughts and speaking loving words, we are sure to bring into our experience the feeling of that great love that is beyond description—the very love of God.

It is popularly taught and believed that there is but one

love; that God is love and that all love is from Him, hence that all love is God's love.

Love is a divine principle and man can know it in its purity by touching it at its fountainhead. There it is not tinged in any way by man's formative thought, but flows forth a pure, pellucid stream of infinite ecstasy. It has no consciousness of good or evil, pure or impure, but pours itself out in great oceans of living magnetic power, to be used by whosoever will.

Man has a faculty through which he receives love from Being; this faculty is commonly called the heart. The heart, however, is but the visible expression of an invisible center of consciousness. Sense discerns that man has a heart, but soul discerns an inner faculty in man through which he may express an attribute of Being. By his word, man calls his powers into activity, that through them he may manifest God.

Jesus was the orderly man of God, manifesting under divine law the attributes of Being. Jesus "called unto him his disciples"; that is, by His word He spiritually quickened and educated His twelve faculties. Peter, faith active in the thinking faculty, is the first disciple called. Peter is the rock foundation of that consciousness which is the church of Christ. You will find that the character of your whole consciousness depends upon how you think. You may have great love, but unless you guide it with right thoughts it will not build up a harmonious consciousness. Love poured through the heart of a mother who has fear in her thought, shatters the body of a delicate child. The thinker must be strong and sure in his grasp of right thoughts. The second disciple is Andrew, brother to Peter; he represents strength. James represents judgment, discrimination, the faculty that chooses the good and eschews the evil. This faculty must be brought out before love in its fullness is safe in the life of man. Love has not will and volition, except as they are infused into it by the other faculties. John is love, and he leaned on the Master's bosom. This is to symbolize the innocence, tenderness, and dependence of love. Peter is bold, impetuous, executive—affirms his undying allegiance to the Master one moment and denies Him the next—but the loyalty and the constancy of love were dominant in the character of John.

We find that these four faculties, evenly balanced, will form the foundation of a harmonious body and mind.

You must think, and think with faith in both God and yourself—that is Peter.

You must think with strength and power—that is Andrew.

You must think with judgment and discretion—that is James.

You must center all your thought, your strength, and your judgment in love—that is John.

To Peter (the faithful thinker) is given the key to the kingdom of heaven, but he can never open the gate until he has reconciled all the other faculties. Many people in this day have found how much depends upon right thinking, and they are counting on getting into the kingdom of health and harmony by holding good thoughts only. They have not always taken into consideration the fact that the thinking faculty is merely the executive power in the consciousness, and that it depends upon many other faculties for the material out of which its thoughts are formed.

To think without strength is to bring forth weakly—without effect. To think without judgment is to bring forth malformed mental creations, good and evil, spirit and matter, sickness and health, life and death, and the thousand other Babylonish conditions found in the world. To think without love is to bring forth hate, discord, and inharmony.

So it is not thought alone that opens the way into the kingdom, but a right use of all the powers of mind and body centered in thought.

Thinking gives color, tone, shape, character, to all creation, but the essences or materials of creation are drawn from the realm of Spirit.

In the world we find love so turned awry by wrong thinking that it does not represent God. In its beginning it came forth from God, but it has been taken into "another country" of error thought and there wasted in riotous living.

Error thought has put greed into love, and we find that the love of money is "a root of all kinds of evil." Error thought has said to love, "We are flesh and blood; this is my child, this is my husband, my father, my mother, my sister, my brother. We are separate from others." Thus error thought has made love to serve it in family selfishness.

"And he stretched forth his hand towards his disciples, and said, Behold, my mother and my brethren! For whosoever shall do the will of my Father who is in heaven, he is my brother, and sister, and mother." This is the love of God in its purity, fresh from the fountainhead.

Wherever love is tainted with selfishness, we may know that error thought has made muddy its clear stream, so that it no longer represents the purity of its source.

Love is the drawing power of mind. It is the magnet of the universe, and about it may be clustered all the attributes of Being, by one who thinks in divine order.

Many who have found the law of true thinking and its effect wonder why supply does not come to them after months and years of holding thoughts of bounty. It is because they have not developed love. They have formed the right image in mind, but the magnet that draws the substance from the storehouse of Being has not been set into action.

To demonstrate supply, we must think supply, and thus form it in the consciousness. We must conserve all the ideas of substance in the mind—and also the fluids of the body, their representatives—because we must have a base for our form. We must vibrate the love center in thought, word, and act. Then there will come to us on the wings of invisibility that which will satisfy every need. This is the secret of demonstrating plenty from the ethers.

"Love . . . taketh not account of evil." Love never sees anything wrong in that which it loves. If it did, it would not be pure love. Pure love is without discriminating power. It simply pours itself out upon the object of its affection, and takes no account of the result. By so doing, love sometimes casts its pearls before swine, but its power is so great that it transforms all that it touches.

Do not be afraid to pour out your love upon all the so-called evil in the world. Deny the appearance of evil, and affirm the omnipotence and the omnipresence of love and goodness. Take no account of the evil that appears in your life and your affairs. Refuse to see it as evil. Declare that what seems evil has somewhere a good side, which shall through your persistent affirmation of its presence be made visible. By using this creative power of your own thought you will change that which seemed evil into good, and divine love will pour its healing balm over all.

Sickness is not good, because it is not of God; but if, through past ignorance in thought or act, a person finds himself in its grasp, he can hasten his deliverance by affirming the experience to be a good lesson that he will take to heart and profit by. If he bemoans his sad fate, he throws the shadow of gloom into the healing waters of love, thereby corrupting them and weakening their restorative action for him.

Always remember that love is the great magnet of God. It is, of itself, neither good nor evil. These are qualities given to it by the thinking faculty in man. Whatever you see for your love, that it will draw to you, because as a magnet it attracts whatever you set your desire upon. To focus your love about self and selfish aims will cause it to draw around you the limited things of personality and the hollow shams of sense life. To focus your love upon money and the possessions of the material world will make you the slave of mammon, and will make your life a failure and a disappointment. To focus your love upon anything less than All-Good will eventually cause you to fall short of your highest aspiration, and will keep you outside the kingdom of heaven.

"Love suffereth long, and is kind." Love does not resent injuries. It does not take affront and insult into account. Pure love does not recognize personality; hence when a person is in the consciousness of love, he cannot be hurt at what may be said to him or about him. "A soft answer turneth away wrath" is ever on the lips of love, and whoever makes this his thought focus will be able to reduce to peace and harmony the tides of impatience and anger that may be surging about him.

One with strong love and the right focal idea may control turbulent multitudes by his silent thought alone.

When we speak of the power of love, it should be understood that we mean power exercised through love. Power is a faculty of mind. It associates itself with some other faculty and in conjunction with that faculty it is made manifest. In the relation of man's faculties in Divine Mind, power and love are associated in action, but in man's present concept of relations he has associated intellect and power. From this wrong relation arise the tyranny and oppression so evident in the world.

Power should never be exercised except through love. Whoever associates his power and his intellect and attempts in a blind way to force his desire to fulfillment will always bring about discord and unrighteous oppression.

Power cannot be used successfully through intellect, because intellect lacks wisdom. Wisdom associates itself with love, and can be found in its purity only at the heart center, hence we speak of the "still small voice" within. Elijah found that the voice of God was not in the wind, not in the earthquake or the fire—these being of the intellect—but in the "still small voice."

Intellect is not wise. Wisdom is not its office. Intellect is the executive officer of wisdom, and can do right only when faithfully carrying out the instructions of its principle.

We see how dangerous to the welfare of man it is for intellect to assume knowledge and to call upon power to help it in carrying out its unsubstantial ideas. Power is the faculty in mind that propels outward, and it must necessarily have balance in some other faculty in order to hold its equilibrium. There is but one other faculty that has opposite action, and that is love, whose office is attraction. When power and love are associated, the centrifugal and the centripetal forces of Being are equalized; man unifies all the work that the Lord God has given him to do, and his dominion over the forces of Being is exercised in peace and harmony. Peace and harmony are the focalizing ideas that chord with the divine nature of love, and when they are associated in the mind there is no limit to man's power. It is said by those who know the power of spiritual forces that one man developed large enough in love might dissolve this planet with his word. But one so developed would never do anything to interfere in any way with the life and the rights of another. Love does not offend or take offense.

Among a certain class of Hindu mystics are those called Bhakti, or Disciples of Love. They know the power of love to protect and to care for them, and they cultivate it until all nature is in love with and befriends them. Thousands of the common people of India are killed annually by serpents and wild animals, yet these mystics have so brought forth the power of love in themselves that serpents and savage animals do not injure them. They live in the wildest jungles;

during periods of silent devotion, lasting sometimes weeks and even months, they make the open forest their home. It is recorded that birds have built their nests in the hair of such devotees during their period of silence. They respect the rights of the tiniest insect, and under no circumstances kill anything or interfere with it in any way. When put to practical test, love always proves its divine origin and power.

You may trust love to get you out of your difficulties. There is nothing too hard for it to accomplish for you, if you put your confidence in it and act without dissimulation. But do not talk love and in your heart feel resentment. This will bring discord to your members and rottenness to your bones. Love is candor and frankness. Deception is no part of love; he who tries to use it in that sort of company will prove himself a liar, and love will desert him in the end.

There is no envy in love. Love is satisfaction in itself, not that satisfaction with personal self, its possessions and its attractions, which is vanity, but an inner satisfaction that sees good everywhere and in everybody. It insists that all is good, and by refusing to see anything but good it causes that quality finally to appear uppermost in itself and in all things. When only good is seen and felt, how can there be anything but satisfaction?

The one who has made union with divine love through his inner consciousness, who lets it pour its healing currents into his soul and his body, is fortunate beyond all description. Instead of envying another, he desires to show others the great joy that may be theirs when they have opened the floodgates of their love nature. Truly, "love envieth not."

Yet with all these glorious possessions, beyond the power of man to describe, "love vaunteth not itself, is not puffed up." Love does not brag about its demonstrations. It simply lives the life, and lets its works speak for it.

Love does not seek its own. It does not make external effort to get anything, not even that which intellect claims belongs to it. It is here that love proves itself to be the invisible magnet that draws to man whatever he needs. But instead of leaving this department of the work to love, intellect sees what it wants and in its blundering way goes about getting it. Thus the real begetting power in man has been ignored until its true office has been forgotten and its power has been suppressed.

When love, the universal magnet, is brought into action in the consciousness of our race, it will change all our methods of supplying human wants. It will harmonize all the forces of nature and will dissolve the discords that now infest earth and air. It will control the elements until they obey man and bring forth that which will supply all his needs, without the labor that is called the sweat of his face. The earth shall yet be made paradise by the power of love. That condition will begin to set in for each one just as soon as he develops the love nature in himself.

When love has begun its silent pulsations at one's solar center, no one can keep one in want or poverty. From the invisible currents of the inner ether, love will draw to man all that belongs to him; and all belongs to him that is required to make him happy and contented.

This mighty magnet is a quality of God that is expressed through man, and it cannot be suppressed by any outside force. No environment or external condition can keep back love, when once you have firmly decided in mind to give it expression. The present unloving condition of the world is no bar to your exercise of love; in fact, it is an incentive. You will know, as you begin to make love manifest, how great a sinner you have been, how far you have fallen short of making yourself the man or the woman of God. This will show you by comparison how greatly you have missed the mark of the high calling that is yours in Christ.

We have been taught the beauties of love and its great power in the world, but no one else has explained that it has a center of action in the body, a center that was designed by the Creator to do a specific work. The man or the woman who has not developed the love center is abnormal, is living in only partial exercise of consciousness. The love center has its nerves and muscles in the body. Through neglect these have become atrophied in nearly the whole race, but they are just as necessary to the perfect man as are legs and arms. In fact they are more necessary. With the love center active, one might live happily and successfully without legs and arms; one might even grow new legs and arms in an adherence to the completeness of life in which love proves to be the fulfillment of the law of perfection.

The body is the instrument of the mind; no one has even seen his real body as it is in the sight of God, except through the mind. The body of flesh, bones, and blood that the eye of sense beholds is not the true body any more than the heart of flesh is the true organ of love.

The true body is an ethereal body, an indestructible body; the body of flesh is the grosser vibration that the sense consciousness beholds. The Spirit body is not absent or dead, but is simply inactive. When, through purification of his ideas and acceleration of his mental energies, man comes into sight of the real forces of Being, his whole body is quickened into new life, and the body of flesh responds to its vibrations. He does this work through the mind—by thinking right thoughts and doing right things also, because man is, in the ultimate, a unit, and the thinking and the doing cannot be separated.

To develop the love center, begin by affirming: *From this time forth and forevermore I shall know no man after the flesh. I shall not see men and women as body and mortal thought. I shall always behold them with the eye of love, which sees only perfection.* Ask daily that love be made alive in you, that it take up its abode at your magnetic center, and make it alive with strong, steady pulsations of spiritual energy.

Let your attention rest for a few moments every day at the heart center in your body, the cardiac plexus, while you declare silently: *You are the abode of love. You are filled and thrilled with the mighty magnetic forces that love uses in doing its work. You are powerful and active to do only good, and you see only goodness and purity everywhere.*

Many people say that they cannot see love in others who are not manifesting it clearly—that they themselves do not feel loving and therefore cannot exercise love. But this development of one's own love center will make one see it, just as the eye sees light. It is difficult to feel love with a dormant love organ, but exceedingly easy when that organ begins to exercise its true inherent potentialities.

Love is in the world in a diluted form as affection between husband and wife, parents and children, friend and friend, but it can be made manifest in its original strength and purity by each man and woman's opening the fountainhead and letting its mighty currents stream forth.

Sex lust has diverted the vital forces in the body away from the love center, the cardiac plexus, which is almost inactive in many men. When a pure-minded woman sends forth her desire for love, such men interpret it sexually and are excited to lust. Love is disappointed, and loathing of the ignorant animal eventually follows. Love is not sex lust.

The love of God for His children is beyond description—a love so tender and so deep that it cannot be mentioned in the same breath with the ordinary love as known by the world. The great love of Being is deeper and wider than the thoughts and the words of man have compassed since the beginning of language. It can be known only on its own plane, and man must awaken within himself the capacity to feel a mighty love before he can comprehend how great is the love of God.

But only the meek and lowly in heart may know the depths of the Father's love. It is not revealed to the self-sufficient, because they do not open the way through their own childlike, innocent hearts.

The Father yearns to have His love felt by every one of us. He has given us the capacity to feel it, and He waits until we develop the love faculty and open our lives to the flood of good that He pours out to us through His all-sufficient love.

Father almighty! *We bow before Thy goodness, and invoke in prayer and supplication Thy silent presence as love.* May its steady currents of power draw us into Thy mighty arms, where we shall rest secure from all the buffets of the world. *We come as little children into the sacred precincts of Thy love, knowing full well that no hand of force ever finds a welcome there.* Open to us the inner peace and the inner harmony that are born of love. Let all fear depart from our mind as the shadows from the morning light. Let us bask forever in the sunshine of perpetual love, Thy love, Thy never-failing love!

Chapter 23

JUDGMENT AND JUSTICE (1909)

"**J**UDGE NOT, that ye be not judged. For with what judgment ye judge, ye shall be judged: and with what measure ye mete, it shall be measured unto you."

—Matthew 7:1, 2

"And thou shalt put in the breastplate of judgment the Urim and the Thummim; and they shall be upon Aaron's heart, when he goeth in before Jehovah: and Aaron shall bear the judgment of the children of Israel upon his heart before Jehovah continually" (Ex. 28:30).

"The Urim and Thummim (Lights and Perfections). These were the sacred symbols (worn upon the breastplate of the high priest, upon his heart) by which God gave oracular responses for the guidance of His people in temporal matters. What they were, is unknown; they are introduced in Exodus without explanation, as if familiar to the Israelites of that day. Modern Egyptology supplies us with a clue; it tells us that Egyptian high priests in every town, who were also its magistrates, wore round their necks a jeweled gem bearing on one side the image of Truth, and on the other sometimes that of

Justice, sometimes that of Light. When the accused was ac-
quitted, the judge held out the image of him to kiss. In the
final judgment, Osiris wears around his neck the jeweled Justice and Truth. The Septuagint translates Urim and Thummim
by 'Light and Truth.' Some scholars suppose that they were
the twelve stones of the breastplate; others that they were
two additional stones concealed in its fold. Josephus adds to
these the two sardonyx buttons, worn on the shoulders,
which he says emitted luminous rays when the response was
favorable; but the precise mode in which the oracles were
given is lost in obscurity."—*Bible Glossary of Antiquities.*

The law as given by Moses is for the guidance of man in
the evolution of his faculties. The figures, personalities, and
symbols represent potentialities developed and undeveloped
on various planes of consciousness. The high priest stands for
spiritual man, officiating between God and sense man. The
breastplate in an armor protects the most vital part, the
heart. The heart is love, the affectional consciousness in
man; it may be subject to the force of weak sympathy, unless balanced by another power in which is discrimination,
or judgment.

The breastplate had on it twelve precious stones, representing the twelve tribes of Israel. This clearly means that the
twelve faculties of the mind must be massed at the great
brain center called the solar plexus. It means that all the intelligence of man's faculties must be brought into play in the
final judgments of the mind. The Urim and Thummim
(Lights and Perfections; under the Egyptian symbology,
"Truth and Justice") are the oracular edicts of Divine Mind
that are intuitively expressed as a logical sequence of the divine principles, Truth and justice.

A modern metaphysician would interpret all this as signifying the omnipresence of Divine Mind in its perfect idea,
Christ. Truth is ready at all times to give judgment and jus-

tice. As God is love, so God is justice. These qualities are in Divine Mind in unity, but are made manifest in man's consciousness too often in diversity. It is through the Christ Mind in the heart that they are unified. When justice and love meet at the heart center, there are balance, poise, and righteousness. When judgment is divorced from love, and works from the head alone, there goes forth the human cry for justice. In his mere human judgment, man is hard and heartless; he deals out punishment without consideration of motive or cause, and justice goes awry.

Good judgment, like all other faculties of the mind, is developed from Principle. In its perfection it is expressed through man's mind, with all its absolute relations uncurtailed. Man has the right concept of judgment, and ideally the judges of our courts have that unbiased and unprejudiced discrimination which ever exists in the Absolute. A prejudiced judge is abhorred, and a judge who allows himself to be moved by his sympathies is not considered safe.

The metaphysician finds it necessary to place his judgment in the Absolute in order to demonstrate its supreme power. This is accomplished by one's first declaring that one's judgment is spiritual and not material; that its origin is in God; that all its conclusions are based on Truth and that they are absolutely free from prejudice, false sympathy, or personal ignorance. This gives a working center from which the ego, or I AM, begins to set in order its own thought world. The habit of judging others, even in the most insignificant matters of daily life, must be discontinued. "Judge not, that ye be not judged," said Jesus. The law of judgment works out in a multitude of directions, and if we do not observe it in small things, we shall find ourselves failing in large.

Judging from the plane of the personal leads into condemnation, and condemnation is always followed by the fixing of a penalty. We see faults in others, and pass judgment upon them without considering motives or circum-stances. Our judgment is often biased and prejudiced; yet we do not hesitate to think of some form of punishment to be meted out to the guilty one. He may be guilty or not guilty; decision as to his guilt or innocence rests in the divine law, and we have no right to pass judgment. In our ignorance we are creating thought forces that will react upon us. "With what judgment ye judge, ye shall be judged." "With what measure ye mete, it shall be measured unto you." Whatever thought you send out will come back to you. This is an un-changeable law of thought action. A man may be just in all his dealings, yet if he condemns others for their injustice, that thought action will bring him into unjust conditions; so it is not safe to judge except in the Absolute. Jesus said that He judged no man on His own account, but in the Father; that is, He judged in the Principle. This is the stand which everyone must take—resting judgment of others in the Ab-solute. When this is done the tendency to condemn will grow less and less, until man, seeing his fellow man as God sees him, will leave him to the Absolute in all cases where he seems unjust.

The great judgment day of Scripture indicates a time of separation between the true and the false. There is no war-rant for the belief that God sends man to everlasting pun-ishment. Modern interpreters of the Scripture say that the "hell of fire" referred to by Jesus means simply a state in which purification is taking place.

The word *hell* is not translated with clearness sufficient to represent the various meanings of the word in the original language. There are three words from which hell is derived: *Sheol,* "the unseen state"; *Hades,* "the unseen world"; and *Gehenna,* "Valley of Hinnom." These are used in various re-lations, nearly all of them allegorical. In a sermon Archdea-con Farrar said: "There would be the proper teaching about hell if we calmly and deliberately erased from our English Bibles the three words, 'damnation,' 'hell,' and 'everlasting.' I say—unhesitatingly I say, claiming the fullest right to speak with the authority of knowledge—that not one of those words ought to stand any longer in our English Bible, for, in our present acceptation of them, they are simply mistranslations." This corroborates the metaphysical interpretation of Scripture, and sustains the truth that hell is a figure of speech that represents a corrective state of mind. When error has reached its limit, the retroactive law asserts itself, and judgment, being part of that law, brings the penalty upon the transgressor. This penalty is not punishment, but discipline, and if the transgressor is truly repentant and obedient, he is forgiven in Truth.

Under our civil law, criminals are confined in penitentiaries where it is intended that order, regular habits, and industry be inculcated, and that what seems punishment may prove to be educational. Men are everywhere calling for broader educational methods in our prisons, and this demand is an acknowledgment of the necessity of purification through discipline and training in morals. This purifying process is the penalty taught by Jesus—the judgment passed on sinners—the "hell of fire." When it is received in the right spirit, this fire burns up the dross in character and purifies mind and body.

Metaphysicians have discovered that there is a certain relation between the functions and organs of the body and the ideas in the mind. The liver seems to be connected with mental discrimination, and whenever man gets very active along the line of judgment, especially where condemnation enters in, there is disturbance of some kind in that part of the organism. A habit of judging others with severity and fixing in one's mind what the punishment should be causes the liver to become torpid and to cease its natural action; the complexion becomes muddy as a result. "There is therefore now no condemnation to them that are in Christ Jesus . . . who walk not after the flesh, but after the Spirit." This statement held in mind, and carried out in thought and act, will heal liver complaint of that kind. Another form of thought related to judgment is the vacillating of the mind that never seems to know definitely what is the proper thing to do: "A double-minded man, unstable in all his ways." There must be singleness of mind and loyalty to true ideas. Everyone should have definite ideas of what is just and right, and stand by them. This stimulates the action of the liver, and often gives so-called bad people good health, because they are not under self-condemnation. Condemnation in any of its forms retards freedom of action in the discriminative faculty. When we hold ourselves in guilt and condemnation, the natural energies of the mind are weakened and the whole body becomes inert.

The remedy for all that appears unjust is denial of condemnation of others, or of self, and affirmation of the great universal Spirit of justice, through which all unequal and unrighteous conditions are finally adjusted.

Observing the conditions that exist in the world, the just man would have them righted according to what he perceives to be the equitable law. Unless such a one has spiritual understanding, he is very likely to bring upon himself physical disabilities in his efforts to reform men. If his feelings come to a point of "righteous indignation," and he "boils" with anger over the evils of the world, he will cook the corpuscles of his blood. Jesus gave this treatment for such a mental condition: "For neither doth the Father judge any man, but he hath given all judgment unto the Son." This Son is the Christ, the universal cosmos; to its equity, man should commit the justice that he wishes to see brought into human affairs. Put all the burdens of the world upon the one supreme Judge and hold every man, and all the conditions in which men are involved, amenable to the law of God. By so doing, you will set into action mind forces powerful and far-reaching.

If you think that you are unjustly treated by your friends, your employers, your government, or those with whom you do business, simply declare the activity of the almighty Mind, and you will set into action mental forces that will find expression in the executors of the law. This is the most lasting reform to which man can apply himself. It is much more effective than legislation or any attempt to control unjust men by human ways.

Jealousy is a form of mental bias that blinds the judgment and causes one to act without weighing the consequences. This state of mind causes the liver to act violently one day and to be torpid the next, finally resulting in a "jaundiced eye" and yellow skin. We speak of one "blinded by jealousy," or "blinded by prejudice." We do not mean by this that the physical eyes have been put out, but that the understanding has been darkened. Whatever darkens the understanding interferes in some way with the purifying processes of the organism, and the fluids and pigments are congested and the skin becomes darkened in consequence.

The remedy for all this is dismissal of that poor judgment which causes one to be jealous, and a fuller trust in the great all-adjusting justice of God. In this there should be active trust, which is a form of prayer. The disturbing elements that come into life should be definitely placed in the hands of God. This is much more than mere doubtful trust, or negative expectancy that things will be made right. The Spirit of justice should be appealed to and prayed to with the persistency of an Elijah or of the Gentile woman whose importunity was rewarded. When the metaphysician sits by his patient with closed eyes he is not asleep, but very much awake to the reality and mental visibility of forces that enter into and make the conditions of the body. This spiritual activity is necessary to the demonstration of the law.

Success in the world is largely dependent on good judgment. A prominent businessman was once asked what he considered the most valuable trait of mind in an employee, and he replied: "Good judgment." Everywhere businessmen are looking for people who have judgment equal to the making of quick decisions, on the spur of the moment. Years ago a passenger train was wrecked near a little town in Texas. The station agent in the little town showed his good judgment by settling, right on the spot, with the injured. He did this without authority from headquarters, but he showed such excellent judgment that his ability was recognized and he was rapidly advanced until he became president of one of the largest railroad systems in the United States.

By clearing your understanding and acknowledging the one supreme Mind in which is all discrimination, you can cultivate the ability of your mind to arrive quickly at right conclusions. Take the stand that it is your inheritance from God to judge wisely and quickly, and do not depart therefrom by statements of inefficiency in matters of judgment. When you are in doubt as to the right thing to do in attaining justice in worldly affairs, ask that the eternal Spirit of justice shall go forth in your behalf and bring about and restore to you that which is your very own. Do not ask for anything but your very own under the righteous law. Some people unconsciously overreach in their desire for possessions. When they put the matter into the care of Spirit, and things do not turn out just as they had expected in their self-seeking way, they are disappointed and rebellious. This will not do under the spiritual law, which requires that man shall be satisfied with justice and accept the results, whatever they may be. "There is a divinity that shapes our ends"; it can be cooperated with by one who believes in things spiritual, and he will thereby be made prosperous and happy.

JUDGMENT AND JUSTICE STATEMENTS

- "Teach me thy way, O Jehovah; and lead me in a plain path."
- *The righteousness of the divine law is active in all my affairs, and I am protected.*
- "Stand therefore, having girded your loins with truth, and having put on the breastplate of righteousness."
- "The meek will he guide in justice."
- "I will sing of loving kindness and justice."
- *My judgment is just, because I seek not my own will, but the will of the Father.*
- "Judge not, that ye be not judged."
- "Behold now, I have set my cause in order; I know that I am righteous."
- *I believe in the divine law of justice, and I trust it to set right every transaction in my life.*
- "There is . . . now no condemnation to them that are in Christ Jesus."
- *I no longer condemn, criticize, censure, or find fault with my associates; neither do I belittle or condemn myself.*

Chapter 24

HEALING POWER
OF JOY (1939)

*J*REJOICE AND AM GLAD *because Thy harmonizing love makes me every whit whole.* All healing systems recognize joy as a beneficent factor in the restoration of health to the sick. "The joy of Jehovah is your strength." This statement is based on a principle recognized by all who help to bring about strength of mind and health of body. An old country doctor used to tell how he healed a woman of a large cyst by telling her a funny story; at which she laughed so heartily that the fluid broke loose and passed away.

The mind puts kinks in the nerves in ways beyond description. A thought of fear will stop the even flow of life in some nerve center deep down in the body, forming a nucleus where other fears may accumulate and finally congest the blood concerned in some important function. The impact of energy of some kind is necessary to break the dam. Physical exercise will sometimes do it, or massage, or electricity; but these are temporary remedies. None of them has touched the cause, which is mental: fear.

There are various methods of erasing fear from the mind and preventing its congestions in the body. One of the most direct and effective shatterers of fear is laughter. Laugh your fears away. See how ridiculous they are when traced to their source. Nearly all persons have some pet fear, and they give up to it without trying to find its source.

The nerves surrounding the heart are most sensitive to thoughts of fear, and when mind and body are strenuously excited the fearfully charged nerve cells grab the heart and hold it like a vise. Businessmen who live in a world of sharp competition and constant risk of loss with few exceptions are subject to this kind of fear.

Christian metaphysicians of course know that the only permanent cure for the ailment is a heartfelt trust in God as the one and only source of good to man. A daily prayer for wisdom and divine guidance in the conduct of one's affairs will restore peace and harmony to mind and body, and health must of necessity follow.

I will sing unto the Lord a new song of harmony and health.

That there is an intimate relation between happiness and health goes without question. When you feel good you sing either audibly or silently. Singing promotes health because it increases the circulation, and a good circulation is a sign and promoter of health. If the blood stream were never congested and all the nerves and pores were open and free and were swiftly carrying forward their appointed work, there would never be an abnormal or false growth in the body. It follows logically then that we should cultivate those mind activities which stimulate naturally the currents of life in the body. One of these, and a very important one, is joy.

No one likes to take medicine even when sugar-coated, because there is an instinctive feeling that it will do no good. Besides it usually tastes bad. But nearly anyone can sing a little song, and those who have tried it right in the face of suffering will tell you that it is a marvelous health restorer.

The reason that singing restores harmony to tense nerves is that its vibrations stir them to action, thus making it possible for the ever-waiting healing Spirit to get in. The organ of the human voice is located right next to the thyroid gland, the accelerator of certain important body functions. To a greater or less degree every word you speak vibrates the cells up and down the body, from front brain to abdomen.

The Spirit of health, or as the doctors call it, the restorative power of nature, is always right at hand awaiting an opportunity to enter in to make whole and to harmonize all discords in the body. Back of every true song is a thought of joy. It is the thought that counts in the end, because it is the thought that invites the healing Spirit. Consequently we should sing with the thought that the Lord is right with us and that His joy is giving our words the healing unction; as Jesus said, "that my joy may be in you, and *that* your joy may be made full."

When men think a great deal about spiritual things and especially about God as an indwelling spiritual presence, both mind and body are thrilled with joy, a feeling of satisfaction, and a tendency to break out in songs of gladness. This is not confined to Christians; persons everywhere, in every age, have told of an inner glory and happiness when they got into the habit of concentrating their mind on God. The great philosopher Spinoza wrote so much about God that he was known as the "God-intoxicated man."

Pythagoras taught that the universe is God's symphony and that all the suns and planets sing as they swing their way through the heavens. All nature has a language and a song for those who listen. Shakespeare says:

"And this our life, exempt from public haunt,
    Finds tongues in trees, books in the running brooks,
    Sermons in stones, and good in everything."

Shakespeare often quoted from the Bible, and he may have got his idea that trees have tongues from I Chronicles 16:33: "Then shall the trees of the wood sing for joy before Jehovah."

"My mind is cleansed by Christ;
My life flows swift and strong;
The peace of God wells up within,
My soul bursts forth in song."

Some people think it almost a sacrilege to sing when they feel bad. They think that that is the time to groan, and they usually do. That is the way the mortal looks at it, and that is the way you may happen to feel, but you can quickly be released from the prison of pain or grief if you will sing and praise and pray.

First sing in your soul—you can sing 'way down inside of yourself—then you will soon be singing with your voice. So we lay down the metaphysical law that everybody should know how to sing. Everybody can sing. It does not make any difference what your previous thoughts have been about your ability to sing, it does not make any difference what you think about it at present, and it does not make any difference whether you can sing or not; cultivate the singing soul and you will some day break forth into a singing voice.

This is a creative law, and it is a law that everyone should know and use, because through the vibrations of the voice joined with high thinking every cell in the body is set into action, and not only in the body but out into the environing thought atmosphere the vibrations go and break up all crystallized conditions.

The whole universe is in vibration, and that vibration is under law. Chaos would result if the law were not supreme. Each particular thing has its rate of vibration. Heat, light, and color are different rates of vibration in one field of primal energy. Different colors are caused by the different frequencies of the vibrations as they strike the eye. But what causes vibration? We answer Mind.

The cells of the body are centers of force in a field of universal energy. There are no solids. That which appears solid is in reality the scene of constant activity. The eye is not keyed to the pulsations of this universal energy and is therefore deceived into believing that things are solid. All energy and life are governed by laws of spiritual harmony. If the mind that receives sound vibrations is in spiritual consciousness, the body responds to the higher activity. If our mind were trained to think thoughts that harmonized with Divine Mind, we could hear the music of the spheres.

You can drive away the gloom of disappointment by resolutely singing a sunshine song. I believe that we could cultivate the power of music in connection with the understanding of Truth and thus rend all the bonds of sin, sickness, and death. The world needs a new hymnal, with words of Truth only and music so strong and powerful that it will penetrate to the very center of the soul.

Our body is now tuned to the divine harmony; we shall find the keynote by listening in the silence to the singing soul.

The new life in Christ fills me with zeal to live, and I am healed.

In putting on Christ—that is, developing the supermind— every faculty has to be raised to supermind proportions. The exact mathematical degree of power necessary to "synchronize" oneself with the "kingdom of the heavens" in which the supermind functions has not been revealed to human consciousness, if indeed it can be. An eminent British astronomer says that he has discovered that God is a great mathematician, and the logical conclusion of all wise philosophers is that everything in the universe both seen and unseen is under mathematical law. "The very hairs of your head are all numbered," said Jesus.

Jesus also said that He came to bring more life to slow-moving humanity. More vital force now is and always has been the crying need of people everywhere. Disease germs run riot in anemic persons. The cause of such conditions is mental: there is a lack of vital interest in life and a disinclination to assume its responsibilities.

Ralph Waldo Emerson once said that no great work was ever accomplished without enthusiasm. Enthusiasm is another word for zeal, and zeal is a great stimulator of man. You cannot think of or repeat the word zeal without evoking a certain mental thrill that spurs you to action in some direction if you repeat it over and over. This brings us back to the point we mentioned about everything having a mathematical infusion; that is, everything is impregnated with mathematics. Every word we speak goes forth from our mouth charged with atomic energies that vibrate at a definite numerical rate. According to science every atom is composed of protons and electrons, the number of electronic elements in an atom determining the character of the substance. Now we see that modern science is proving the truth of Jesus' statement that we shall be held accountable for every word we speak. Our minds determine the character of our words and what the mind determines the mouth obediently utters, its words loaded with constructive or destructive electrons all mathematically arranged to build up or blow up both ourselves and our aims and ideals. We are perfectly aware that some persons are overzealous, that they consume their vitality by talking and acting without wisdom: "The zeal of thy house hath eaten me up." Such persons are so enthusiastic in externals that they lose contact with the source of things, the inner mind, and they destroy the body, the temple of the living God. However these are the minority. The great majority lack zeal in doing even the most ordinary things, and even the overzealous would find a

much-coveted and needed poise by linking their minds with
the Christ.

The beginning of the culture of the mind that enables it to
make contact with the realm of creative ideas is faith, and
faith is superenthusiasm. You must have such confidence in
your ability to make union with creative Mind that you fuse
the two and the invisible elements melt and fall into the
mold you have made for them.

When we know that every word is mathematically linked
with certain creative ideas and that Divine Mind has made
it possible for every one of us to draw upon these ideas mentally, we have the key to all creative processes. "Whosoever . . .
shall not doubt in his heart, but shall believe that what he
saith cometh to pass; he shall have it." Here in a nutshell
Jesus has stated the law and its fulfillment. The one and
only reason that we do not always succeed in our demonstrations is that we do not persist in our mental work. If we
have never tested our faith in God and His mathematical
laws, we must begin to discipline our minds and raise our
thoughts to the point where they abandon the slow inertia
of the natural man for the speed and spring of the spiritual
man. This is accomplished by prayer, meditation, and the
repetition of true words. It is not the vain repetition of words
over and over, parrotlike, but the quiet realization that there
is a listening Mind and a ready host of great ideas at all times
waiting for us.

*I am at peace because I trust divine justice to regulate my mind,
body, and affairs.*

The mind may be compared to the sea, which is calm or
stormy according to the wind that moves it. Thought utilizes
the substance of the mind and forms that which man ideates.

A restful state of mind is greatly to be desired because of
its constructive character. When the mind is lashed by a
brainstorm the cells of the whole organism are shattered

and exhaustion ensues. Nervous prostration is the result of exhausted nerve force.

Man's whole character is determined by the thoughts for which he allows a place in his mind. A strong man or a weak man is what he is because of repeated thoughts of strength or weakness. Steadfast affirmations of peace will harmonize the whole body structure and open the way to attainment of healthy conditions in mind and body. The reason that prayers and treatments for health are not more successful is that the mind has not been put in a receptive state by affirmations of peace.

The Mind of Spirit is harmonious and peaceful, and it must have a like manner of expression in man's consciousness. When a body of water is choppy with fitful currents of air it cannot reflect objects clearly. Neither can man reflect the steady strong glow of Omnipotence when his mind is disturbed by anxious thoughts, fearful thoughts, or angry thoughts.

Be at peace and your unity with God-Mind will bring you health and happiness.

We all should practice delightful, happy, joyous states of mind. It is such thoughts that open the way for the ever-present Father-Mind to pour out its splendid resources into our mind and through us into all our affairs.

Thou art my life unfailing, and I rejoice in Thy abundant, buoyant health.

No one can understand the real character of God without a metaphysical study and analysis of mind and its properties. To think of God as an enormously enlarged man, as most persons do, entangles one in a maze of wrong conclusions concerning the nature and creative processes of Being.

Think of Being as an aggregation of ideas with potential creative capacity but governed in its creative processes by unalterable laws. Mentally see those ideas projected into action in a universe evolving a self-conscious creature possessed of free will called man. As man develops through the combination of those original ideas, behold him arriving at a place in his evolution where he realizes his power of self-determination and consciously begins to choose as his own field of action the many pleasant activities of the universe and to combine them in his own way.

This phase of man's development is symbolized in the Edenic allegory as Adam and Eve eating of the fruit of the tree of the knowledge of good and evil. The tree that bears the fruit of pleasure in the midst of man's body garden is the sympathetic nervous system. Satan, sensation, tempts Adam and Eve—man—to appropriate or eat of this tree without listening to the voice of wisdom, Jehovah God. The result is unbridled and unlawful development of the sympathetic nervous system with excess of pleasure (good) followed by a corresponding reaction of pain (evil).

Jesus regained this lost Eden and showed us how to regain it by likewise identifying our minds with God-Mind. His prayer was "Not my will, but thine, be done."

Christ is the name of the God-Mind imaged in everyone. When we identify ourselves with that image, we rise superior to the Adamic man and become unified with the spiritual man. It is in the strength of this supermind that we can say to the man of flesh, "I will; be thou made clean." This is the decree of the Christ in you to your conscious mind and its visible body; it is the exercise of the authority given to every child of God. "Decree a thing, and it shall be established unto thee."

And manifest substance flows from a realm of light, according to the most modern conclusions of physical science. James says, "Every good gift and every perfect gift is from

above, coming down from the Father of lights." God ideas
are the source of all that appears. Accept this mighty and all-
productive truth and consciously connect your mind with
the Father-Mind, and you will realize abundant health and
true joy.

*The Holy Spirit life heals me, and I radiate health to everybody
and everything.*

Some persons think that when they quit lying they are
demonstrating Truth. To quit lying is commendable but falls
short of fulfilling the complete reformation of the Spirit of
Truth. In chapter after chapter of the Gospel of John, Jesus
repeats the promise that He will send a Comforter, whom He
names "the Spirit of truth," to those who believe on Him. In
the 15th chapter we read, "But when the Comforter is come,
whom I will send unto you from the Father *even* the Spirit of
truth, which proceedeth from the Father, he shall bear witness of me." In the 16th chapter we find these words: "I have
yet many things to say unto you, but ye cannot bear them
now. Howbeit when he, the Spirit of truth, is come, he shall
guide you into all the truth." "And I will pray the Father, and
he shall give you another Comforter, that he may be with
you for ever, *even* the Spirit of truth . . . for he abideth with
you, and shall be in you."

The Spirit of Truth is the mind of God in its executive capacity: it carries out the divine plan of the originating Spirit.
It proceeds from the Father and bears witness of the Son. We
have in the operation of our own minds an illustration of
how Divine Mind works. When an idea is fully formulated
in our minds and we decide to carry it out, our thoughts
change their character from contemplative to executive. We
no longer plan but proceed to execute what we have already planned. So God-Mind sends forth its Spirit to carry
out in man the divine idea imaged in the Son.

It is very comforting to know that Spirit is cooperating

with us in our efforts to manifest God's law. God in His divine perfection has seemed so far removed from our human frailties that we have lost heart. But now we see that Jesus taught that God is intimately associated with us in all our life's problems and that we need only ask in His name in order to have all needs fulfilled.

The Spirit of Truth is God's thought projecting into our minds ideas that will build a spiritual consciousness like that of Jesus. The Spirit of Truth watches every detail of our lives, and when we ask and by affirmation proclaim its presence, it brings new life into our bodies and moves us to observe hygienic and dietary laws that restore health.

Again the Spirit of Truth opens our minds to God's law of supply and support, to the existence of a universal etheric thought substance prepared for man's body sustenance by infinite Mind. We have thought that in answer to our prayers God in some mysterious manner brought about the marvelous demonstrations that we had. Now we see that there has been prepared from the beginning an interpenetrating substance that, like a tenuous bread of heaven, showers us with its abundance.

But we must not only ask but bring the Spirit into our consciousness by affirming its abundance to be the source of all our good. Then perfection will begin to be manifested right in the face of apparent negation. Remember the invitation of the Master "Hitherto have ye asked nothing in my name: ask, and ye shall receive, that your joy may be made full."

Part Seven
ESCHATOLOGY: THE FINAL THINGS

ESCHATOLOGY: THE FINAL THINGS

ESCHATOLOGY IS an area of theology that deals with "final things." Christian eschatology has traditionally involved discussions of the state of the soul after death, the second advent of Jesus Christ, the "Final Judgment," and the Resurrection. In other words, eschatology has traditionally consisted of speculations about the future.

Some theologians like Albert Schweitzer have argued that Jesus expected the Final Judgment to take place during the lifetime of Jesus himself or immediately after the Crucifixion.[1] Obviously there was no literal final judgment and so if Jesus did have those expectations, he was clearly wrong. If Jesus was wrong, that would seem to indicate that he was not the Messiah.

Other theologians claim that Jesus' followers misunderstood him and that it was the disciples of Jesus who expected the Final Judgment and Resurrection to come soon.[2]

Up through the nineteenth and twentieth centuries, some Christians have sincerely believed and expected the end of the world. Adventist groups, the Worldwide Church of God, and others continue to advocate the belief that the end is near. All that can be said about these groups is that so far, they have been mistaken.

Another tradition, infrequently occuring and small in numbers, has held what is called a "realized eschatology." Realized eschatology claims that the Kingdom of God is always with us, but most do not have the spiritual discernment to realize it. According to the Gospel of Thomas, Jesus himself held a realized eschatology, saying, "the Father's imperial rule is spread out upon the earth, and people don't see it."[3]

Charles Fillmore belongs to the tradition of realized eschatology, as can be seen in the first chapter of this section, "The Restoration of God's Kingdom" (from *Talks on Truth*). While some passages in this section sound like Fillmore is talking about something about to happen, the following passage makes his view clear:

"The fact that the kingdom of heaven is at hand and 'within you,' the sense man totally ignores. . . . It is here all about you; the knowledge of its presence only awaits the opening of your interior eye, the single eye, as Jesus taught."

Fillmore's whole teaching ultimately revolves around the idea that the Kingdom of God is latent within us, as a potentiality to be discovered and developed in our consciousness and expressed in our experience. So it is here, now, but we must discern and express it.

Fillmore does not specifically describe his own vision of "heaven on earth" in terms of human government, education, and economics. Rather, he maintains that through focusing on developing spiritual consciousness each one will find his or her role in the kingdom. What he does consistently teach is that following Christ Jesus all the way will lead to the development of the powers and virtues ascribed to Jesus in The Gospels, including an immortal body which will ascend from mortal sight just as Jesus did. What is more, Fillmore holds that this development is the ultimate destiny of all humanity, no matter how long we put it off.

What Charles Fillmore believed about death and immortality is clearly and concisely put forward in "Attaining Eternal Life" (also from *Talks on Truth*). In this chapter, he sets forth the proposition that any denial of God's life, including weakness and loss of vitality, is death. Consequently, he holds that most people are "dead" now and can awaken to the more abundant life of Christ. Death as it is ordinarily conceived is just the most extreme form of death as loss of physical vitality. The soul then sleeps, dreams of being embodied again and eventually is re-embodied. Each return of soul to a body brings with it the progress that has been made in past incarnations. This process continues until we put on true immortality, "continuous conscious existence in the body."

"Reincarnation" (from *Keep a True Lent* with the original article published in *Unity* in November 1938), argues for the necessity of reincarnation as a way provided by divine mercy for humanity to attain full regeneration, the immortal body referred to in Fillmore's other writings. For Fillmore, reincarnation is not something to be *hoped* for, and in that respect, his view is like the Hindu teaching that the goal of life is to get off the wheel of birth, death, and rebirth. On the other hand, Hinduism holds that reincarnation is essentially a *consequence* of the law of karma, while Fillmore sees reincarnation more as a *gift*, another opportunity to fulfill our Christ potential. His view has nothing to do with the view popularized in American tabloids and popular consciousness that reincarnation provides an opportunity to speculate about what historical personalities we might have been in past lives.

We close the section on eschatology and the book with

"The Church of Christ" (from *Talks on Truth*). This chapter summarizes once again Fillmore's view that the goal of Christianity is the overcoming of death, which makes a fitting conclusion. But more significantly, this chapter contains Fillmore's critique of both "historical Christianity" and the metaphysical Christianity of his time. Part of his critique is that Jesus did not attempt nor intend to set up a church organization with "creeds, tenets, or textbooks" or with human authority at its head:

> Whoever formulates a creed or writes a book, claiming it to be an infallible guide for mankind; whoever organizes a church in which it is attempted, by rules and tenets, to save men from their evil ways; whoever attempts to offer, in any way, a substitute for the omnipresent Spirit of God dwelling in each of us, is an obstructor of the soul's progress.

Fillmore himself did not intend to set up his own teachings as dogmas to be ascribed to or tests of orthodoxy. To truly capture the spirit of what Charles Fillmore was about, we must let go of the idea that he is some kind of ultimate authority on Christianity or that Unity, as an organization, is intended to be "the True Church."

Like Emerson, Fillmore points us back within ourselves when we look to him for "leadership." We might well respect his views and practice the disciplines he taught, but if that leads to mere parroting of his words and an inner life opposed to our own temperment and most basic intuitions of Spirit, it would be better to ignore him altogether. He had strong convictions and spoke them untenatively, with authority. Nevertheless, he also consistently held that all of us have Christ and the spirit of God within us as the ultimate authority. If we open our minds to both the words and spirit of Charles Fillmore and let him inspire us, provoke us, and challenge us, his works can direct our attention to a higher nature within us. If we open our minds to that higher nature, we can find it. From that higher nature, we discover Truth for ourselves, find our own bliss, and live more abundantly.

Chapter 25

THE RESTORATION OF GOD'S KINGDOM (1926)

O NCE TO EVERY MAN and nation comes the
        moment to decide,
        In the strife of truth with falsehood, for the
        good or evil side;
Some great cause, God's new Messiah, offering each the
    bloom or blight,
Parts the goats upon the left hand, and the sheep upon the
    right,
And the choice goes by forever 'twixt that darkness
    and that light.

—Lowell

The promise that the Garden of Eden will be restored on earth is older than the Bible. Other bibles of other peoples far antedating the Hebrews prophesy a time when man shall possess the earth in peace and plenty; a time when the elements shall be subdued, disease and death eliminated, and immortal life in the body again set up. It should be observed that all prophecies to this end that come through mystical channels say that this is a state to be regained. They do not hint at evolution, as understood in modern thought. But the students of physical science arrive through their deductions at virtually the same conclusions concerning the ultimate condition of humanity.

They also agree that this condition of peace and happiness will be brought about through causes originating largely with man and his acts. In other words, its consummation will depend upon the wisdom and the energy with which men act at certain crises in history. These prophets, both ancient and modern, say that we are now at one of the most vital turning points in our experience. They get at it in a variety of ways, and they differ widely in minor points, but they are unanimous in their conclusions that now is the time foretold by prophets of old, and reiterated by prophets now.

But it does not require a prophet's perception to discern the signs of these times. The dissolution of the old and the birth of the new are manifest in every walk of life. For instance, the thought that has been held inviolate for thousands of years about the opaqueness of matter has been shattered. The materialist and his world are no more. This, however, is only a minor example of the astounding swiftness with which the material sense of things has been dissolved in recent years. The past half century has witnessed more of this than the history of all the world records before. The past few years have accelerated this dissolution at a tremendous pace, and a prominent scientist says that the changes have been so many that the textbooks of nearly every science will have to be rewritten. Yet those who are watching the mental realm know that still greater changes are going on there. The religious world of a few years ago does not exist today. There is but one sect in all Christendom that stands by its creed and carries forward its work on the old lines. All the others are shaken to their foundations. Their creeds and dogmas are skeletons in their closets, which they do not care to talk about.

In politics and in government the same upheavals are at work. The rights of men are no longer theories; they are about to become real conditions in the world of affairs. So from any plane of observation that may be chosen, we can assert with conviction that a crisis is here. Something is happening. All along the line are evidences of the birth of the Prince of Peace. A higher state of consciousness is bursting full-blown upon the whole race. It is everywhere, and those who are most open to its influx are being rewarded. The power is abroad in the earth, and it calls to men and to nations, "Come up higher."

All this presages a new state of consciousness for the whole race. It is the beginning of the visible reign of the Christ, whose seed man was Jesus of Nazareth. Every state of consciousness is first planted as a seed idea by some individual. So Jesus of Nazareth planted the seed thoughts that are now springing up in so many forms and shapes. It was He who went into all the domains of thought and formulated ideas that have waited for a people who could comprehend and utilize them. We are that people. The dawn of the millennium is in our keeping. We possess the keys that open the gates of the New Jerusalem.

It should not be assumed that this refers to any sect or class; it refers to all the people of this great time who are open to spiritual understanding. The keys are presented to those who come into a perception that all is mind and that all things and conditions represent states of consciousness, produced through the free action of the I AM in every man and woman. This is the key that is being intrusted to many in this great day of the Lord.

But the possession of this key is not all. A key is for use. We may know all about the way in which mind formulates states of consciousness and all about our relation to God, but unless we have made a change in our consciousness and realized, in a measure at least, the presence of God in our mind, we are not using the key. Theory is one thing; practice is another.

The balanced mind no longer seeks to do evil, and the factor of evil no longer enters into its problem; but a proper discrimination between the enduring, permanent things of existence, and the transient and evanescent is not so common. To choose wisely in this respect requires wisdom and spiritual perception. Those who are unconsciously building on the shifting sands of the material world are many. They try to perpetuate the existing state of things by calling it spiritual, and their ideals are but little removed from the materialistic. The new heavens and the new earth are not to lie darkened or cumbered by any conditions that exist today. All things are to be made new. This is the promise of all the prophets of all the ages. There is to be no more war, nor sorrow, nor crying, nor pain, nor poverty; hence, all conditions that cause these must be destroyed.

Our ideal world must first be formed in mind on a very high plane. We may choose to build it from the standpoint of the most transcendent dreams of humanity's perfection. Nothing less will answer, and all attempts to bring forth the new civilization in conformity to any lower ideal will mean failure to the true metaphysician of the Jesus Christ school. Jesus Christ has a distinct school. He has His ideals; they have been sown in the minds of men, and will surely come to fruitage. He saw a people here on earth with all the powers of the gods, but He did not look to governments, or churches, or industrial movements to bring about the civilization that He planned.

His kingdom is now ready to be set up. The conditions are ripe for it. It is open to all, but only those may come in who are willing to give up for it all their ideas of earthly possessions. "Seek ye first his kingdom, and his righteousness; and all these things shall be added unto you." This admonition still holds good, and its fulfillment is capable of visible realization by those who are willing to accept the conditions. But it is not to be attained in the Ananias and Sapphira way. There can be no reservation. Every earthly link must be broken, every mortal love crucified. This was the way by which Jesus of Nazareth got into this kingdom, and His way is the way that we must employ.

It is not for us to quarrel with the conditions of the world, nor to take upon ourselves the burden of righting them. That is a long, circuitous route into the kingdom, and those who are choosing it face many weary years of waiting. We are to accept that which is now prepared for us. The feast is ready and the invitations are out. This is no longer a parable, but an exact statement of that which really exists in the very atmosphere of this planet. There is a state of consciousness that can be attained and is being attained by men, where all things are provided to fulfill the desires of the regenerated souls. It is not removed to some problematical heaven, nor is it on some distant planet; but right here in our midst are the form and the substance of the condition promised by Jesus Christ.

The day is not distant when this kingdom will have its place in the geography of this people, and those who have chosen it will be known to exist under laws and through means beyond the ken of the Adam man. The way into this kingdom is through the mind, and its doors all open in response to words.

If the "kingdom of heaven," to which Jesus so often referred, is a city with golden streets, in the skies, He could easily have located it; but He did nothing of the kind. On the contrary, He again and again gave illustrations to show His listeners that it is a desirable condition which can be brought about among them by the power of Spirit. He did not speak of it as situated anywhere in particular, or say that it could be attained quickly. For instance, in Luke 13: "Unto what is the kingdom of God like? and whereunto shall I liken it? It is like unto a grain of mustard seed, which a man took, and cast into his own garden; and it grew, and became a tree; and the birds of the heaven lodged in the branches thereof." And again: "It is like unto leaven, which a woman took and hid in three measures of meal, till it was all leavened."

It is a great mystery how these comparisons of heaven ever came to be construed to refer in any way to a locality in the skies. What relation to a city with streets of gold has a mustard seed planted in the earth and springing forth into a tree? Or a little cake of yeast fermenting a baking of bread? A remarkably strange lot of comparisons this wise one used, if He had in mind a place where the good were to go after death!

But He never pretended to represent any such thing. His command to His disciples fully carries out His idea of the kingdom of heaven. It was a condition to be brought about in the affairs of men. It was to grow from small beginnings, like the mustard seed or the yeast cake. His disciples were sent forth to sow this seed in a definite way, by carrying into the midst of men the signs that evidence the power of Spirit through which the kingdom of heaven is to be established right here on this planet. There is no basis for any other view. All the visionary theories about a place called heaven are founded on John's symbolical description of the New Jerusalem, which was a picture, an imagination, of the fulfillment on earth of the very movement inaugurated by Jesus and by Him described as having such small beginnings. The city that John saw was among men. "Behold, the tabernacle of God is with men, and he shall dwell with them, and they shall be his peoples, and God himself shall be with them, *and be* their God: and he shall wipe away every tear from their eyes; and death shall be no more; neither shall there be mourning, nor crying, nor pain, any more: the first things are passed away." This all describes what is to take place here among us. No reference is made to its being among angels, nor is it stated that it was established at the time that John saw the vision. It means that heaven is to be consummated in new conditions on earth.

If the kingdom taught by Jesus is in the skies, why did He direct His disciples to pray, "Thy kingdom come. Thy will be done, as in heaven, so on earth"?

The fact that the kingdom of heaven is at hand and "within you," the sense man totally ignores. He does not see beyond the range of the three limitations of space, hence cannot cognize that which lies within and is interlaced with phenomena on another plane. The kingdom of heaven is not only an ideal realm in which all possibility is freely transformed into externality, but it also has its externality, as tangible to the higher faculties as are the aspects of nature to the sense man. It has its working plans, and it executes them with a fidelity and an accuracy not comprehended by the lax methods of the lower plane. So you who have looked upon the kingdom of heaven as a potentiality to be realized by the power of your word should change your base and see it as it is—a real place already formed, and waiting for you, as a bride adorned for her husband.

It is here all about you; the knowledge of its presence only awaits the opening of your interior eye, the single eye, as Jesus taught. When you look with this eye your whole body is made full of the light that is neither of the sun nor of the moon, but of the Father.

As a disciple, it is not necessary that anyone should know all the intricacies of the metaphysical law; he has simply to act on his inspiration. He need only preach the kingdom of heaven as being at hand, and it will manifest itself. Electricians do not know what electricity is; they have merely utilized some of its laws. They have found that an unknown principle in nature is made manifest when they observe certain conditions. They simply make the mechanical apparatus, set it in motion, and the invisible unknown becomes visible as light, heat, power.

In the world of ideas the metaphysician has discovered that there is a realm having potentialities whose depths he has not sounded. This realm is to him the greatest storehouse of wisdom and of life, and he finds that his own center of consciousness is like it. He is essentially one with it. His thinking faculty represents the mechanical device through which this all-Principle is made manifest. His word sets the machinery in motion, and results follow in the realm of ideas that parallel those in the realm of dynamics. When you know this, you have the working plan upon which is based discipleship. Then go forth and preach, "The kingdom of heaven is at hand." As to defining what that kingdom is like, you must be guided by the Spirit of Truth alone.

The Master could not describe it to men on the sense plane except in symbols. He said that it was like a pearl of great price, to possess which the discoverer sold all that he had. He compared its growth in the mind to a small seed or a little leaven. He summed it all up in the words "The kingdom of God is within you."

You cannot understand mathematics until you have studied mathematics; neither can you understand what the kingdom of heaven is like until you have studied that kingdom on its own spiritual plane.

"Awake! thou that sleepest" in the sense mind! Rouse yourself, for the kingdom of heaven is at hand. You are a king! Bestir yourself; the Christ of God is born in you, and the hour of your reign is at hand!

Chapter 26

ATTAINING ETERNAL LIFE (1926)

HESE QUERIES often come to us: "What do you teach about death?" "Where do people go when they die?" A succinct answer to these questions is found in a statement made by Paul: "The mind of the flesh is death." According to the Bible, all men are "dead through . . . trespasses and sins."

Adam, as originally created, was in illumination. Spirit continually breathed into him the inspiration and knowledge that gave him superior understanding. But he began eating (or appropriating) ideas of two powers—God and not-God, good and evil. The result, so the allegory relates, was a falling away from life and all that it involves. This was the first death.

Men do not think of the first death in its relation to the second death. The latter enters when the soul loses control of the body, when the functional activities cease and the physical organism dissolves. If the scriptural statements given above express facts, sinners (men who believe in two powers, good and evil) are already dead. They do not have to wait until the body stops acting, to know the conditions that prevail in death. Why should we worry about the condition of men who go through the second death? The first death is death of the light and the life of Spirit in our consciousness, and the result is a withdrawal of the soul from the organism. The soul of the carnal-minded does not live in the body, but outside of it. Because of his sins, man has been driven out of the body Eden.

What is death? Briefly stated, it is cessation of vital force and action in the body. Jesus referred to the dead as having "fallen asleep," as also did Paul. There are various degrees of this sleepy condition into which the body falls. Students of physiology find that the body has unused resources that can be temporarily awakened. Through deep breathing they bring into action certain centers in the lungs that give additional purity to the blood; by the quickening of other centers in the body, weak persons can be made strong. This is not the regeneration taught by Jesus, but it demonstrates that the body is not living up to its capacity in even a material way. Some physiologists say that in our thinking exercises we use only a small part of the brain. Nearly the whole nervous system of man is in a sleepy, inactive state. These investigators tell us that if some substance could be poured in through our nervous systems that would wake us up all over, we should be transformed into new beings.

That is exactly what the new life in Christ does for us. "Be ye transformed by the renewing of your mind." We are to be transformed not by deep breathing, or by muscular exercise, or by having our nerves shocked by electricity; but by a new process of thought and spiritual energy we are to awaken our sleepy body, we are to get back to the original state in which we consciously receive the inspiration of Spirit and charge our body with the life of the Infinite.

This is the teaching of pure Christianity, and it is borne out by the discoveries of modern science. Both agree that men must have more life and greater vitality in order to carry forward the demands of mind and its aspirations. Jesus went so far as to claim that men who do not lay hold of the larger consciousness of life which He brought to the race, have no life in them.

What shall we do to escape the second death? We must take the life of the Christ man, which is potentially here in every one of us, and concentrate it into our brain and body. This is accomplished by the power of the word. We can take the first step, that of quickening the circulation, by directing living thoughts and words into the blood channels of the body.

This quickening was taught by Jesus. He said, "I came that they may have life, and may have *it* abundantly." What is the nature and the work of these little canals that carry the blood through all parts of the body? They are the rivers of life, flowing from the one head, divine life. They carry the blood corpuscles, which physiology tells us are little batteries, each with a positive and a negative pole. If these little batteries of your body have the life element in them, they constantly electrify your organism; but if through the power of your thought and word you affirm the opposite of life and talk about the absence of life, what are you doing? You are robbing the batteries of their natural life element; you are slowing down their vitality by giving them an element of negation. This treatment will produce death in the corpuscles, and eventually will bring death to the organism, which they ought to supply with life. By such a process of denial as this the body becomes separated from its sustaining life principle. To hold negation in the mind is to stamp negation on the body. There is no duality in God. We intuitively know that God is good and that God is all. We intuitively know that life is the one real expression of God. To demonstrate the God life, we must plant the knowledge of that life in the flesh. To keep on living, we must supply the God substance, out of which the body will be renewed.

There is no need of any state or condition called death. The word "death" is a denial of God's idea of life. If we would accept life as God offers it to us, we are obliged to refuse the conditions that man has attached to it.

If we would realize the larger life, we must believe in it; we must begin to affirm it as ours here and now. And what kind of life do you conceive this eternal life to be? A life that goes and comes? Affirming eternal life, would you say, "I feel tired and weak; I wish I had a little stimulant to tone me up"? Certainly not. You would meet the feeling of weakness with an affirmation of strength; you would meet every evil suggestion with a denial of its reality and a strong word of Truth. Sound words quickly tone up the mind and body, and there is never a reaction of weakness following their use.

It does not make any difference to the loyal Christian how many people "fall asleep." We know that the sleepers awaken again, that what men call the sleep of death is just a long dream. Some people have more vivid dreams than others, so some who fall asleep in the second death may dream of returning life until they quickly take up again the construction of an organism. The early Christians considered it a great advantage to have a knowledge of Jesus before falling asleep.

It is possible to think about the absence of life until death seems real and lasting. This makes the dream dense and dark, and the awakening slow. Christianity shows how to come right back into life, and that is the only salvation for man. If you believe faithfully in the Christ life, you will never die. That is the promise of Jesus, and our understanding of the laws of mind substantiates His assurance in this respect. The mind can be so filled with thoughts of life that there will be no room for a thought of death. Death can never take possession of the body of one whose mind is thoroughly charged with ideas of life.

This will answer the question "If a man die, shall he live *again*?" Eternal life means continuous conscious existence in the body. Every man lives just to the extent of his appreciation of eternal life. Not only must we live, but we must live wisely. In the Genesis allegory it is written that, for fear that man would eat of the tree of life and live forever in his sinful mind, the Lord God sent him forth from the Garden of Eden. This means that man does not consciously live in his organism, which is the real Garden of Eden. In his unregenerated state, man reflects his mind into his body. But when the baptism of fire, the descent of the Holy Spirit, takes place, there is a reunion of mind and body, and the thrill of divine life is again felt by Adam. The return of the soul to the interior of the organism is part of the symbology portrayed in the history of Jesus of Nazareth. Man must seek and know the law of life before he can live forever. Living without conforming to the law is tragedy.

The law of life is revealed to the mind of man through conscious thinking. Give attention to the omnipresent intelligence and it will make you wise. The "*light* which lighteth every man, coming into the world" is here, as the atmosphere is here. "The light shineth in the darkness; and the darkness apprehended it not." Why? Because men do not realize the Truth about Spirit and its laws. Spirit is like mind—in fact it is the highest realm of mind. There is an ever-present, all-knowing One. Put yourself into conscious unity with this presence through the power of your thought and your word, and you will gradually become mentally open to a world of causes of which you never before dreamed.

Physiology says that the body has two sets of cells, live cells and dead cells. The live cells have a little electric light at their center and the dead ones are dark. In good health there is a preponderance of the light cells; in ill health the dark cells predominate. Metaphysicians have found that man can light up the body cells by affirming life and intelligence for them. Metaphysicians tell their patients to make affirmations such as this:

I am alive with the life of Christ. I am intelligent with the intelligence of Christ.

Take these words and use them, day after day, night after night. Affirm them when you go to bed, and affirm them when you awake in the morning; make them part of your consciousness, and you will take a very important step in demonstrating eternal life.

The body is shocked to death by the violent thought voltage of the unwise mind. Selfishness leads to strife, which is followed by anger and hate. These emotions generate currents of thought whose volts burn up the body cells in the same way that a live wire sears the flesh. Hate currents burn out the connections in the glands, exactly as an excessively high current burns out a fuse in your house lighting system. Then the lights go out and death of the body sets in. Love, peace, and harmony are the only remedies that count. "God is love," and to live in God-Mind, man must cultivate love until it becomes the keynote of his life. We must love everybody and everything, ourselves included. Some people hate themselves. Self-hate is destructive. You must love yourself. Affirm the infinite love as your love, and you will find that there will be generated in your mind and body an entirely new element. Love is the cementing element of all things. You could not have an organism without the help of the cementing power of love. Love is the magnet. You must have love. You cannot live without it. Then begin to live in the thought of love. Personal love is part of the law, but divine love fulfills the law. Center your love thoughts upon God, and you will find love for your fellow man growing marvelously.

We must have substance in its purity in our body. All about us are elements, out of which, if we knew how to use them, we could make any form that we desire. We have not cultivated faith in the invisible substance idea, and it therefore has not been incorporated into our flesh. But now that we know that it exists and that through our affirmations we bring it into expression, we begin at once to affirm divine substance. By this practice we put our body under a refining process that we may continue until we are transfigured into the likeness of the divine man that John saw on Patmos.

The pure substance of Being is a universal solvent. Man can take the substance idea into his mind and, by the presence of its native purity, cleanse everything upon which he concentrates his thought. Do you know what makes an impure cell in your organism? Simply the thought of impurity. That is the point of origin. Impurity is not altogether the result of the impure food that you eat. That has something to do with it, but the desire for impure food begins in the mind, a hungering of the impure thought for that whereon to feed and grow. Coughing and expectorating are ways by which the body forces out the corrupt cells which unclean thinking has formed. When you find yourself trying in this manner to eliminate impurities, stop and affirm the one, infinite, pure substance, as the only substance in existence.

Jesus said that His body was living substance, and He told His followers to eat it. You eat the purified substance of the body of Christ by affirming it to be the real substance of your body. You can send the thought of pure substance to every part of your body, and it will affect the mucous membrane until the catarrhal condition, the cold, and all other diseases resulting from inactive cells, will be purified or eliminated. This process will stop the coughing and the wheezing, if you hold steadily to the one proposition that there is a universally pure substance and that that substance is the one element out of which the Christ body is formed in you.

In the regeneration we thus daily put on the body of Christ, until finally every cell becomes so related to its neighbor that each reflects the other, as diamond reflects diamond, and the redeemed body literally shines. "They that are wise shall shine." The wisdom that shines is the wisdom of Spirit, the knowledge that life is spiritual Being, complete here and now.

The whole secret of the demonstration of Christ is that we shall come to realize our original sinlessness. Sin and the consciousness of sin are the cause of all darkness and death. No amount of physical health can overcome the sins of the carnal mind. Unless he is regenerated under the Jesus Christ teaching, man is a whited sepulcher, "full of dead men's bones." So you are not really alive, wholly alive, safely alive, eternally alive, until you get right where Jesus Christ was and is. He cultivated and demonstrated these thoughts which are the foundation of mental harmony, and if we study His life we shall see just how we must follow Him into His life, become part of it, and live in eternal life, here and now.

If we are not spiritually alive, if we have not the Christ Mind, we are not alive at all. That is the teaching of Christianity. If we believe in the Bible we must believe these propositions. In order to be alive, really alive, we must be sanctified, purified, and regenerated. We must be perfect, even as Jesus was perfect. There is no other way. We may as well face this proposition, because we cannot get away from it. It is true. If I am in any degree a sinner, I have in that degree a corruptible, dead body. I must then be guilty of the carnal mind. And what is the remedy? I must get rid of carnality; that is all. The quicker I do that, the quicker I shall become alive. I should not expect that through my further dying the good Lord will make me alive. I can find in the Scriptures no hint of a promise that warrants such a presumption. "God is not *the God* of the dead, but of the living."

In a parable (Luke 16:19-31) Jesus describes the states of consciousness of one who passes through the change called death. The rich man and Lazarus represent the outer and inner consciousness of the average worldly-minded man and woman. The outer consciousness appropriates the attributes of soul and body and expresses them through sense avenues. "He was clothed in purple and fine linen, faring sumptuously every day." This condition typifies material riches.

Material selfishness starves the soul and devitalizes the psychical body. This body is described thus: "A certain beggar named Lazarus was laid at his gate, full of sores, and desiring to be fed with the *crumbs* that fell from the rich man's table." The soul life is put out of the consciousness and fed with the dogs.

When death overtakes such a one, the inner as well as the outer life changes environment. The material avenues are lost to the outer, and the soul finds self in a hell of desires without the flesh sensations through which to express itself. "And in Hades he lifted up his eyes, being in torments."

Lazarus, the beggar, was "carried away by the angels into Abraham's bosom." The inner spiritual ego, drawn by its innate spiritual ideas, finds a haven of rest in the bosom of the Father, represented by Abraham.

When man loses the material avenues of expression and has not developed the spiritual, he is in torment. Appetite longs for satisfaction, and in its anguish for a cooling draught, calls to its spiritual counterpart (Lazarus). But the body consciousness, the place of union for all the attributes of man, has been removed, producing in the life consciousness a great gulf or chasm that cannot be crossed, except by incarnation in another body.

Then the sense man is contrite, and would have his five brothers warned of the danger of sense life. These five brothers are the five senses. Abraham says, "They have Moses and the prophets; let them hear them"; that is, they understand the law (Moses) and they know what will follow its transgression (prophets). The rich man rejoins: "Nay, father Abraham: but if one go to them from the dead, they will repent." "And he said unto him, If they hear not Moses and the prophets, neither will they be persuaded, if one rise from the dead." The personal consciousness, which has been formed through material attachments, cannot be reached except through its own plane of consciousness. The phenomenal manifestations of spiritualism do not cause people to repent of their sins.

When one understands the disintegration that death produces in man, this parable is perceived to be rich in its description of the process and of the new relation of the segregated parts of the complete man.

Man is Spirit, soul, and body. The Spirit is I AM, and I AM is the ego of Deity. Jehovah told Moses that His name was I AM. Jesus said, "I am the way, and the truth, and the life." Every time that man says "I am," he is speaking the name of Being.

Soul is the sum total of man's experiences gathered throughout the ages. Soul has its inner and its outer avenues of expression. In this parable Lazarus represents the inner, and the rich man the outer, first united in the body, then separated through body dissolution.

The body is the meeting place of the life and substance attributes of Being, consequently body is an important factor in consciousness. Body is not matter; it is substance and life in expression. Expression takes the character of the presiding ego. When the ego attaches itself to life and substance alone and ignores the higher attributes of Being, it becomes gross and material in thought and in manifestation. This condition is typified by the man rich in sense consciousness with a beggar soul.

Every form in the universe has within it a thought picture or pattern. The form may be destroyed, but the picture endures. Man's body is first a mental picture imprinted upon the ether or universal substance. When the body goes into dissolution, the picture remains and stimulates the consciousness of the five senses (five brothers), if it has had no higher activity. It is this sense-body shade that appears to the average psychic. These shades often float about like empty shells, without animation or intelligence. However, if intense interest or intense feeling has been projected into the body at the time of dissolution, it will be reflected in the shade or ghost. The moving picture of a tragedy may be repeated in the astral until the film is broken up. These are the "demons" of Bible times and the "evil spirits" of today. The Christ Mind has supreme dominion over them and can cast them out at will.

To the oft-repeated question "Where is my loved one who is dead?" there can be no comprehensive answer until there is a broader and deeper understanding of man. If all of man were the physical, then the question could easily be answered. But man is very much more than body, even more than intellect. The central reality of man is Spirit, then comes soul, then come intellect and sense consciousness, out of which body is formed. When the body is destroyed, the house of these various component parts of man is no more, and they are left homeless. Then they separate, each going to its own state of consciousness. The spiritual ego reverts to its original essence in the bosom of the Father; soul falls asleep until the next incarnation. Body and sense consciousness are earth-bound, and in due season they disintegrate. Those who have lived honestly and purely find peace and happiness for a time in the rest which follows sincere observance of the divine law.

But the goal of man is eternal life, and in each incarnation that goal is brought nearer if Spirit is given an opportunity to express itself. When this is done, the true spiritual body will replace the physical body and all men will become like Jesus Christ. This is to be accomplished here in the earth. With the eye of a prophet, John saw the redeemed earth, as described in Revelation, Chapter 21: "And I saw a new heaven and a new earth: for the first heaven and the first earth are passed away; and the sea is no more. And I saw the holy city, new Jerusalem, coming down out of heaven from God, made ready as a bride adorned for her husband. And I heard a great voice out of the throne saying, Behold, the tabernacle of God is with men, and he shall dwell with them, and they shall be his peoples, and God himself shall be with them, and be their God: and he shall wipe away every tear from their eyes; and death shall be no more; neither shall there be mourning, nor crying, nor pain, any more: the first things are passed away. And he that sitteth on the throne said, Behold, I make all things new."

Chapter 27

REINCARNATION (1938)

THE WHOLE MAN—Spirit, soul, and body—must be lifted up into the Christ consciousness of life and perfection, which is the goal of man's existence.

The Western world in general looks on re-embodiment, or reincarnation, as a heathen doctrine. Many people close the door of their minds to it, without waiting to find out what message it may bring when interpreted in the light of Truth. It is the object of this article to set forth the Unity teaching concerning reincarnation; to show why we consider it reasonable and to explain its relation to, and its place in, the Christ doctrine.

The teaching of Jesus is that all men shall, through Him, be made free from sin and be saved to the uttermost—Spirit, soul, body. But until this salvation is attained, there is death. To give men opportunity to get the full benefit of salvation, life is necessary, and a body through which to express life is also necessary. So, when man loses his body by death, the law of expression works within him for re-embodiment, and he takes advantage of the Adam method of generation to re-gain a body. Divine mercy permits this process in order that man may have further opportunity to demonstrate Christ life. But generation and death must give place to regeneration and eternal life. The necessity of rebirth must, therefore, pass away with all other makeshifts of the mortal man. It will have no place when men take advantage of the redeeming, regenerating life of Christ and quit dying.

Re-embodiment should not be given undue importance, because it is merely a temporary remedy to be followed by the real, which is resurrection. The whole man—Spirit, soul, and body—must be lifted up into the Christ consciousness of life and perfection.

Jesus teaches that rebirth or reincarnation is the unifying force of nature at work in its effort to restore man to his original deathless estate. Man, through his disregard of the law of life, brought death upon himself, as taught in the 3d chapter of Genesis. But a single span of life, from the birth of an infant to the death of an old man, does not constitute all of man's opportunity for living. Life is continuous and in harmony with the wholeness of Being only when it is expressed in a perfect body; hence man must have a body in order to gain an abiding consciousness of life. Through repeated trials at living, man is finding out that he must learn to control the issues of life in his body.

The objections that the natural man raises to re-embodiment arise largely from the fact that he lives in the personal consciousness and cannot see things in the spiritual and universal. He thinks that by re-embodiment he loses his identity. But identity endures. Personal consciousness does not endure. The personal man is not immortal, and he dies. This is clear to anyone who is willing to give up his belief in the reality and importance of the personal consciousness.

The personal man with all his limitations, all his relations, must give way to the universal, the Christ man. The privilege is ours to give up or forsake everything—father, mother, husband, wife, children, houses, lands—for Christ's sake and so enter into the consciousness of eternal life. By doing this we come into the realization of eternal life and receive a hundredfold more of the very things that we have forsaken. If we refuse or neglect to make this "sacrifice" and prefer to live in the narrow, personal way, and cling to the old personal relationships, there is nothing for it but to meet the result of our choice, and to sever all those relations by death. It is just a question of giving up a little for the all and gaining eternal life. So if re-embodiment frees one from the old, personal relationships, it is not such a dreadful thing after all, for it gives us new personal relationships. Rising out of these into the universal is a work that everyone must do willingly for himself. Death and re-embodiment do not give redemption. Reincarnation serves only as a further opportunity to lay hold of redemption.

The pure, incorruptible substance of Spirit, built into the organism through true, pure, spiritual thought and word, makes the body incorruptible and eternal. As the mind changes from error to Truth, corresponding changes take place in the body, and the ultimate of these changes is perfection and wholeness in every part. Therefore those who are trying to lay hold of eternal life have ground for their faith in the promise that they will be saved from the grave.

Knowing that Spirit, soul, and body are all necessary to man and that he cannot truly be said to live except in their conscious union and expression, the error of believing that death is the open door to a higher life, the gateway to heaven, is easily seen. There is no progress in death. Death is negation. The demonstration of eternal life can be made only in life—soul and body together working out the problem and together being lifted up.

Sense consciousness has no power to lift itself out of ignorance and sin, so the mere matter of repeated births has not taken the race forward. It is the descent of Spirit from time to time, as the people have been able to receive it, that has made all progress. As men's growth has made it possible, new truths have been discerned and new dispensations have come. When the time was ripe, Jesus came and brought the good news of salvation from death. But His words had to work in the race consciousness for nearly two thousand years before anyone was sufficiently awakened and quickened to believe in a complete redemption and to strive to lay hold of it. The promise is that the leaven of the Word will finally leaven the whole of the human family and that all people will come into the light of spiritual life.

From the standpoint of creative Mind it is plain that reembodiment serves a purpose in affording opportunities for spiritual development. All that is gained in spiritual growth in one's life experience becomes part of the individual's real identity; and if he is faithful, he will finally gather such a store of spiritual power and wisdom that he can demonstrate salvation of his body through Christ, who is "able to save to the uttermost." But, we would repeat, reincarnation is only an opportunity.

"The hour . . . now is." Right now the resurrection work is going on, and men and women are awakening to a new consciousness of life, understanding, and bodily perfection. This resurrection work must extend to every member of the Adam race, whether he is what we call alive or whether he, as Jesus said of the dead, sleeps. All must be awakened and be unified in soul and body.

Many of the present-day ideas of resurrection have come down from past centuries of ignorance and have been accepted without question because they seem to be supported by a literal interpretation of certain Bible texts. But in these, as in all Scripture, we should go back of the letter and see the spiritual meaning of the parables and the symbols used to teach the Truth about the raising of the dead. Thus we shall find unfolding day by day in ourselves the awakening and resurrection of thought that we once supposed would come in a single day to the bodies of those in the grave. When this raising of our dying and dead thoughts has gone far enough in us, we shall find ourselves gradually slipping into continuous health; that is, we shall realize that our bodies are self-renewing and therefore naturally immortal. Such a mighty and far-reaching work would be included in the promise "Greater *work* than these shall he [man] do."

Mention is also made in John's Gospel (King James Version) of "the resurrection of damnation." Damnation is condemnation. Paul makes it very clear that, by Adam's transgression, condemnation came on all his race. As death has no power to help anyone, the condition of the Adam man is not bettered by dying. Therefore, when people are re-embodied they "come forth . . . unto the resurrection of damnation," in other words, condemnation or correction. Everyone begins where he left off. But though one may have died in condemnation and been re-embodied in that state, he has opportunity, when re-embodied, to come up into Christ (in whom is no condemnation), identify himself with the Christ race, and demonstrate through Him the deathless life. So is proved the divine justice of including all in sin in Adam, that all may be delivered in one, even Jesus Christ.

Everyone who would demonstrate that he is risen with Christ must first lay hold of life by faith and affirm without wavering that he is raised out of sin and condemnation and death into eternal life. Then the word of life carries on day by day the resurrecting, redeeming work in the mind and in the body. "I die daily," I am raised daily. Every day some old limitation or error loses its hold and passes away and the imperishable, incorruptible substance of Truth becomes a little more firmly established in consciousness. In this way the body is transformed and raised up in honor, incorruptible, immortal. This is the raising of the dead, as commanded by Jesus.

However some of the details of this great work must of necessity be, at this time, mere speculation. It is not profitable to allow our minds to dwell on mortal questionings about how the work of Spirit is to be done in and through us. It is our place to hold ourselves in a positive life thought, realizing always the omnipresence and perfection of life in God, thus bringing perfect life more and more into manifestation in ourselves and in others. When we realize how much our faithfulness means to the race, we shall rejoice in being true to the great principles of Truth that will bring to pass the time when death and the grave will be no more. "And death shall be no more; neither shall there be mourning, nor crying, nor pain, any more: the first things are passed away."

That you do not remember your past lives proves nothing. Neither do you remember the day on which you were born, but you do not on that account question the fact of your birth. Comparatively little of your present life is remembered, but this does not alter the fact that you have lived. Memory, to the natural man, is a matter of physical brain records, photographic or phonographic in character. The memory of experiences in past lives is not clearly recorded in the new brain structure of the infant. Such memories are usually in the nature of vague impressions; the sense of identity is blurred. But in the book of life, the great Mind of the universe, all identity is sharply marked, and as the individual becomes quickened and raised out of personal consciousness into the universal, he will be able to bridge over the breaks in personal experience. He will come to himself.

Realizing his spiritual identity as a son of God, he will not entangle himself with either present or past personality, but will claim and demonstrate his divine sonship. He will no longer limit himself to a brief span of life, beginning with birth and ending with death, but will live in the consciousness of eternal life, which has neither end nor beginning.

Chapter 28

THE CHURCH
OF CHRIST (1926)

"HE CAME UNTO HIS OWN, and they that were his own received him not."
—John 1:11

The pure doctrine of Jesus Christ has never been popular with those who like formality and rites in religion.

The disciples of Jesus were from the ranks of the common people, unlearned in the lore of the scribes and without reputation, religiously or otherwise. They, in their turn, became filled with the Holy Spirit, and did unusual works in healing and teaching, yet their converts were not largely from orthodox circles. It was the "common people" who gladly heard them and their Master. The aristocracy and the organized church opposed them at every turn. They were stoned, quartered, and burned, and their doctrines never became the popular religion. Pure Christianity was literally killed in less than three hundred years after the Crucifixion. What is called Christianity is a combination of paganism, Israelitism, and the letter of Jesus' doctrine without the spirit.

This heterogeneous mass became acceptable because it

was sanctioned by kings and enforced as the church of the state. As it had a little from all the religions, it offered balm to the forced worshipers from each sect, and thus quickly became popular. It is not the doctrine of Jesus Christ, however, and never has been, in any of its many forms and sects. Here and there a gleam of Truth has come to spiritually awakened devotees, and they have broken away from the institution and formed newer and higher standards of Truth; but all have been far short of the original doctrine set forth by Jesus and His disciples.

Jesus never organized a church on earth, nor did He authorize anyone else to do so. He said to Peter, "Upon this rock I will build my church." He did not tell Peter that He was to be the head of the church, with a line of popes to follow. He said, "I will build my church" (*ecclesia*, assembly, or called-out ones). Jesus Christ is still the head of His "assembly," and its only organization is in Spirit. Whoever attempts to organize it on earth, with creeds, tenets, or textbooks of any kind or description as authority, is in direct opposition to His word and His example. He gave but one guide, one source from which His followers should receive their inspiration: "The Holy Spirit, whom the Father will send in my name, he shall teach you all things, and bring to your remembrance all that I said unto you."

The puerile claim that this promise was for His immediate disciples only is hardly worth considering, because of so many texts in which He plainly states that His ministry and words are for the world. He further said, "He that hath my commandments, and keepeth them, he it is that loveth me: and he that loveth me shall be loved of my Father, and I will love him, and will manifest myself unto him."

It was this same Spirit of Truth in Peter that perceived the Christ, and of which He said, "Flesh and blood hath not revealed it unto thee, but my Father who is in heaven." This revealment of Truth direct from Spirit is the rock upon which the one and only church of Jesus Christ is built. All other authorities are spurious.

That the one and only true Church of Christ is without authority or head on earth is evident from the accepted words of Jesus Himself. He never authorized the history of His life as recorded in the Gospels, so far as known; yet, accepting them as such history, on their face they bear out the claim of a spiritual church, with only the Holy Ghost as mediator between man and God. It is evident that Jesus saw the tendency among men to make idols of the Scriptures, and it was His aim to do away with that sort of idolatry. Instead of a command to "search the scriptures," as given in the Authorized Version, the American Standard Version tells us that Jesus reprimanded the Pharisees (John 5:39) in these words: "Ye search the scriptures, because ye think that in them ye have eternal life; and these are they which bear witness of me; and ye will not come to me, that ye may have life."

It is the eternal binding of the thoughts to some external authority in book, creed, or tradition that keeps men in bondage to the lower world. When the mind is perfectly free to search out the higher truths of existence, there flow into the consciousness a vigor and a virility that set in motion all the crystallized thoughts, and fresh life stirs the whole man. Instead of confining the infinite God in the little being of parts and passions conceived by some good but ignorant church father of bygone ages, the open mind flows forth in its own native freedom, and its God is a whole universe, larger in every way than was his of the limited concept. So it is with all the questions of doctrine that form the stock in trade of hereditary religion. What our forefathers discussed for a lifetime, fought bitter battles over and left undecided, the free-minded man sees through in a moment's consideration. He sees through it with unerring accuracy, because his point of view is far removed from the narrow bigotry engrafted by creeds and dogmas into the susceptible mind of the infant churchman.

The mind of man is like a clear stream that flows from some lofty mountain. It has nothing at its point of origin to corrupt or to distort it, but as it flows out into the plain of experience, it meets the obstruction of doubt and fear. It is here that dams are built and its course is turned in many ways.

Whoever formulates a creed or writes a book, claiming it to be an infallible guide for mankind; whoever organizes a church in which it is attempted, by rules and tenets, to save men from their evil ways; whoever attempts of offer, in any way, a substitute for the one omnipresent Spirit of God dwelling in each of us, is an obstructer of the soul's progress.

But those very things are the first attempted by the mind that is not in constant openness to the influx from the Father. Man is by nature an organizer. It is his function in the Godhead to formulate the potentialities of Principle. It is through man's conscious ego that the Father makes Himself manifest to him as infinite externality. The within and the without are one only when man recognizes that he draws all his life, his substance, and his intelligence from infinite Spirit welling up within him.

Many have caught sight of the fact that the true church of Christ is a state of consciousness in man, but few have gone so far in the realization as to know that in the very body of each man and woman is a temple in which the Christ holds religious services at all times: "Ye are a temple of God." The appellation was not symbolical, but a statement of architectural truth. Under the direction of the Christ, a new body is constructed by the thinking faculty in man; the materials entering into this superior structure are the spiritualized organic substances, and the new creation is the temple or body of Spirit. It breathes an atmosphere and is thrilled with a life energy more real than that of the external form. When one who has come into the church of Christ feels the stirring within him of this body of the Spirit, he knows what Paul meant when he said, "There is a natural body, there is also a spiritual *body.*"

Most of the opposition to the church of Christ comes from those who have never felt within them the stirring of this spiritual body, who refuse to believe the experiences of those who have. They live in the intellectual-spiritual, and when the Holy Spirit proceeds to organize an abiding place within them, they refuse Him recognition and call Him "mortal mind," "the Devil," or "an unclean spirit."

It is this blasphemy against the Holy Ghost that Jesus said could not be forgiven. Everything that a man does or has done, the Father freely forgives except the cursing of His Holy Spirit by calling it an unclean spirit. He who understands the law of mental action can easily see why this cannot be forgiven. Mind organizes its states of consciousness according to methods inherent in Being. First is the idea, the center in which the form is generated. This form is projected from that center to a circumference, and in its line of structure in the consciousness of man it proceeds to occupy the place of preexisting forms. The idea of perfection, held in the mind, will build a body having for its attributes all the harmony possible to the organism in which it is born. "God giveth it a body even as it pleased him, and to each seed a body of its own." That "seed" is the true idea held in your mind, through which the Holy Spirit nourishes and grows in you the new body.

If you refuse to receive the sensible ministrations of this Holy Spirit, you, of course, cut off the builder of the eternal temple in which God makes His permanent dwelling place in you.

When you refuse to receive this baptism of the Holy Ghost, your flesh is not quickened, and it must eventually go back to dust. In that case you are again sent to school to learn the lesson in another earthly experience.

This is the law. Let him who has ears hear the law; let him not oppose the construction of the temple that Spirit builds in obedience to the thought held by the mind, and his body shall become an enduring, deathless habitation of the living God. Let us, each one of us, see to it that this opposition to Christ and His methods is not found within us.

If our teaching has been such as to disparage the entertainment of the new sensations in the body when in prayer or in the silence, let us cast those ideas out of our mind and throw ourselves wholly into the care of Spirit. The mind of the flesh vigorously opposes this newcomer in its domain, and if you side with it and ignorantly cast out Spirit, you eventually will find yourself without a body. Having sinned against the Holy Ghost, you become homeless in consequence.

Pronounce every experience good, and of God, and by that mental attitude you will call forth only the good. What seemed error will disappear, and only the good will remain. This is the law, and no one can break it. The Adversary always flees before the mind that is fixed on the pure, the just, and the upright. There is no error in all the universe that can stand for one moment in the presence of the innocent mind. Innocence is its own defense, and he who invokes the Father with pure motive and upright heart need not fear any experience. God has not forgotten His world nor the children of light. It is His will to build in you His eternal habitation, and He will do it in a manner so attractive that you will be delighted with the process after the first few moves have been made. It is not always pleasant to tear down old brick and mortar, but when the new structure begins to go up, there is rejoicing.

So you will find in your experience with the work of the Holy Spirit in reconstructing your organism that the present structure must be literally torn down atom by atom. It is in its present state temporary and without the conscious life of the indwelling Spirit. You, with the race, have separated yourself from God in consciousness; that separation extends to the body, the most remote plane of consciousness. In returning, the Father, the inner Spirit that is and ever has been pure, first recognizes its true estate. This recognition is on the plane of causes, the ideal, and may remain there for a long time. But the law of seedtime and harvest prevails here, as in the natural world, and the idea is the seed that will spring forth from its subjective realm. This, when watered by the Holy Spirit through your receptive thought, grows a new organism that will be a permanent battery from which you will radiate the transcendent powers of Spirit forever and forever.

When this is done, creation is a perfect, homogeneous symphony of life, light, and love. Discord is eliminated; sin, sorrow, and everything that in any way interferes with the highest ideal of existence are dissolved, and man realizes that his dominion is to be the obedient outlet of the inexhaustible inlet. Herein is God glorified and His inexhaustible resources are not limited by man, but allowed full and free flow into a universe without height or depth, without beginning or ending.

The true church of Christ is never organized upon the earth, because the minute that man organizes his religion, he ceases to be guided wholly by the free Spirit of Truth, and to that extent he falls away from the true church.

Many of the Protestant sects were in their incipiency very close to the original church. Wesley was led by Spirit, and his ministry was characterized by a spiritual glow and power that was felt all over the religious world. He was free; he had the freedom of Jesus Christ back of him, yet he and his followers were despised by the organized church, and it was a stinging epithet to be called a Methodist.

The church of Jesus Christ still waits for a ministry that will represent it as it is—an organization in heaven without a head on earth, without a creed, without a line of written authority. This church exists, and must be set up in its rightful place—the minds and the hearts of men. It can never be confined to any external organization; whoever attempts such a movement, by that act ceases to represent the true church of Christ.

There is need of such a church, an imperative need that it be set up. Whoever advocates such a setting up, may for a season expect the opposition of the organized institutions on every hand, but the final outcome must be victory.

There can be but one leader for man in his search for God—the Spirit within him. When he unreservedly gives himself up to this Spirit he finds that the old world of forms and their limitations are no longer of interest. A new world is opened to his vision. What was the goal of his human life becomes a mere toy to his expanded concepts of God and the destiny of man.

He finds that the church of Jesus Christ is not a church at all, under the new definition. He has looked upon his religion as having to do with the salvation of his soul—a sort of school in which he is coached in catechism and creed, that he may be prepared to go to a place called "heaven" after death.

When the true church is revealed to his soul, all this illusion of the animal man is dissolved. He finds that the church of Jesus Christ has to do with the world right here and now; that it is not a religion, as he has been accustomed to regard religion; that it is an organic principle in nature working along definite lines of growth in the building up of a state of consciousness for the whole human race.

Thus the church of Jesus Christ is an exact science. It has its part in the economy of Being, as the organizer of the unorganized. It does not refer to things abstract, but to things concrete. Whoever looks upon it as an abstraction has wholly misconceived it.

God never performs miracles, if by miracle is meant a departure from universal law. Whatever the prophets did was done by the operation of laws inherent in Being and open to the discovery of every man.

Whatever Jesus of Nazareth did, it is likewise the privilege of every man to do. The ability to do such works as He did is simply a question of discernment. Discernment comes through the functioning of an orderly organic structure, which is in the soul of every man. It is first a state of consciousness, a perception of what is in the potential; this then formulates itself into a working structure that becomes in every man the permanent church of Christ.

The church of Christ covers every department of man's existence and enters into every fiber of his being. He carries it with him day and night, seven days of the week. He lives in it as a fish lives in water; as he becomes conscious of its enveloping presence, he is transformed into a new creature. Life becomes an ecstasy, and his cup is full to overflowing.

The burdens of the human drop out of sight just as fast as the organic church is constructed. The construction of this church is orderly, definite, and exact. It is not done in a moment, but little by little the man is built from the within to the without, a new creature in consciousness and in body.

This means that your body will be so transformed within and even without that it will never go through the change called death. It will be a resurrected body, becoming more and more refined as you catch sight of the free truths of Being, until it will literally disappear from the sight of those who see with the eye of sense.

This is the way in which the last enemy, "death," is to be overcome. The corruptible shall put on incorruption right here and now. Be careful not to defer this change to some future state, some day of judgment, some sound of a last trump, but recognize it in the light of an organic change occurring in and through your body, from day to day, until you literally shine with the glory of the noonday sun.

This is the promised New Jerusalem, a city in which neither the sun nor the moon is necessary. This is the city of God within you, and your body shall become so illuminated by the brilliancy of your mind that the light streaming forth will be brighter than that of the sun. This is not a fanciful sketch, but a statement of facts based upon spiritual dynamics of which the body is the dynamo.

Metaphysicians in this age have caught sight of the possibilities that are man's when he consciously recognizes his relation to God and proceeds to carry out in thought, and to act right here, that which he perceives to be true in Spirit; but many of them are not wise in their methods of attaining the ultimate organic building. They have made connection with the realm of ideas, but are loath to comply with the requirements of organic growth from the generative idea to its concrete structure. This growth is the construction of the church of Jesus Christ in each one of us, and it is a most delicate and intricate process. No external architect is here allowed; only Spirit can tell what is necessary from day to day, and Spirit can be heard only by the attentive ego.

If you have any ideas of your own as to how this new body is to be constructed, drop them immediately. If you have been before the public as a teacher of divine science, and have set up in consciousness abstract theories about the unreality of the body and its sensations, you will be willing to give them all up before you can be received into the regeneration. Although you may have served Truth long and faithfully, do not be rebellious if all your labors seem as dust and ashes. The rebellious Israelites never entered the Promised Land. You must be obedient. You must be willing to give up all your plans, your hopes, and your ambitions. Spirit wants all your attention. If you have done good, you will be rewarded, but you must not claim your good as a merit card that gives you any preference in the regeneration. You must be willing to become as nothing in the sight of men—virtually crucified for your good works. Then your personal mentality loses its center, the atoms of your being swiftly change their polarization from the material to the spiritual plane, and you come forth from the tomb of sense with a body of light.

APPENDIX
WAYS TO USE THIS BOOK

There are many ways this book can be used as a resource for studies and personal development. The following are some examples.

- ### AN AID TO PRAYER, MEDITATION, AND PERSONAL DEVELOPMENT

Almost every chapter in this book contains suggestions for prayer, meditation, and personal development. It is not necessary to understand or agree with the more theoretical aspects of Fillmore's ideas in order to apply his teachings on affirmative prayer. The reader can simply look through the chapters for ideas to use and affirmations to hold in mind during prayer or at various times of the day.

- ### A TEXT FOR AN OVERVIEW OF CHARLES FILLMORE'S TEACHINGS

This book is intended as an overview of Charles Fillmore's teachings to be used in the context of a class or for independent personal study. The introductory commentaries are intended to provide historical context and helpful summaries of ideas and themes found in each section. To cover the whole book thoroughly in the context of a class, it is suggested that the teacher or class leader cover only one or two chapters an hour. Any attempt to discuss more than two chapters an hour would probably be confusing and excessive for the class members. Independent study, of course, can be done at one's own pace. It is also suggested that the ideas in the chapter be thought of as points for discussion and reflection, rather than as dogmas to be memorized. To dogmatize would clearly be in opposition to both the letter and spirit of Fillmore's work. Fillmore's attitude toward religious and metaphysical ideas was that each person should test the ideas to see what results might be attained in one's life.

- *A Text for an Introduction to Unity*

Unity ministers might find this book to be useful as a resource for an "Introduction to Unity" class for prospective new Unity church members. When people are thinking about joining a new church, they may have questions such as these: What does your church teach about God? about Jesus? about the Bible? In addition, the minister or leader of the class might want to focus on Unity teachings on prayer, spiritual healing, prosperity, or eternal life. Once the teacher becomes familiar with the contents of this book, it should be relatively easy to choose chapters or parts of chapters that provide the desired and appropriate introductory information. Useful chapters for an introductory class would be the following: Chapter 5, "The True Character of Being"; Chapter 6, "Reform Your God Thought"; Chapter 9, "Being's Perfect Idea"; Chapter 10, "Jesus Christ's Atonement"; Chapter 14, "Holy Spirit Fulfills the Law"; Chapter 16, "The Omnipotence of Prayer"; Chapter 21, "Indispensable Assurance"; Chapter 22, "The Development of Divine Love"; Chapter 24, "Healing Power of Joy"; and Chapter 25, "The Restoration of God's Kingdom." This particular set of chapters would cover the topics of the nature of God, Jesus Christ, prayer, faith, love, healing, joy, and divine purpose.

- ## *A TEXT FOR EXPLORING UNITY TEACHINGS ON CHRISTIAN THEOLOGY*

If your interest is in what Unity teaches about God, either as a matter of religious studies or from the perspective of a student of Unity, Parts Two, Three, and Four are the most appropriate sections for study. The chapters in these three parts of the book are arranged in the chronological order in which they were written. Thus studying these parts in order gives a sense of how Fillmore's thought developed regarding the nature of God, especially in terms of the Trinity. The introductions to these sections should be helpful for understanding this development and for providing a broader context to which one can relate the development of Fillmore's theological ideas.

- ## *A TEXT FOR EXPLORING UNITY TEACHINGS ON METAPHYSICS*

If the reader wants to focus specifically on Unity metaphysics, there are chapters that are particularly helpful. Since Charles Fillmore always had both biblical and practical concerns, all chapters will have those elements as well, but it is still possible to pull out and focus on the metaphysical teachings. The appropriate sections for such a study would be the introductory section for Part One, Epistemology; the introductory section for Part Two, Metaphysical Theology; Chapter 5, "The True Character of Being"; Chapter 7, "Spiritual Substance"; Chapter 9, "Being's Perfect Idea"; the introductory section for Part Five on Cosmology; Chapter 15, "Spiritual Man," which deals with the creative process; and Chapter 18, "Right Giving, the Key to Abundant Receiving," which deals with cause and effect.

- ### *A TEXT FOR A COURSE ON PRAYER AND HEALING*

Every chapter in this book has something to say about prayer and healing, but some chapters are especially focused on these ideas. While the teacher may want to read the entire book and choose chapters that are especially meaningful to him or her, the following chapters are recommended for a course on prayer and healing: Chapter 6, "Reform Your God Thought"; Chapter 8, "God Presence"; Chapter 11, "I Am the Way, and the Truth, and the Life"; Chapter 16, "The Omnipotence of Prayer"; Chapter 17, "Realization Precedes Manifestation"; Chapter 21, "Indispensable Assurance"; Chapter 22, "The Development of Divine Love"; and Chapter 24, "Healing Power of Joy." This set of chapters would also be an appropriate alternative for an introductory class to Unity.

- ### *AN AID TO STUDYING HOW CHARLES FILLMORE'S THOUGHT DEVELOPED*

Considering how much writing Charles Fillmore did over a course of almost 60 years, his thought and use of language were remarkably consistent. However, the selection of chapters in this book does give some evidence of change and enrichment of his ideas. Parts Two through Four are especially revealing in that regard. It is recommended that the student who has an interest in how Fillmore's thought developed pay special attention to the introductions to those parts as well as the contents of the chapters in those sections. For more depth on the development of Fillmore's thought, one could use Fillmore's books *Christian Healing* (1909) *Talks on Truth* (1926) and *Jesus Christ Heals* (1939). For those who would be even more thorough, the library at Unity School of Christianity in Unity Village, Missouri, contains everything Fillmore wrote— magazine articles and books—from 1889 to 1948.

- ## A Resource for Exploring Unity History

This book is not intended as a history of Unity; there are several good works on that, notably *The Story of Unity* by James Dillet Freeman, *The Unity Way of Life* by Marcus Bach, *Myrtle Fillmore: Mother of Unity* by Thomas Witherspoon, *Charles Fillmore: Herald of the New Age* by Hugh D'Andrade, and *Torch-Bearer to Light the Way* by Neal Vahle. However, this book does contain some historical information of interest. The introduction to this book and Part One on epistemology have the most information relevant to how Unity developed historically. Chapter One, "Not an Answer, but an Opportunity," contains some autobiographical references by Charles Fillmore that have not been published since the original magazine article in 1894. The full text of Chapter Two, "The Pure Reason and Honest Logic of Practical Christianity," has not been published since 1920. Chapter Three, "Faith Precipitations" has been available in the book *Atom-Smashing Power of Mind*, but the version included here from the November 1946 *Unity Magazine* is somewhat different and interesting to compare to the version as edited for *Atom-Smashing Power*. Chapter Four, "Unity of Religion and Science," has not been published in book form since the 1959 *Unity's Seventy Years of Faith and Works*.

- ## An Aid to Developing a Historical Perspective on Unity

The introductory commentaries were written specifically as a way of providing historical context for Fillmore's ideas; therefore they can be used by themselves as an aid to studying not only this book but any Fillmore book. These introductory sections may also prove a useful resource for studying other Unity and New Thought books.

- ## *A Resource for Exploring New Religious Movements in America*

There is a growing interest in new religious movements in religious studies departments of academic institutions. This book is partly intended as a resource for those who have an academic interest in new religious movements. Religious studies students looking for some detail specifically on Unity should find this book useful. It is hoped that the introductory sections may also provide clues for research in religion in nineteenth- and twentieth-century America.

- ## *A Resource for Discussion of Christian Theology*

Unfortunately, much discussion of different Christian theologies in church classes degenerates into sarcastic polemics against denominations who do not hold to the "correct" (read "our") theology. This book is not likely to change that aspect of theological discussion in the churches. However, there are places, here and there, where people are seeking to understand and appreciate the diversity of ideas and traditions within Christianity. It is hoped that these open-hearted Christians and other students of religion will find in this book resources for constructive dialogue on the meaning and value of Christian faith. It is hoped that eventually we will all learn to celebrate the richness and profundity of the spiritual traditions on our little planet. It is hoped that this book can make some small contribution to that quest.

- ## *A Resource for Re-thinking Christian Theology*

Many of Charles Fillmore's ideas about Christianity can be seen as a revival of some early forms of Christian theology. For example, Origen's ideas about universal salvation and the role of reincarnation find renewed expression in Fillmore's writings. The emphasis in Fillmore's writings on mystical union with God and having the mind of Christ are consistent with mysticism in the early Church and the Eastern Orthodox ideas about the "deification" of humanity. These are ideas that are worth revisiting and may have some value for our more open and democratic age. Some of Fillmore's speculations about Christ are worth consideration and dialogue if the concept of "the Christ of faith" (as distinguished from the Jesus of history) has any merit for contemporary Christianity. Fillmore's independence and creativity of thought are at least provocative for discussion and can lead to a deepening of one's spiritual life and quest for Truth and self-knowledge. Any and every chapter in this book could be used for discussion and reflection on Christian theology.

- ### A RESOURCE FOR EXPLORING THE INFLUENCE OF EASTERN RELIGION ON WESTERN RELIGION

The introductory sections of this book and some knowledge of Eastern religion can help provide a background for considering how Eastern ideas have begun to enter into the mainstream of Western religious thought. Fillmore's writings show some evidence of that influence, especially the chapters on "Being's Perfect Idea," "The Development of Divine Love," and "Reincarnation."

ENDNOTES

INTRODUCTION

1. A. Powell Davies, *The First Christian* (New York: The New American Library, 1957), pp. 112–124.

2. Ibid., pp. 108–112.

3. *The New Oxford Annotated Bible With the Apocryphal Deuterocanonical Books* (New York: Oxford University Press, 1991), p. 1344 (see footnote on Acts 17:28).

4. Hugh D'Andrade, *Charles Fillmore: Herald of the New Age* (New York: Harper & Row, 1974), pp. 62–64.

5. Ernest C. Wilson, *If You Want to Enough*, compiled and edited by Ronald and Beverly Potter, Englewood, CO: Quality Press, 1984, p. 127.

6. Charles S. Braden, *Spirits in Rebellion* (Dallas: Southern Methodist University Press, 1963), p. 91.

7. For a more detailed biography of Charles Fillmore, see James Dillet Freeman, *The Story of Unity* (Unity Village: Unity Books, 1978), and Hugh D'Andrade, *Charles Fillmore: Herald of the New Age*.

8. For more information on nineteenth-century religion in America, see Catherine L. Albanese, *America: Religions and Religion* (Belmont, Ca.: Wadsworth Publishing Co., 1992).

9. Braden, p. 35.

10. Ibid., p. 9.

11. William James, *The Varieties of Religious Experience* (New York: The Modern Library, 1929), pp. 100–119.

12. Braden, p. 92.

13. Horatio W. Dresser (ed.), *The Quimby Manuscripts* (Secaucus, N.J.: The Citadel Press, 1961), p. 159.

14. For a detailed history of New Thought, see Braden, *Spirits in Rebellion*.

15. For concise descriptions of Fillmore's views on these and other doctrines, see *The Revealing Word* (Unity Village: Unity Books, 1994) and *Metaphysical Bible Dictionary* (Unity Village: Unity Books, 1995).

16. John Hamlin Dewey, *The New Testament Occultism* (New York: J.H. Dewey Publishing Co., 1895).

17. James W. Teener, *"Unity School of Christianity," a doctoral dissertation*, Chicago, University of Chicago, 1939, p. 200.

18. Williston Walker, *A History of the Christian Church* (New York: Charles Scribner's Sons, 1985), pp. 90–91.

19. Ibid., p. 199.

20. Ibid., p. 413.

21. See Paul Davies and John Gribbin, *The Matter Myth* (New York: Simon & Schuster, 1992), and Paul Davies, *The Mind of God* (New York: Simon & Schuster, 1992).

PART ONE

Epistemology: How to Know the Truth

1. Donald Davidson, *Essays on Actions and Events* (Oxford: Clarendon Press, 1986), pp. 207–225. See "Mental Events."

2. See Plato's dialogue "Meno."

3. Fulton H. Anderson (ed.), *The New Organon* (Indianapolis: Bobbs-Merrill Educational Publishing, 1960), p. 129.

4. Robert O. Becker, *Cross Currents* (Los Angeles: Jeremy P. Tarcher, Inc., 1990) pp. 32–39.

PART TWO

Metaphysical Theology: The Nature of God

1. Richard McKeon (ed.), *The Basic Works of Aristotle* (New York: Random House, 1941), pp. 693, 779.

2. For Gnostic references, see James Robinson (ed.), *The Nag Hammadi Library in English* (New York: Harper & Row, 1981), "The Gospel of Truth," pp. 41, 46; "The Thunder, Perfect Mind," p. 272;

"Tripartite Tractate," p. 58. The "Church Father" Ignatius of Antioch wrote: "there is one God, who has manifested himself through Jesus Christ his Son, who is his Word that proceeded from silence." See Edgar J. Goodspeed, *The Apostolic Fathers: An American Translation*.

PART THREE

Metaphysical Christology: Divine Humanity

1. Williston Walker, *A History of the Christian Church* (New York: Charles Scribner's Sons, 1985), p. 55.

2. Ibid., pp. 260–261.

PART FOUR

Pneumatology: The Nature of the Holy Spirit

1. Robinson, "The Gospel of Truth," "The Apocryphon of John," "The Gospel of the Egyptians," "Sophia," "The Dialogue of the Savior."

2. *Julian of Norwich: Showings*, Trans., Edmund Colledge, O.S.A and James Walsh, S.J (New York: Paulist Press, 1978), pp. 292–305.

PART FIVE

Cosmology: Laws of Mind

1. Andrew Dickson White, *A History of the Warfare of Science With Theology in Christendom* (New York: Appleton and Co., 1910).

2. Joseph Campbell (ed.), *The Portable Jung*, (New York: Penguin Books, 1976), p. 329.

3. Ibid.

PART SIX

Spiritual Development: Putting on the Christ

1. For Jung's view, see Violet Stuab De Laszlo (ed.), *The Basic Writings of C. G. Jung* (New York: The Modern Library, 1959), the essay "The Religious and Psychological Problems of Alchemy," pp. 448–451.

2. Socrates' perspective on love, as expressed in Plato's "Sympo-

sium was that it is the Spirit that ultimately *draws* us to the knowledge of the Good and immortality. In that sense of *drawing*, we have something analogous to the idea of love as a magnet.

3. Ralph Waldo Emerson, *Emerson's Essays* (New York: Thomas Y. Crowell Company, 1926), the essay "Compensation."

4. Norman Cousins, *Anatomy of an Illness as Perceived by the Patient* (New York: W. W. Norton & Company, 1979).

Part Seven

Eschatology: The Final Things

1. Albert Schweitzer, *The Quest of the Historical Jesus* (New York: The Macmillan Company, 1950), pp. 370–371.

2. See the work of The Jesus Seminar as in *The Five Gospels* (New York: Macmillan Publishing Co., 1993), pp. 3–4.

3. *The Five Gospels*, p. 531.

INDEX

ABOUT THE AUTHOR

The Reverend James Gaither is chairperson of metaphysical studies and skills at Unity School for Religious Studies at Unity Village, Missouri. He teaches metaphysics, church history, and comparative religions as well as supervises the development of the metaphysics curriculum for both the ministerial and continuing education programs.

A graduate of Augustana College in Rock Island, Illinois, Jim earned a bachelor's degree in sociology and political science. Later he earned a master's in philosophy from the University of Kansas in Lawrence where he also has done some doctoral work.

Jim was ordained as a Unity minister in 1979 and served Christ Unity Church in Collinsville, Illinois, for five years before moving to Unity Village. Jim also served as chairperson of historical studies and skills for Unity School for Religious Studies.

A contributing author to *How Different Religions View Death and Afterlife* (2nd edition, The Charles Press, Philadelphia, 1998), Jim writes articles and a monthly column, "Metaphysical Musings," for *Unity Magazine*.

Jim lives in Lee's Summit, Missouri, with his wife Christine and two of their three daughters, Rachel and Gretchen. Their third, Joanna, is grown and married.

The Charles Fillmore Reference Library

Three Other Enlightening Volumes That Build a Solid Foundation for Unity's Teachings and Beliefs by Charles Fillmore, Unity Cofounder and Teacher

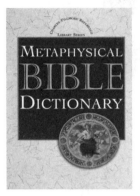

Metaphysical Bible Dictionary

A one-of-a-kind book presenting the esoteric meanings of names and people, places, key words, and phrases found in the Bible.

$19.95, hardcover with dust jacket, 706 pp.
ISBN 0-87159-067-0, #78

The Revealing Word

A special dictionary containing metaphysical meanings of 1200 words and phrases frequently used in Unity publications and in the Bible.
$12.95, hardcover with concealed spiral binding, 216 pp., ISBN 0-87159-006-9, #103

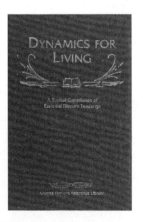

Dynamics for Living
A Topical Compilation of Essential Fillmore Teachings

Selected and arranged by Warren Meyer

This guide provides easy reference to Charles Fillmore's most influential teachings and combines three decades of writing in one handy publication.
$12.95, hardcover, 367 pp.
ISBN 0-87159-110-3, #138

Unity Classic Library Series

Timeless Titles of Spiritual Renewal

Every book in this series has earned the "classic" status due to its popularity, durability, and uncompromising quality. Each brings a special viewpoint and understanding of Unity's beliefs and principles. These books are respected additions to any metaphysical collection.

By Charles Fillmore:

Atom-Smashing Power of Mind
$11.95, hardcover, 206 pp., ISBN 0-87159-109-X, #132

Jesus Christ Heals
$11.95, hardcover with dust jacket, 218 pp., ISBN 0-87159-197-9, #55

Keep a True Lent
$11.95, hardcover with dust jacket, 231 pp., ISBN 0-87159-073-5, #96

Mysteries of Genesis
$11.95, hardcover, 432 pp., ISBN 0-87159-219-3, #92

Mysteries of John
$11.95, hardcover, 215 pp., ISBN 0-87159-204-5, #38

Prosperity
$11.95, hardcover, 217 pp., ISBN 0-87159-107-3, #106

Talks on Truth
$11.95, hardcover, 200 pp., ISBN 0-87159-234-7, #109

By Charles & Cora Fillmore:

Teach Us to Pray
$11.95, hardcover, 213 pp., ISBN 0-87159-203-7, #47

The Twelve Powers
$11.95, hardcover with dust jacket, 309 pp., ISBN 0-87159-238-X, #31

Printed in the U.S.A.   76-471-75C-8-99

DATE DUE